THE
HEAVYWEIGHT CHAMPIONSHIP

THE

HEAVYWEIGHT

An Informal History of Heavyweight

NAT FLEISCHER

CHAMPIONSHIP

Boxing from 1719 to the Present Day

G. P. PUTNAM'S SONS, NEW YORK

CONTENTS

ILLUSTRATIONS

INTRODUCTION

FIGHTING with the fists probably began the day the first anthropoid creatures came down from the trees and started lumbering about on their hind legs. Undoubtedly men (and women too) continued to use their fists, in addition to rocks and clubs, as they fought their way through the thousands of years that elapsed between their subsavage state and a condition of primitive civilization.

Boxing as a sport or entertainment naturally developed much later, after certain more gifted and favored sections of the human race had progressed far enough to secure for themselves a measure of physical and economic safety sufficient to give them leisure for games, contests, and spectacles. But late as that development may have come in terms of human evolution, it must have come very early in relation to surviving myth, legend, and history. Excavations at Knossos on the island of Crete, where a high civilization flourished as early as 1500 B.C., give evidence that a form of boxing was known there. The epics of Homer, which may first have been sung three thousand years ago, contain references to the sport. Boxing was practiced by the athletes of Athens and other Greek city states and was included in the ancient Olympic Games. In Rome, boxers frequently took part in the gladiatorial combats in the Colosseum.

The early Greek boxers were unpaid athletes, amateurs in the true sense, and many illustrations of their bouts survive on vases and other pottery that may be seen in museum collections. As wealth and luxury increased, boxers were hired, or more frequently, they were slaves specially trained as pugilists. Greek boxers wore a leather covering to protect their fists and forearms, and one might conclude that these fighters were regarded as valuable property, to be used over and over again. A fine bronze of a seated Greek boxer in the Museo delle Terme in Rome shows him prepared for a match; the statue also shows the distinctive mark of his trade, a pair of cauliflower ears.

By the first century of the Christian Era, when the Roman Empire reached the fullness of its military and political power and simultaneously, under the successive reigns of Caligula, Claudius, and Nero, entered its decadence, boxing had come into a new phase of development. Fighters no longer covered their fists with leather in order to protect them. They now wore the cestus, a sort of elbow-length glove studded with iron or brass pointed knobs. They had, literally, become killers. These boxers, who, like gladiators and other performers in the arenas, were all slaves, had no choice. They stood toe to toe and slugged until, mauled to a bloody pulp by metal-studded fists, one, sometimes both, fell dead. The Roman crowd demanded that its entertainers leave the stage as corpses, and boxers adapted their art to the fashion of the day.

As the political star of Rome descended, the ability to pay for lavish spectacles also declined, and the gladiators and boxers gradually passed out of circulation. Another reason for the abandonment of the arenas was the growing influence of the Christian religion. With the crumbling of the empire and the increasing audacity of barbarian invaders, the Church of Rome became more and more the central authority in the lives of men—and it was an authority that sternly forbade all earthly vanities.

So far as records are concerned, boxing as a sport or show had no existence for well over a thousand years. But there can be no question that men continued to use their fists to settle their arguments, or to establish their authority, or to keep themselves in condition between seasons of war, or just because they liked a fight. Specific historical evidence is lacking, in all probability, because fist fighting was largely confined to the lower social levels. Knights and gentlemen fought with swords, and the troubadours of the Middle Ages sang exclusively of their romantic deeds—a ballad or madrigal celebrating the encounters of vulgar peasants would almost certainly have bounced these wandering minstrels outside the castle gates without their supper.

The resurgence of boxing as a form of public entertainment was dependent upon the rise of the modern city and in particular upon the rise of London. It is beyond the scope of this book to inquire into how and why the English capital rather than Paris or some other continental city should have been most favorable to the new growth, but the fact remains that the sprawling seaport on the Thames, with its diversified population, its crowded slums, and its twisting, dirty streets did have the necessary ingredients. By the beginning of the eighteenth century boxing was a popular sport in London and a few other English cities, and by 1719 interest in it had grown to the point where one man, James Figg, through his victories over the most able fighters in the kingdom, won common acceptance as champion of England.

Bouts were conducted with extreme informality in those early days. They were rough-and-tumble fights rather than boxing matches. Opponents, in addition to punching with ungloved fists, used their open hands to catch hold of each other as in wrestling, and men were thrown to the floor or turf more often than they were knocked down by solid punches. Rules evolved as certain practices came to be regarded as undesirable. In all probability, the preferences of spectators had a lot to do with the changes. The Fancy * demanded lively action two centuries ago, just as they do today.

What lifted boxing from little more than cuffing and scuffling to a standardized method of physical encounter between two men was a code of rules, of which Jack Broughton, champion for sixteen years, was the author. Broughton's Rules (given in the Appendix) defined the fundamental conditions of a fight

---

* This designation was applied to the elegant gentlemen who provided the bulk of attendance at early sporting events. That certain members of the gentry thought of themselves as "fancy" may be amply proved by the existence of various clubs named Corinthians. This word, used to classify the most elaborate and ornate of the classic orders of architecture, was deliberately chosen by the rich and the well born to describe themselves in relation to their sporting activities.

and the conduct of the fighters, and they provided for the selection of umpires. So satisfactory were these rules that for nearly a hundred years after their acceptance in 1743 no substantial alterations were deemed necessary.

For several generations the only boxers of note were Englishmen, and it was to England that fighters from other parts of the world had to go in order to gain any sort of recognition. The first invaders were Irishmen, those traditionally great lovers of every kind of fighting, and a little later an occasional American appeared in the British ring. It is significant that the first American boxer of distinction was a Negro, a former slave, who had won his freedom in consequence of his victory over a slave owned by another master.

Toward the close of the eighteenth century, after a period in which a number of second-rate and corrupt fighters brought boxing into very low repute, the sport was revitalized by the rise of a brilliant new champion. Daniel Mendoza, an English Jew of Portuguese descent, was more than the best boxer of his time. He was the first great ring general, the tactical ancestor of such champions as Corbett and Tunney.

Other worthy champions followed Mendoza in the British ring, and meanwhile interest in boxing was developing rapidly in America. In 1816 Jacob Hyer won the first fight to attract public interest in the United States. This bout was not in any sense a championship match, although it has erroneously been so described. It was important primarily because it was conducted under British rules, thus establishing the pattern of future ring combat in the New World.

As steam navigation improved both the speed and comfort of transatlantic travel, not only did American fighters invade England with increasing frequency, but English and Irish boxers made the westward journey in greater and greater numbers. It was not until 1860, however, that the first international match to decide a championship was arranged. In that year John C. Heenan—the "Benicia Boy"—who claimed the championship of the United States, met Tom Sayers, the English champion. On April 17, in London, they fought a forty-two-round draw.

The last of the great fighters to be reared in the English school of pugilism was Jem Mace, one of the most scientific, as well as one of the most courageous, of them all. Though really never more than a middleweight, Mace won the heavyweight crown in 1861. He lost it to Tom King the following year, but when King refused to meet him again, Jem reclaimed the title and was generally accepted as king of the British heavies.

Mace fought frequently in both England and the United States, and in 1870 he beat English-born Tom Allen in Louisiana for the American title. Thus Mace became bare-knuckle champion of the world. He was the last man to hold that title. After Mace's retirement, the only Englishman who succeeded in winning the world championship was Bob Fitzsimmons—but he, though born in Cornwall, had been brought up in New Zealand, learned his fighting in Australia, and made his world mark in the United States after becoming a citizen of this country.

It was a son of that American stronghold of learning and culture, Boston, who engaged in the first heavyweight championship bout with gloves. But John L. Sullivan held only the bare-knuckle championship of the United States at the time. It was not until his conqueror, James J. Corbett, took the measure of Charlie Mitchell of England that the United States had its first undisputed world champion.

But though Sullivan never held, or claimed to hold, the title of world champion, it would have been barely worthy of him. He was above titles. The Boston Strong Boy knew, and all the world agreed, that he was the greatest fighter on earth. He repeatedly went out of his way to proclaim his greatness and, whenever possible, to prove it both in and out of the ring. He fought in the United States and abroad and during his ten-year reign only Charlie Mitchell even held him to a draw. When Corbett beat Sullivan at New Orleans in 1892, the whole world was stunned and saddened.

Since Corbett's day, the championship of the United States and of the world have been identical. The reason is readily apparent: It was here in the United States that the money was to be made, and it was here that fighters came eagerly from other parts of the world. Boxing exhibitions, barely two generations ago regarded as brutal and degenerate to the extent of being outlawed in most states, rapidly achieved the conditions of legality, respectability, popularity, and big business.

With Jack Dempsey's overwhelming victory over Jess Willard in Toledo in 1919, exactly two hundred years after James Figg won recognition as first champion, prizefighting was solidly established as a leading spectator sport and as an important industry. And eight years later, in Chicago, when Gene Tunney successfully defended his title against Dempsey, boxing provided the biggest gate ever known in the history of sport—more than two and a half million dollars.

Since 1928, when Tunney retired undefeated, six men, including a German and an Italian, have held the championship. The great Negro fighter Joe Louis, champion 1937–1949, is at least in one respect the greatest of all time. No other fighter in more than two centuries of boxing has ever approached his record of twenty-five bouts in defense of the heavyweight title.

This book is the story of the champions and their important fights. In addition, for quick reference, it contains a chronological list of all the modern heavyweight championship bouts, beginning with Sullivan's victory over Paddy Ryan in 1882. There is also a glossary of boxing terms and ring slang. And finally, the rules of boxing, showing the evolution of the sport from Broughton's day until the acceptance of the Queensberry code, are set down.*

The one thing that is not contained here is discussion of trivial discrepancies—variations in the spelling of names, differences in dates, places, and the like—that are repeatedly found when one compares the early printed accounts on boxing. In every case where the discrepancy is immaterial, it is so treated, without explanation or even mention. Significant differences, either of records or opinions, are of course given appropriate exposition.

I suddenly realized some months ago that eight years had passed since I began writing this informal history of the heavyweight championship. What had started in my mind as a simple

---

* No fundamental changes in ring conduct have been introduced since the Marquis of Queensberry Rules were written. With minor variations, they still govern boxing in all parts of the world.

compilation of the material in my library and files, some of it going back as far as the first half of the eighteenth century, augmented by personal observations that began while Jim Jeffries wore the crown, was threatening to continue indefinitely as a hobby. And so, with real reluctance, I decided the time had come to turn over my manuscript to the publisher. I can wish nothing better for my book than that the people who read it will find half the enjoyment I experienced in writing it.

NAT FLEISCHER

New York City
March, 1949

THE
HEAVYWEIGHT CHAMPIONSHIP

CHAPTER 1

BOXING'S BEGINNINGS
IN ENGLAND

ON A September day about the year 1730, the people of London—or at least such among them as frequented taverns and public houses—learned that "at Figg's Great Tiled Booth on the Bowling Green, Southwark, during the time of the Fair," entertainment would be provided in "the manly arts of foil play, backsword, cudgelling, and boxing." Their source of information was a printed handbill. So far as present records show, this was the first advertisement of boxing as a public spectacle.

But if this was the earliest boxing advertisement, boxing itself had for some time been a popular sport in London and elsewhere in England. Several years before this particular Southwark Fair, James Figg, a native of Oxfordshire, had beaten enough of his contemporaries to gain recognition as champion of England. The year is uncertain, although 1719 is generally accepted.

Surviving records are very sketchy. In 1727 Figg successfully defended the championship against Ned Sutton. He may or may not have held the title continuously until 1734. Vague mention is made of several other "champions" in the early 1730's—Gretting, Tom Pipes, and Jack Hammersmith. But whether or not any or all of these three had legitimate claim to the championship, it is significant that when the Earl of Bath in 1733 imported from Italy a ferocious character named Tito Alberto di Carni, the man chosen to defend the honor of England was James Figg. Although fourteen years had passed since he first held the title, Figg had little trouble with his opponent, and Carni, who was known professionally as the Venetian Gondolier, departed for his native land almost as soon

3

as he regained consciousness. The following year Figg retired from the prize ring.

If it should seem strange that the first champion fought only twice during the fifteen years after he won the title, two circumstances will explain this. First of all, boxers fought with bare

JAMES FIGG

knuckles, and after a long, hard match many months usually elapsed before a man's hands had completely healed. The winner normally was in worse shape than the loser, for his hands had taken the heavier beating. Broken noses and battered ears healed quickly. Broken fingers and torn tendons did not. The other reason why the early champions fought so infrequently was that financial incentive was lacking. Purses were small at best and usually nonexistent. A fighter's best chance to make real money was through a side bet—and that required capital or a rich backer willing to share generously with his man. Few challengers were able to post the necessary cash, and, conversely, a champion, who could make a decent living giving lessons and appearing occasionally in exhibitions, was likely to be very cautious about risking the title that brought him a livelihood.

Figg had, on the whole, rather a good thing of it for more than twenty years. After his retirement he opened a sort of theater in Tottenham Court Road, where exhibitions of pugilism were regularly given. Among his patrons were Jonathan Swift, Alexander Pope, and William Hogarth, the artist. The great Hogarth not only immortalized the champion's muscular figure and stern face in two of his most celebrated works, "Rake's Progress," and "Southwark Fair," but designed his professional card. Not an inconsiderable distinction for an illiterate roughneck.

Figg died in 1740. A history of him and his career was published in 1747 by Captain John Godfrey, a noted athlete, in his book entitled *A Treatise Upon the Useful Science of Defence.* Godfrey makes it clear that boxing was only one of the arts in which Figg excelled. Commenting on his own experience in both cudgel play and boxing, he wrote, "I have purchased my knowledge with many a broken head and bruises in every part of me. I chose to go mostly to Figg, and exercise with him, partly as I knew him to be the ablest master, and partly as he was of a rugged temper, and would spare no man, high or low, who took up a stick against him." Remarking on Figg's boxing skill, Godfrey wrote, "There is a majesty in his countenance and blaze in his actions beyond all else I have ever seen. James Figg is the most perfect example of self-defence of his day. Seconded by his strength and temper, his skill renders him invincible."

After Figg retired from the ring, in 1734, one of his pupils, an alumnus of the Southwark Fair booth, inherited his championship. His name was George Taylor, and there is substantial difference of opinion about his career. According to one source of information, Taylor held the title for six years; according to another, he lost it almost immediately. There is, however, no disagreement about the identity of his successor, and it is not even of trifling consequence today whether Jack Broughton won the crown in 1734 or 1740. His importance lies in his contribution to boxing.

Until Broughton came along, boxers had stood toe to toe, like the ancients, and slugged it out. If the chance presented itself, one fighter might catch hold of his opponent and toss

JOHN BROUGHTON

him to the ground or floor, then fall upon him if he failed instantly to roll away. It was considered manly and proper to kick a man when he was down—the word "purring" was employed to describe this activity—and eye-gouging was common practice with the fighters and hugely enjoyed by the spectators. The use of fists was relatively incidental.

Broughton, though highly adept in the arts of throwing his opponent, jumping on him, gouging, and purring, found by experience that his own most potent weapon was his fists. He revolutionized boxing by introducing science and deception into the ring. Pierce Egan, in his *Boxiana*, said of this champion:

> Broughton, like all great masters, generally exhibited something new in every performance; and those pugilists who had witnessed his contests, and afterwards entered the lists against him, expecting to find that he would fight upon the *old suit*, were most terribly deceived; as contrary to most other boxers, he did not depend upon any particular blow, although he was distinguished for giving some remarkable hits, which were scarcely ever forgotten. Broughton, when necessary in the conflict, by putting in his stomach-blow, has often decided the battle; and his lunge under the ear generally produced terrible consequences to his opponent. The eye of Broughton was most lively and acute, soon perceiving the weakness of any adversary; and his arm, keeping pace with that valuable assistant, protected him from the most destructive blows; and his quick penetration made him always aware of any direct intent pursued by his adversary, as immediately to render it futile and unavailing. His guard was considered so complete that his frame appeared as well secured as if in a fence. Uncommon strength and *bottom* often fell before him; and his expertness in the cross-buttock was great. His various attitudes in the fight were fine and impressive, and his countenance always animated and cheerful.

Broughton's mastery of boxing technique gave him a position of authority in all matters relating to the sport that no other fighter before or after him ever quite held. In addition to being the greatest fighter of his day, Broughton was the unquestioned arbiter of the ring, and in 1743 he wrote a code of rules. With minor modifications, Broughton's Rules governed boxing until 1838.

Another contribution of Broughton's was the "mufflers"—the forerunner of present-day boxing gloves—for sparring exhibitions. Broughton was a good businessman, with a sharp eye toward the money to be made by giving boxing lessons to "persons of quality and distinction." At his "academy" in Haymarket, he announced, in 1747, instruction would be given "with the utmost tenderness and regard to the delicacy of the frame and constitution of the pupil. For which reason mufflers are provided that will effectually secure them from the inconveniency of black eyes, broken jaws, and bloody noses."

Jack Broughton fought his last fight in 1750. Champion since 1740 (or perhaps 1734), he agreed to meet Jack Slack for the crown. The fight was a short one. Temporarily blinded after fourteen minutes of heavy battling, Broughton lost not only his title but a fortune for his patron, the Duke of Cumberland, who had backed him at ten-to-one odds.

Broughton fully deserves to be known as "the Father of the English School of Pugilism." It was his skill and intelligence that gave form to the sport and fixed its direction. Broughton was an advocate of fair play. He understood the importance of training and clean living. He was a decent and honest man.

Jack Slack, who won the championship from Broughton, was a man of different stripe. Known as the Norwich Butcher, from the trade he had followed before he became a professional fighter, he relied upon strength rather than skill. "He had but little method in his striking," according to an eighteenth-century account. "He exceeded all others in the force of his blows, and a *slack* was commonly used to signify a blow given with great strength." Another of Slack's favorite blows was the "chopper," which appears to have been the rabbit punch of his day. "Bringing his fist to his breast, and projecting his elbow, he threw off a blow and instantly describing a circle, the center of which was the elbow, he unexpectedly struck his antagonist in the face with the back of his hand. This mode was completely his own, but has since been adopted by numbers."

Slack was not only a fighter who employed dirty tactics but a crooked promoter as well. During the ten years he wore the crown, though fighting infrequently himself, he staged a number of shady bouts. In consequence, the sport that Broughton had raised to such a high level of popularity sank rapidly in public esteem. Perhaps it was in the hope of re-establishing the integrity of boxing that an appeal was made to noble patrons to lend their names to a fight for the championship. In any case, the same Duke of Cumberland who had lost so heavily when Broughton was beaten appeared now as Slack's patron, and the Duke of York publicly supported the challenger, Bill Stevens, who was known as the Nailer.

There is no evidence that this contest, which took place June 17, 1760, was "thrown" by Slack—he was then ten years older

JACK SLACK

than he had been when he won the title from Broughton—but the emergence of Stevens as champion did nothing to raise confidence in the honesty of boxers. The Nailer had long been notorious for his participation in fixed fights, and the most important immediate effect of his victory over Slack was profound disgust on the part of boxing enthusiasts. For a time the sport was almost completely neglected.

Naturally enough, the principal victims of this neglect were the boxers themselves, and Stevens decided to make the supreme sacrifice—for a price. He agreed to lose his title to a relatively unknown fighter, George Meggs, a protégé of Jack Slack. The results, it was reasoned, could be none other than salutary. First, the three worthies concerned could, by fixing the fight, bet heavily and be certain of the outcome. Second, the elimination of Stevens would restore public confidence in the sport.

In accordance with the arrangements, Stevens lost the fight to Meggs, and both of them, along with Slack, won substantial bets; Slack also received fifty guineas from Meggs for concluding negotiations with Stevens. But they failed in their objective of rebuilding faith in the sport, and that was at least partly the fault of Bill Stevens, a man admirable for his candor if nothing else.

When reproached by a supporter who had lost a large bet, the Nailer exclaimed in great good humor, "Why, Lord bless you! I got double as much for letting Meggs beat me as I got for thrashing Slack."

After this sordid affair both Stevens and Slack were ostracized. Meggs apparently was not too severely blamed for his part, and he continued to fight. But boxing was in a bad way, and for the next few years the championship was in an unsettled state. After Meggs came "Baker" Milson, Tom Juchau, Bill Darts, and "Waterman" Lyons. But the title meant so little, by way of either fortune or fame, that after two weeks as champion Lyons returned to his more honorable and profitable career of ferrying travelers across the Thames. Darts reassumed the championship (without objection by the contented ferryman) and held it until Peter Corcoran of Ireland took it away from him in the shortest bout on record. The contest lasted less than one minute.

Corcoran, the first of his race to become champion of England, was born in 1740 at Athey, County Carlow. Strong and toughened by a boyhood on the farm, he came to London and took up fighting. He won easily from Bill Turner in his first important match, September 4, 1769.

One of the spectators was a countryman of Corcoran's, Colonel O'Kelly, who was well known for his successes in horse racing and his enthusiasm for other sports. Impressed by Corcoran's easy win over Turner, O'Kelly offered to get him a match for the championship. The Colonel was not inspired wholly by altruism. Taking his time, he arranged the bout to be held at the site of one of the big race tracks on the day of an important race. O'Kelly's shrewdness was rewarded. The combination of a horse race and a fight for the championship drew a throng of several thousand. It was on May 18, 1771, that Corcoran beat Bill Darts in the first round by crashing his head against one of the heavy posts that supported the ropes.

Meanwhile the discredited Slack had set up shop at Bristol in the west of England, and there he discovered in Harry Sellers a potential champion. On October 10, 1776, at the Crown Inn at Staines, near London, Corcoran and Sellers met for the title. Sellers won. But once again the sport of boxing lost, for, justified or not, there were strong rumors that Slack had fixed the fight.

On September 25, 1780, at Slough, not far from Staines, Sellers defended his dubious title against another Irishman, Duggan Fearns. When Sellers lost after only a minute and a half of fighting, the gallery loudly accused both combatants of engaging in a swindle. Fearns never fought again, and Sellers, though continuing in the ring, was never afforded another chance at a match of any consequence. Boxing in England was now at its nadir.

Jack Harris, a man of very ordinary ability, then claimed the title. But so great was public apathy that no attempt was made to find a challenger. By the time Tom Johnson (whose real name was Tom Jackling) came forward, Harris had passed into the limbo of forgotten fighters, and it was Johnson who was acclaimed as champion in 1783 when he won a decisive victory over Jack Jarvis. Johnson's strength and science made him a popular figure, and his popularity increased as he met and defeated one challenger after another. In the eight years of Johnson's reign the sport regained much of the prestige it had lost in the dreary years following the dethronement of the great Broughton. When Johnson finally lost the championship to Big Ben Brain (also known as Brian and Bryan) in 1791, after eighteen rounds of furious fighting, the title passed with unquestioned honor for the first time in more than forty years.

This first period of English boxing, 1719 to 1791, may properly be described as belonging to three men: to Figg, the boxer who contributed the ingredients that got it started; to Broughton, who gave science to the ring and wrote a code of rules; and to Johnson, who rescued the sport from disrepute.

CHAPTER 2

DANIEL MENDOZA AND
HIS CONTRIBUTIONS

IT WAS THE rise of a brilliant new fighter, a man who did as much to advance the science of boxing in the 1790's as Jack Broughton had done half a century earlier, that marks the beginning of the second phase of English boxing. But before looking into the career and contributions of Daniel Mendoza, it might be well to get a general view of the sport in the last years of the eighteenth century and the early years of the nineteenth.

Most fights were held on the turf, a smaller number indoors on a stage or platform. There were normally no seats for spectators. Instead, the Fancy moved about more or less at will, placing bets and generally behaving with the arrogance that marked the true Georgian gentleman. It was to check the movements of the spectators, as much as for any other reason, that a ring—actually, as it is today, a square—was marked off by heavy corner posts and rails or ropes. Even with a ring, there was likely to be interference with the fighters, and Broughton's Rules of 1743 stipulated that only "the principals and their seconds" were to be permitted in the fighting area. Though Broughton did not define the fighting area, his rules provided that "a square of a yard" be marked and that at the beginning of a fight and following every fall thereafter each second was to bring his man "to the side of the square and place him opposite to the other." Broughton's rules further provided that after a fall, that is, after one of the combatants had either been dropped by a punch or thrown to the ground, half a minute should be allowed the victim to return to his side of the square. Failing, he was to be "deemed a beaten man." The rules also provided that neither adversary should strike his opponent when he was down, "or seize him by the ham, or breeches, or any part below the waist; a man on his knees to be reckoned down."

There were no rounds in the modern sense of three-minute fighting periods followed by one-minute rest periods. All fights were continuous, each round lasting until a fall had been scored, each battle ending only after one of the fighters was unable or unwilling to return to the side of the square within the time permitted. But lest anyone marvel unduly at the stamina of those early warriors of the ring who not infrequently fought a hundred rounds or more over a period of several hours, consider that many of those rounds lasted only a few seconds and that a tired fighter, simply by dropping to one knee at the mere touch of his opponent's fist, could rest for thirty seconds before continuing. Many bouts were excessively slow and uninteresting.

The typical encounter, however, was a lively and rather bloody affair. Specifically forbidden only to seize an opponent below the waist and to strike him when down, a fighter could employ his strength and guile in a variety of ways now unknown to the ring. He could trip his man, toss him with a cross-buttock, or grasp his head and beat it against one of the corner posts; he could pull his hair (and surely did if it was long enough), tweak his nose, and twist his ear; and in addition to punching his adversary, he could elbow him or poke him in the eye with a thumb. Almost the only limiting influence on a fighter's tactics was the attitude of the umpires. Boxing was usually rough, tough, and ugly.

Even a greater test of stamina in some ways than a fight for the championship was the training a fighter was expected to undergo. Indeed, one of the marvels of the ring was that the more conscientious athletes were able to come to the side of the square at all. Boxers, wrestlers, jockeys, and foot racers were all subjected to the most violent conditioning regimen. Even more debilitating, if possible, than the barbarous medical treatments customarily prescribed by contemporary physicians, training had by the turn of the nineteenth century become a cult. And a little later, with Captain Robert Barclay, a Scottish gentleman who had received his education at Cambridge University, as high priest, the ritual of training was followed almost as if its authority derived from holy writ.

In his *Boxiana* Pierce Egan describes Captain Barclay's recommendations for bringing athletes to a state of competitive perfection:

The skillful trainer attends to the state of the bowels, the lungs, and the skin; and he uses such means as will reduce the fat, and, at the same time, invigorate the muscular fibres. The patient is purged by drastic medicines; he is sweated by walking under a load of clothes, and by lying between feather-beds. His limbs are roughly rubbed. His diet is beef or mutton; his drink, strong ale; and he is gradually inured to exercise. . . . [He] enters upon his training with a regular course of physic, which consists of three doses. Glauber Salts are generally preferred; and from one ounce and a half to two ounces are taken each time, with an interval of four days between each dose. After having gone through the course of physic, he commences his regular exercise. . . . He must rise at five in the morning, run half a mile at top speed uphill, and walk six miles at a moderate pace, coming in about seven to breakfast, which should consist of beef-steaks or mutton-chops under-done, with stale bread and old beer. After breakfast, he must again walk six miles at a moderate pace, and at twelve lie down in bed without his clothes for half an hour. On getting up, he must walk four miles, and return by four to dinner, which should also be beef-steaks or mutton-chops, with bread and beer as at breakfast. Immediately after dinner, he must resume his exercise, by running half a mile at the top of his speed, and walking six miles at a moderate pace. He takes no more exercise for that day. . . .

After having gone on in this regular course for three or four weeks, he must take a four-mile sweat, which is produced by running four miles, in flannel, at the top of his speed. Immediately on returning, a hot liquor is prescribed. . . . It is termed the sweating liquor, and is composed of the following ingredients, viz. one ounce of caraway-seed; half an ounce of coriander-seed; one ounce of root liquorice; and half an ounce of sugar-candy; mixed with two bottles of cider, and boiled down to one-half. He is then put to bed

in his flannels, and being covered with six or eight pairs of
blankets and a feather-bed, must remain in this state from
twenty-five to thirty minutes, when he is taken out and
rubbed perfectly dry. Being then well wrapt in his great
coat he walks out gently for two miles, and returns to breakfast, which, on such occasions, should consist of a roasted
fowl. He afterwards proceeds with his usual exercise. These
sweats are continued weekly. . . . If the stomach be foul, an
emetic or two must be given, about a week before the conclusion of the training, and he is now supposed to be in the
highest condition.

Besides his usual or regular exercise, a person under training ought to employ himself in the intervals in every kind
of exertion, which tends to activity, such as cricket, bowls,
throwing quoits, &c. so that, during the whole day, both body
and mind may be constantly occupied.

Captain Barclay was a firm believer in meat as the best training food. He permitted no vegetables to be eaten "as they are
watery, and of difficult digestion." Butter and cheese were forbidden, "the one being very indigestible, and the other apt to
turn rancid on the stomach." Only the yolks of eggs (raw in
the morning) were given a place on the training table, and
milk was condemned "as it curdles on the stomach." Soups and
other warm fluids were outlawed. The trainee had discretion in
only one matter: of the foods allowed, he could eat as much or
as little as his appetite dictated.

Such was the broad pattern of fighting and training when
Daniel Mendoza appeared. Born in the Whitechapel section of
London's East End in 1763, he was the first Jew to attain fame
in the ring. His first fight, so far as records show, took place at
Mile End in 1784 against a behemoth known as Harry the Coal-
heaver. Mendoza won after a forty-minute battle. It was not
until three years later, however, that his name began to be
well known. After he had disposed of Martin the Bath Butcher
in April, 1787, his reputation was firmly established. By accom-
plishing in just twenty minutes a task that Richard Humphries,
"the gentleman boxer," already noted for his mastery of ring

science, had needed an hour and three quarters to perform, Mendoza established himself as the most skillful boxer of his day. Men whose recollections went back half a century unhesitatingly acclaimed him as greater than the now legendary Broughton.

RICHARD HUMPHRIES

It is futile, of course, to compare fighters of different eras, but there is little room for doubt about Mendoza's superiority in the science of boxing to all who had preceded him. Standing only five feet, seven inches, and probably weighing one hundred sixty at the outside, Mendoza fought the best men of his day. Not only did he win consistently, but even after 1795, when he lost the championship, he continued for years to be regarded as the greatest exponent of his art.

As early as 1790 a writer observed, "Mendoza is a pugilist better initiated in the theory of boxing than perhaps any of his contemporaries, and has produced some exceedingly expert pupils. In his manner there is more neatness than strength, and it has been said, more show than service; his blows are generally deficient in force, but given with astonishing quickness, and he is allowed to strike oftener, and stop more dexterously, than any other man; he is extremely well formed in the breast and arms, but his loins are very weak; his wind is good, and he possesses excellent bottom."

On the strength of this comment and others in like vein, as well as on what is known about his small stature, it is apparent that Mendoza took the measure of his opponents by a series of darting attacks balanced with strategic retreats. He introduced footwork of a sort previously unknown. He demonstrated that a light jab frequently landed could be a destructive blow and, conversely, that a roundhouse swing was worthless against a man who wasn't there. And he made it clear, both for his contemporaries and those who came after, that a medium-size boxer who was clever with his feet as well as his hands could always beat a slow-moving slugger, no matter how big he might be. Scientific boxing had been born.

According to Mendoza's own statement, supported by Pierce Egan, his ring career comprised thirty-five bouts. He won the championship on November 12, 1791, by defeating Bill Warr; he lost it April 15, 1795, to Gentleman John Jackson in nine rounds. But Mendoza's dethronement did not force him into retirement. Eleven years later he was still good enough to win a fifty-three-round battle from a rising young boxer, described as "an elegant sparrer," named Harry Lee, and in 1820, at the age of fifty-seven, he met Tom Owen for a purse of fifty guineas. That time Mendoza lost, and he never again entered a ring. He lived to the age of seventy-three, passing his last years as keeper of the Admiral Nelson, an inn very popular in his native Whitechapel.

Mendoza not only revolutionized boxing. He popularized the sport in a measure previously unknown. In 1791, the year in which he became champion of England, he signed a contract with Philip Astey, one of the leading horsemen of his day, to give boxing demonstrations. Astey was proprietor of the first traveling circus, and Mendoza's tour with this show provided many sections of England with their first view of a first-rate fighter in action. The circus also toured Scotland. After nine profitable months on the road, the champion was persuaded by his employer to risk a tour of Ireland. The risk was not so much financial as physical. At that time it was a dangerous venture for any Englishman to cross the Irish Sea and set foot in the land of the shamrock. Such an undertaking was doubly hazardous if the Englishman was, as in this case, a Jew.

Trouble began during the crossing when a small craft drew alongside the little ship on which Mendoza had embarked and made fast. Men began to board, with intentions that were clearly piratical, and it was the prompt activity of Mendoza, more than anything else, that drove them off. The champion went in swinging—he recognized the inadequacy of science in a gang fight— and in a moment he had knocked two of the attackers overboard. One of them drowned, and the rest, intimidated by the one-man hurricane, jumped back into their boat and made off.

Possibly this story was slightly exaggerated, but it had the useful effect of enhancing Mendoza's reputation, and when the champion reached Dublin he found a number of gentlemen eager both to see him in action and to test his skill. Prior to his arrival boxing in Ireland had been the activity almost exclusively of ruffians and plug-uglies, but so great was the renown of the trim, handsome fellow from London who had repeatedly demonstrated that brawn was not a prerequisite to success in the ring that the gentry thronged to study his technique. Mendoza soon opened a school, where he gave instruction to sons of the elite, and his gymnasium became the nucleus of the amateur sporting clubs which soon appeared in other parts of the country.

At this time one Squire Fitzgerald was known for his skill and daring in all branches of sport. In addition to being a fine amateur boxer, he was a fearless horseman, a crack shot, a noted foot racer, an accomplished swordsman, and a man of prodigious strength. Jealous of the attention that was being paid to Mendoza, he determined to enter the ring against him. A forthright man, he proceeded to Daly's Club, where the Englishman was giving an exhibition, and at once began to comment loudly and unfavorably on Jews in general and Mendoza in particular. Fitzgerald called Dan a trickster who had been fooling the public far too long and stated flatly that the Jew wouldn't stand a chance against a real fighter equipped with courage and determination. He concluded his remarks by issuing a challenge for a fight to the finish with bare fists.

When Mendoza declined to box without gloves, Fitzgerald exclaimed, "Gloves be damned! I've come here to show ye what an Irishman can do with his bare fists to a Jew and I demand action."

"So that's what you've come for," Mendoza replied with cold scorn. "Well, I must beg to decline having a set-to with a novice as you, except with gloves."

"Refuse and I'll brand you as a coward and faker throughout Ireland," snarled Fitzgerald.

"Me a coward!" shouted Mendoza angrily. "No man has ever dared to offer such an insult to me before, and you'll not go away to brag of it."

"Then you'll fight me, will you?" inquired the squire.

"Yes, I'll fight you," Mendoza answered, "and I'll give you the worst thrashing an Irishman ever received. But I shall continue to insist that we fight with gloves."

After a short conference among the Irishman's friends and backers, the Duke of Leinster stepped forward.

"Mr. Mendoza, we have come here expecting to see a set-to between you and our countryman," he stated. "We will give you fifty guineas if you will agree."

The promise of gold gave the match a brighter aspect, and Mendoza consented to fight then and there. The room was cleared of all persons except the immediate backers of the two men, the doors were locked, and the contestants stripped for action.

During the early part of the battle, Fitzgerald attacked vigorously, but he was quite unable to penetrate Mendoza's guard. Mendoza, taking care not to underestimate his adversary, confined himself to defensive tactics.

"Why don't you fight, you cowardly Jew?" Fitzgerald taunted.

"I thought you were a fighter and a champion. Are you the best England can produce?"

"I'm only playing with you," laughed Mendoza. He was waiting for the Irishman to lose his temper.

"Don't stand there grinning at me," shouted Fitzgerald. "Fight, I say, and don't try your cursed Jewish tricks on me."

"Well, if you'll have it, you shall have it," came back Mendoza, his smile suddenly vanishing. With that he whipped a right and a left to Fitzgerald's face, bringing blood and closing his left eye. After a further series of jabs and hooks had brought blood from both nose and mouth, the Irishman began for the first time to comprehend how fast and hard a professional could strike. He went to his knees under a terrific blow straight to the chin.

There was now dead silence in the gymnasium. When Fitzgerald regained his feet, Mendoza asked him whether he was ready to give up.

"Quit, shall I! Let me get at him," bellowed Fitzgerald, pushing his seconds aside. "I'll finish him yet."

He rushed in, and this time Mendoza dropped his opponent with a tremendous right between the eyes. Mendoza now altered his tactics, just by way of variety, and twice in succession threw Fitzgerald heavily to the floor. By that time the Irishman had nothing left but his gameness and a capacity for taking further punishment. But he was too proud to quit and he stood up to a beating that continued for more than half an hour. Then his backers and seconds succeeded in convincing him that he had lost honorably.

Bitter during the fight, Fitzgerald now showed himself to be a true sportsman. Taking Mendoza's hand and holding it aloft, he said to the winner, "You beat me fairly, and I may tell you that you are the only man who has ever done so, or even floored me. In the heat of the battle I used offensive expressions, and I ask you to forgive me. You are a great fighter, a true son of the Fancy, a credit to the sport and to your race. I'm proud to shake the hand of the bravest and most skillful fighter I've ever met."

When word of the fight got out, Mendoza was indeed a great hero. Before, he had been merely the champion of England. Now he was champion of Ireland—a matter of real con-sequence. To the other debt that boxing owes Mendoza must be added the one of arousing enthusiasm among the Irish. It would be hard to imagine the subsequent development of the sport without their participation on both sides of the Atlantic.

CHAPTER 3

GENTLEMAN JACKSON
AND HIS TIMES

T HE NEXT bright fistic star to shine after Daniel Mendoza was John Jackson, who won the championship in 1795. His entry into the ring was prompted by a spirit of adventure and an eagerness to occupy a place in the limelight rather than by the need, as with most fighters, to improve his economic position. Though his family, being engaged in a useful occupation, could not be classified as "gentry," the nineteen-year-old Jackson was on elbow-rubbing terms with the blue bloods. He was known to the Fancy as Gentleman Jackson, and he had the unique distinction of being referred to in British ring histories and other publications as *Mister* John Jackson.

Jackson's professional career began June 9, 1788, against a 230-pound giant from Birmingham named William Fewterell. Standing five feet, eleven inches, and weighing 198, Jackson was believed to have little chance to win from the veteran of eighteen fights who opposed him, and the betting odds reflected the popular conviction. But Jackson, possessed of "all those athletic requisites which constitute the beau ideal of perfect manhood," as the rich prose of the period painted him, was quite undisturbed by Fewterell's reputation. He met his early rushes with straight lefts and repeatedly rocked the bigger man with right crosses to the head. By the time five rounds had been fought, Fewterell was beginning to realize that his opponent, though a boy in years, was very mature in ring generalship. Jackson continued his methodical work, and gradually Fewterell weakened. After sixty-seven minutes of milling, Fewterell reached the stage of complete exhaustion and was obliged to retire from the battle.

Nearly a year passed before young Jackson again appeared

professionally. His opponent was George Ingleston, known as the Brewer, who was greatly admired for his hard hitting. The ring was set up in the court of an Essex inn. The date was March 12, 1789.

Ingleston had the advantage in weight, height, and reach, but Jackson was far more skillful. He dropped the Brewer to win the first and second rounds. In the third, just as he was closing in for the finish, Jackson skidded on the floor that had been soaked by a heavy rain several hours before the fight and turned his ankle. In spite of his courage, he was unable to continue, and Ingleston, on the verge of being knocked out, was declared winner.

Jackson brooded about this fight—it was unmistakably a case of the better man losing—and was so disturbed by its effect on his spirits that he decided to quit the ring forever. Many people concluded that he was prompted more by a growing dislike of his occupation than by his loss to Ingleston, but those who knew him well were aware that the true cause was a morbid fear that his reputation had been permanently destroyed. He did not fight again professionally for six years. It was only after Mendoza had enjoyed long acclaim as the greatest fighter of the ages that Jackson shook off his neurosis and challenged the champion.

The two great boxers met at Hornchurch on April 15, 1795, and at the end of just eleven minutes Jackson was champion of England. But though the victory was quick and complete, Jackson's triumph was not untainted. During a hot exchange of blows he had suddenly seized Mendoza's heavy hair, snapped his head down, and beat him into submission with the other hand. There was no technical violation—Broughton's Rules still governed and they prohibited only the seizing of an opponent below the waist—yet such an act as Jackson's had never been known in a championship fight, if only for the reason that experienced boxers wore their hair cropped close. Opinion was more or less evenly divided. One group held that Jackson had taken an advantage that was, to say the least, questionable. The other side maintained that Mendoza, like Absalom of biblical fame, had come to a deserved end through pride in his flowing curls.

Having won the championship, Jackson at once made it clear that he had been interested in only one thing: to prove to the world that he was the greatest living master of the ring. He immediately announced his retirement from competition in spite of strenuous efforts to persuade him to fight Mendoza and others, and thereafter he demonstrated his skill only as a teacher. Giving instruction was his true métier, and his boxing academy became famous.

Jackson was also a good deal of a snob, and he was very proud that his clientele was made up largely of young gentlemen, knights, and barons. Nor were the young blades any less proud to take lessons from the retired undefeated champion and to be seen in the company of this man of mighty shoulders and slender waist, who dressed in the height of fashion and vied with Beau Brummell and the Prince Regent for public attention.

One of the young blades was Lord Byron, the poet who "awoke one morning to find myself famous" and became the social lion of London. In spite of a club foot, Byron learned to be more than a merely competent boxer under Jackson's tutelage, and he continued through the rest of his short life to regard Jackson as a warm friend. From Italy Byron later wrote his teacher about being attacked by a thug, of whom he disposed "with a good English punch in the guts." And in *Hints from Horace* the poet paid immortal tribute to his master in the following couplet:

> And men unpracticed in exchanging knocks
> Must go to Jackson ere they dare to box.

In justice to Jackson it should also be noted that his predilection for the society of persons in high station did not destroy his popularity with the masses. When he was past fifty, after the accession of George IV, he was called upon to recruit the leading boxers of the period to help keep order during the time of the coronation. A number of noted fighters responded to Jackson's call, but it was as much the esteem in which the leader was held as the reputation of his strong-arm squad that accounted for the good behavior of the crowd.

It may be debated whether Jackson was ever quite as great

an artist in the ring as Mendoza. But there can be little doubt that he was a worthy champion, and none at all concerning his beneficial influence on the sport of boxing.

Although Jackson never defended the championship he won from Mendoza in 1795, he continued in effect to hold the title for five years, for during that time no one approaching his caliber as a fighter appeared. It was not until 1800 that an acceptable successor appeared. He was a nineteen-year-old of magnificent proportions named Jem Belcher. Just half a century earlier his grandfather, Jack Slack, had won the championship from Broughton.

Authorities vary concerning the year in which Belcher was first recognized as champion, but since he beat all but one of the fighters who opposed him between 1800 and 1803 and fought a draw with the one he failed to beat, the year 1800 is the most acceptable, though it was not until 1803 that he won decisively in seventeen rounds from Jack Bartholomew, the man who had previously drawn with him. In 1805 Belcher lost the championship to Henry Pearce, a mediocre boxer, but a fighter of such courage and persistence that he was nicknamed the Game Chicken; prior to this fight Belcher had been blinded in one eye while playing racquets, and the handicap was too great for him to overcome. It was Jem Belcher who first tied a handkerchief of distinctive color to the post in his corner, and thereafter most boxers flaunted their colors when they entered the ring.

Pearce, the new champion, had a friend named John Gully, a young merchant whose failure in business had landed him in debtors' prison. In that day there was no way for a bankrupt to win release except through discharge of his debts, and Gully might have languished behind bars for the rest of his life if a happy circumstance had not brought attention to his plight. He was visited by Pearce one day, and since he was an able amateur boxer, the two requested permission to stage an informal bout for the entertainment of the jail's inmates. They boxed with gloves, and Gully actually outpointed the champion. The story of the young prisoner's showing spread quickly—aided, no doubt, by Pearce's testimony—with the result that a rich sportsman offered to pay Gully's debts on condition that he agree to fight Pearce for the championship.

The two met on October 8, 1805, but on this occasion, fighting with bare knuckles, the experience of the Game Chicken

JOHN GULLY

was too much for Gully, who lost in sixty-four rounds. Pearce continued to hold the championship until 1808, when poor health compelled him to retire. He nominated his friend as the most worthy successor, and the choice was approved by the Pugilistic Club, which was the boxing commission of the time. But it was not until Gully had whipped Bob Gregson, called the Lancashire Giant, that he was fully accepted by the Fancy.

Once he had received unqualified popular acclaim, Gully resigned his title and turned to the race track. His success on the turf surpassed his fame in the ring. He had two winners of the Derby and won a considerable fortune. Later he became member of Parliament from Pontefract, Yorkshire.

EARLY NEGRO FIGHTERS

Meanwhile an external influence had begun to work on English boxing. That was the Negro fighter. Here and there one can find mention of a black man—generally he was a valet or groom—whose employer had taught him the ring science he himself had learned from a professional. But few of these colored servants, imported almost entirely from the West Indies, possessed the fighting spirit necessary to beat a tough Britisher, and none of them achieved notable success. It was not until Bill Richmond, son of a Georgia-born slave, appeared in England that boxing enthusiasts saw the first Negro fighter of real ability.

Born in 1763, the property of a Staten Island clergyman, Richmond first attracted attention during the occupation of New York by the British in the early part of the American Revolution. Only a boy, he whipped in quick succession three soldiers who had set upon him in a tavern. One of the assailants was Joseph Burns, a pugilist known as the Birmingham Blacksmith, who had fought professionally at home before going out to America in the army. His amazed comrades spread the story of how a black-skinned Yankee had whipped not only the experienced Burns but a couple of his cronies to boot.

The gossip of the private soldiers filtered through to their officers' quarters and in due time reached the ears of the commanding general, Earl Percy, later Duke of Northumberland. An ardent patron of the prize ring, his sporting instincts aroused by this extraordinary tale, Percy ordered the Negro to be brought to him. Finding Richmond might have been difficult had it not happened that later on the same night of his victory over the British trio he had been apprehended as a runaway from his clerical master's household.

When Richmond was brought in, the General sent for the discomfited Burns. Then and there the two were matched in an impromptu contest with gloves. Percy and his officers applauded generously when the Negro, showing wonderful dexterity and hitting powers, compelled the soldier to quit after three minutes of slugging.

Highly pleased with his find, the General took Richmond into his household service. When Percy and his troops embarked for England after the American Revolution, Richmond accompanied the General, and under his patronage the Negro, who was hardly more than a welterweight, defeated several top heavyweights.

Richmond first gained public attention overseas in 1791 at the York races, where Docky Moore, a Sheffield knife grinder who had a reputation as a bully and a troublemaker, decided to test Richmond's mettle. Though the Negro scaled only 150 pounds to 211 for his adversary, he battered Moore into submission in short order.

On his next appearance in the ring at the York races, Richmond gave a well-deserved beating to two Inniskillen dragoons who had insulted him because of his color, and three days later he whipped a blacksmith for the same reason. At the White Conduit House in London, Richmond increased his growing popularity by thrashing Paddy Green and further enhanced his reputation a little later by defeating Frank Meyers, the York Bully.

His first setback came at the hands of George Maddox, who knocked him out after flooring him three times, but in his next fight, with Youssep the Jew, on May 21, 1805, Richmond won handily in six rounds. A number of fighters now sought matches with him, and he agreed to meet Jack Holmes, alias Tom Tough, a coachman who had previously been whipped by Tom Cribb in a bout that lasted one hour.

The contest with Holmes was the first in which Richmond appeared in a twenty-four-foot ring and was his initial test against a fighter of real capacity. This bout took place on July 12, 1805, at Crickenwood and excited great interest, for after fourteen years of fighting in England, the American had become a favorite with the Fancy. The fight was fast and bloody, with hard hitting on both sides. In the twenty-sixth round Richmond cut his opponent's face badly, then put him away with several rights to the jaw. The battle lasted thirty-five minutes.

Now past forty-two, Richmond looked for bigger prey, and his backers made overtures to Tom Cribb, who had his eye on the championship. Tom quickly accepted.

TOM CRIBB

While training for the bout, Richmond became unruly. The former slave, a good-natured, easy-going fellow, had acquired a pronounced liking for fast company and good liquor. He found life in London to his taste in every respect, with the result that he was not in condition when he faced Cribb. Despite this handicap, Richmond fought so desperately and with such courage that an hour and a half elapsed before Cribb knocked him out.

Richmond took his defeat very much to heart. He temporarily retired and didn't appear again in a public ring until he faced

Jack Carter at Epsom Downs on April 14, 1809. One of England's best heavyweights, Carter knocked the Negro senseless in the second round—but Richmond was back on his feet within the thirty seconds allowed, and at the end of twenty-five minutes the Negro had whipped his man. In his next contest the American beat Atkinson of Banbury in twenty minutes and followed that with a victory over Ike Wood, a water man, on July 11, 1809, in twenty-three rounds. On August 9, Richmond faced his former conqueror, George Maddox, now fifty-four years old, who succeeded in going fifty-two rounds before yielding to his younger rival.

Richmond now retired from the ring and opened a tavern, the Horse and Dolphin, where he did an excellent business. But the American was first and last a fighting man, and at the age of fifty-two he entered the Pugilistic Club's tournament and defeated a powerful fighter, Tom Davis, to win the fifty-guinea prize. Richmond's next mill was with Tom Shelton on August 11, 1815, and again he won, this time in twenty-three rounds that lasted twenty-nine minutes.

By now Richmond was enormously popular, and the Horse and Dolphin became the rendezvous of London's leading sportsmen. Lord Byron was a frequenter. Evidence of his friendly interest in Richmond is revealed in *His Lordship's Life and Journals,* edited by Thomas Moore.

In 1818 Jack Carter, who had lost to Richmond nine years before, posted a second challenge, and on November 12 the former slave, despite his fifty-five years, won the fight that was to mark his final appearance in the prize ring. Richmond now retired permanently to the Horse and Dolphin. He died in London at the age of sixty-six.

Richmond was the first native-born American to win high honors in the ring. It was his success that induced another American slave, the celebrated Tom Molineaux, to invade the London field.

Tom, who adopted the surname of his owner, was born in Virginia on March 23, 1784. He was stocky, short, and very muscular, and in his prime weighed about 200 pounds. At the age of fourteen, after his father Zachary had died, Tom became the handy man around his master's estate. Two years later, when Randolph Peyton, a neighbor, boasted that not a slave in any Virginia family could take the measure of his own slave, Abe, Squire Molineaux asked for a volunteer from among his chattels to test his neighbor's boast. Tom eagerly responded. He was matched with Abe and promised his freedom if he won the battle.

A considerable sum was wagered on the outcome. It was up to young Tom to win a fortune for his master and gain his own freedom, and he succeeded. With freedom came a desire to see the world. Tom learned that the ship *Bristol* was in need of a deckhand, and he asked for the job. Two days later he sailed for England.

While at sea Tom got the urge to become a professional fighter. After watching several boxing contests on board the ship, he was sure that he could fight better than any of the men he had seen in action. When he landed, he resolved to follow in Richmond's footsteps. He offered to fight any man in England, and with Richmond's help he found a backer who matched him with Burrows, a protégé of Tom Cribb who himself was to win the championship in 1809. Burrows was hopelessly outclassed by the powerful Negro.

Other matches followed, and as time went on, Molineaux built up a formidable reputation. Fighter after fighter fell before him, and in 1809, he gave "Tom Tough," whom Richmond had beaten several years earlier, a terrific drubbing.

Immediately after this victory, Molineaux discharged a bomb that shook sporting England to its foundations. This was a declaration that he claimed the championship.

In support of his claim, the Negro pointed to the fact that Cribb, who had won the title a short while before, had at once retired. Tom further remarked that he had beaten the best men the Pugilistic Club had selected for him as opponents. If Cribb thought he could defeat him, let him return to the ring and do battle, the Negro insisted.

Molineaux's claim was first regarded as a piece of impudence

—it was unparalleled effrontery on the part of an American and a black American at that. But the claim also was entirely rational. Besides the Fancy had confidence in Cribb, and in response to the insistent demand for his services, he finally agreed to tackle Molineaux. The bout took place on December 18, 1810, at Copthall Common, Sussex. This first international title bout, and the first between a Negro and white man in which the crown was involved, was fought in a cold driving rain, and Cribb was returned the victor at the end of fifty-five minutes.

Unable to force Cribb into a return engagement immediately, Molineaux issued a challenge to any man in England, and Joe Rimmer accepted. Rimmer was so easily beaten by the dark-skinned American that again the cry went up for Cribb to come to the rescue, for Molineaux once more claimed the heavyweight championship.

Thus Cribb again found himself subjected to heavy pressure on all sides to return to the ring. During the months which had elapsed since the bout with Molineaux, the champion had lived a life of careless ease, and the fat had piled up on his frame. He feared it would be impossible for him to get back into condition, but the pressure continued, and at last Cribb consented to a return engagement.

The fight took place at Thistleton Gap, Leicester, before a crowd estimated at 25,000. This time the weather was good, but Molineaux was grossly fat, and it was evident that he must win quickly if he were to win at all.

Molineaux tore into his opponent at the start. He set such a fast pace and carried the fight to his antagonist with such ferocity that for a time it looked as if Cribb would be knocked out. At the end of the eleventh round, however, the Negro, exhausted and unable to stand, gave in. Tom Cribb was still champion. The fight had lasted nineteen minutes and eleven seconds.

Molineaux continued to fight for a time. But excessive dissipation broke down his health, and he contracted tuberculosis. On August 4, 1818, the great Negro fighter who might have been champion died at the age of thirty-four.

Tom Spring, and Others

Tom Spring came into this world under the name of Winter. But, outside the ring, Tom was one of the mildest and most cheerful individuals, and it was said that he changed his name to conform with his temperament. Born in 1795, Tom was only

TOM SPRING

seventeen when he won his first victory over "Hammer" Hollands, a pugilist of great hitting power. In this battle Spring's agility and tactics astonished the experts, especially the then champion, Cribb, who took the young man under his wing and taught him much of the craft and ring generalship for which he was famous.

After defeating Stringer, a pupil of Bill Richmond, in a battle lasting thirty-nine minutes, Spring, through Cribb's influence, was matched with Ned Painter. He won in thirty-one rounds. Painter, partially disabled in the early stages of the contest by a fall, demanded a second meeting. Spring agreed, but this time he was the victim of a first-round punch that closed his right eye. Nevertheless, he battled on desperately through forty-one rounds before yielding.

This was the only time in a long and honorable career that Spring suffered defeat. The youngster, advertised by Cribb as the best lad of his years in all England. kept on milling and whipped in turn Jack Carter, Ben Burn, Bob Burn, Joshua Hudson (known as the John Bull Fighter because he resembled the cartoonists' stock character), and Tom Oliver.

In consequence of these victories, Tom Cribb announced his retirement as champion and named Spring as the man most worthy of holding the title. Cribb's choice pleased the Pugilistic Club and, on the whole, satisfied the fistic brotherhood. But from the town of Bristol, birthplace of Bill Neate, came a roar of protest. Naming as champion a youngster who had never shown much slugging ability but had won his battles simply through flashy sparring and tricky work was an insult to the great Neate—and consequently to Bristol. Public feeling on the subject ran high at Bristol, for Neate had recently knocked out the celebrated Tom Hickman the Gasman, thus achieving undying fame as the hero of William Hazlitt's magazine story, "The Fight."

Neate, although deservedly eulogized by Hazlitt for his gallant victory over the Gasman, was not what boxing fans today would call a first-rater. The Bristol pugilist's name would never have shone above scores of his contemporaries had not a gifted writer been present to chronicle the scene.

Hazlitt's article appeared in the *New Monthly Magazine* in February, 1822, and although the fine art of press ballyhoo was still in its formative stages, Bill Neate's fame expanded enormously. The net result was that Spring and Neate met for the title on Hinckley Downs, May 17, 1823, before thirty-five thousand spectators. Neate surrendered after thirty-seven minutes of fighting. The Bristol man asserted that he had broken his arm and couldn't continue, but what really beat him was Spring's superb science.

The Irish champion, John Langan, now challenged Spring, and the two met on the turf at Worcester race course for the English title. When Spring was declared winner, after seventy-seven rounds and two hours, twenty-nine minutes, the cry went up throughout Ireland that its favorite son had been jobbed, even though Langan admitted that he had failed to come to scratch at the call of time after being floored. But Langan was eager for a return engagement, and Spring agreed to meet him again.

For this fight Langan insisted on a raised platform to protect him from the crowd. Previously the turf ring had been broken by the spectators, and Langan, a fearless, scientific fighter, was anxious for the second fight to go to a finish. He was confident that he would win the championship.

Langan weighed 176 pounds to Spring's 190. The battle was a close one, shifting back and forth for seventy-six rounds, at the end of which Langan was forced to retire. So popular was the Irish champion that even in defeat he was acclaimed.

After this second victory over Langan, Tom Spring decided to retire. Opening an inn, he continued to prosper. He died August 20, 1851, at the age of fifty-six.

Spring's successor to the heavyweight title was Tom Cannon, who was crowned in 1824 by virtue of two victories over Joshua Hudson, the John Bull Fighter, who had previously beaten the promising Jem Ward. But Cannon's reign was short. He was challenged by Ward, born in 1800, who relieved him of the crown July 19, 1825, at Warwick. The temperature was above 90 degrees, and the fight lasted only ten minutes.

For a year and a half the new champion was in undisputed possession of the title. Then along came Peter Crawley, known as Young Rump Steak, to challenge him. Peter, twenty-eight years old, had lost only one fight, to Hickman the Gasman. Crawley and Ward met for the championship January 2, 1827, and in the eleventh round the challenger won by a knockout. Two days later he announced his retirement. Not since the day of Waterman Lyons had anyone been so contemptuous of the championship.

Upon Crawley's retirement, Ward reclaimed the title and offered to fight all comers. For more than a year no one came forward, and then Jack Carter challenged. He and Ward clashed May 27, 1828, Carter losing in seventeen rounds. Then followed Ward's last battle, against Simon Byrne, champion of Ireland. On July 12, 1831, they fought at Warwick, with Jem the winner

TOM CANNON

after an hour and seventeen minutes. Ward announced his retirement a year later, and like so many other champions, he became the owner of a tavern. He lived to the age of eighty-one.

A DEAF CHAMPION

James "Deaf" Burke was Ward's successor as champion. He was the son of a Thames waterman who plied his trade at the Strand Lane stairs, and the Deaf 'Un, as he was later affectionately known to his admirers, grew up along the river front. He learned neither to read nor to write, yet no more decent and courageous fellow ever graced the prize ring than this English-born Irishman who became the first globe-trotter in the history of boxing.

Near the Strand, where young James often passed, stood a tavern called The Spotted Dog, the landlord of which was Joe Parish, formerly a waterman, and a fighter of no mean ability. One day during a heavy rain Burke asked for shelter, and Parish not only took him in but gave him dry clothes and warm food. Learning that the boy had been orphaned, and impressed with his sturdy frame, Parish put him to work and began to teach him ring science.

Only sixteen years old at the time, Burke began to practice in earnest. He visited the training quarters of the leading fighters and progressed rapidly under Parish's guidance. Parish believed in Burke. Waiting until his pupil was nineteen, he matched him with a tough veteran, Ned Murphy.

Burke's first professional encounter went fifty rounds before darkness set in and halted proceedings, an exacting test for an inexperienced, untried youth. Next day the boxing world was agog over the "Irish-Saxon, who bids well to make his name in pugilism."

Burke quickly followed his debut with three victories, for a total of four fights in less than a year. He took on Tom Hands, a butcher, and trounced him in ten rounds. Only two days later, on August 16, 1828, he tackled a giant Negro, Sambo the Black, and stopped him in thirty-three minutes. The following winter, on March 10, 1829, he beat a fighter named Young Berridge in eleven rounds.

Parish felt that the time was now ripe for his charge to face some better talent. He obtained backing for a match with the formidable Irishman, Fitzmaurice, and a bout was arranged to take place during Epsom week, following the running of the Derby. But prize fighting had not yet attained the status of complete respectability, and on the day before the proposed battle the rivals were arrested and placed under bond to preserve the peace for three months.

Just after this, Burke became a London hero by his daring

rescue of several persons from a burning building. According to a newspaper report, "he dashed into the blazing furnace with reckless abandon, making trip after trip, until he had rescued many persons. He carried out a child, then went back and brought out another, and a third time carried a woman to safety. Again and again he returned amongst the debris and succeeded in bringing out two more children, one of whom died in his arms."

Perhaps it was this valiant exploit which caused the magistrates to relent. In any case, Burke was permitted to fight Fitzmaurice only a week after the original match had been canceled. The battle was one of the longest on record, lasting just five minutes under three hours. At the end of 150 rounds both men were on the verge of collapse. In the final session a left to the face caused Fitzmaurice to fall, and his seconds, fearing fatal results, halted proceedings. Burke was declared winner.

One of the few reverses which Burke experienced in his long career took place in his next battle. William Cousens was his opponent. Their fight, on August 25, 1829, in a meadow near Whetstone, went 111 rounds and lasted two hours and five minutes. The following December found Burke again in the ring, this time with a big, clumsy fellow called Young Girdler, to whom he handed an unmerciful lacing. He next defeated Andrew Gow, a raw-boned Scotchman, and a little later he disposed of Bob Hampson, who was vaunted as a coming champion. Timothy Crawley, a clever Irish fighter, fell before him not long afterward.

Other victories followed, most notably the ones over Birmingham Jack Davis, on February 22, 1831, and James Blissett, on May 28 of the same year. Then an injury to one of his legs, caused by a rowing accident, kept Burke on the side lines for nearly twelve months. Fully recovered after a long stay in the hospital, he met the veteran Jack Carter on May 2, 1832, at the Old Barge House, Woolwich, before a select gathering. The Deaf 'Un obtained the verdict in the eleventh round when Carter broke his arm on Burke's tough head.

It was after this encounter that Jem Ward, who had conquered Simon Byrne in their contest for the heavyweight championship of England, publicly announced his retirement from the ring. Burke, having whipped all who cared to test his mettle, laid claim to the title and offered to defend it against all comers. Although Burke's record justified the claim, a gigantic farmer from Hull, Harry Macone, disputed his right to the crown. Macone had distinguished himself by beating several stalwart yokels in his vicinity, and his admirers had bestowed on him the resounding epithet of Yorkshire Hero.

The Hero's challenge was quickly taken up, and a real slugging match followed. Burke was battered hard and frequently floored, but his science triumphed. He took Macone's measure after fifty-nine rounds and so became the acknowledged successor to Jem Ward as heavyweight champion.

Simon Byrne now came forward to contest for the honor he had missed when Ward beat him in 1831. He and Burke battled at St. Albans through ninety-eight rounds that lasted three hours and sixteen minutes, the longest heavyweight championship fight on record.* Burke won, but Byrne died in consequence of the beating he took. The shock was so great that the champion forsook the prize ring for a time, supporting himself meanwhile by giving exhibitions in England, Scotland, and Wales. It was a meager livelihood at best. The Deaf 'Un had slight talent for making money, and poverty did not aid in shaking off the depression which Byrne's death had brought upon him. He decided upon a change of scene. Late in 1833 he began to think about going to America.

Another factor prompted Burke in his decision to cross the Atlantic. That was the presence in the United States of Samuel O'Rourke, who had succeeded Simon Byrne as champion of Ireland. There was great bitterness between O'Rourke and Burke. That story, however, belongs more properly to the history of pugilism in America and will be told in its appropriate place.

* Longer fights have been recorded, but they were not championship bouts.

CHAPTER 4

BOXING'S BEGINNINGS
IN AMERICA

IN AMERICA the sport of boxing developed slowly. One reason why it lagged so far behind in the United States was that lads who were handy with their fists were likely to take ship for England, where a market for their special wares was known to exist. The ones who met with success on the other side had no reason ever to leave the dazzling city of London; those who failed attracted slight attention when they returned home. In other words, the British prize ring was exceedingly remote from wild, uncouth America, and such effect as it exerted was for many years of trifling magnitude.

Even in ports like Boston, New York, Philadelphia, and Charleston, where pugnacious British sailors were not unknown and international brawling along the water front was common enough, there was almost no organized boxing. Such combat was illegal, and the infrequent matches were hidden from the authorities in back rooms of drinking places or private clubs, with only a handful of spectators present. It was not an atmosphere to encourage the sport.

Nearly a century elapsed between the crowning of James Figg as first champion of England and the first ring fight in America under rules prescribed (and accepted and observed by the principals) for bare-knuckle fighting in England. The fight took place in 1816 in New York City between Jacob Hyer and Tom Beasley, and the only thing that can be reported concerning it is that Hyer won. It was his only bout. He retired after his triumph and for the next twenty-five years organized pugilism in this country was dormant. Not until 1841, when Jacob's son Tom beat Country McClusky, was there a recognized champion of the United States.

But though the fight in 1816 between Beasley and Jacob Hyer must be accepted as the first fight held in America under the bare-knuckle code, the honor of having his name first identified with the ring belongs to Zachary Molineaux, whose son Tom distinguished himself in England. The following excerpt from the Philadelphia *Register* in the year 1788 is the earliest known published mention of boxing in the United States:

> Zachary Thomas Molineaux, a Virginia slave who fought for the colonists in the recent strife with England, was haled before our magistrate last Friday to answer a charge of assault brought against him by Silas Freeman, and for the disturbance of the peace in that he engaged in a fight. Molineaux, whose record of loyalty to the colonies did him well at the hearing, was admonished and dismissed from custody after an apology. He is known in Virginia as a Negro whose mauleys have downed many opponents in fist bouts.
>
> This war-like hero who was the conquering pugilist of Virginia is a member of a family that possesses considerable pugilistic excellence and bottom. Before being discharged, Zachary Molineaux promised that he never again would commit assault nor appear on a public highway in a fist fight.

In 1818, two years after the Hyer-Beasley fight, an Englishman named William Fuller, who had once been beaten by Molineaux in London, opened a boxing school in Charleston. He laid claim to the American championship, but since he did nothing but give exhibitions, no one paid great attention to the claim. As an instructor, however, Fuller must be given credit for stimulating interest in the science of boxing during the years he lived in this country.

The first real excitement over an organized match in the United States was provided by two gentlemen of Irish blood. One of them was Deaf Burke, the first holder of the English championship to cross the Atlantic. The other was his mortal enemy, Sam O'Rourke, champion of Ireland.

After the death of Simon Byrne in his bout against Burke, O'Rourke challenged Byrne's killer to a fight for the championship. But since he qualified his challenge by specifying that the match be held in Ireland, Burke, a sensible man, did not respond. It was obvious to the sporting world that O'Rourke's intentions were not wholly serious. But his challenge brought him the publicity he was looking for, and when he set off for the United States a little later, he was more than ready to let the innocent

DEAF BURKE

infer that Burke's failure to fight had constituted a resignation of the title. Safely across the Atlantic, O'Rourke began a campaign of abuse against Burke and thereby succeeded in building up his own reputation.

Meanwhile Burke was preparing to come to the United States himself. When he learned that O'Rourke was vilifying him in New York, he speeded up his preparations. He landed in the New World in February, 1834. Almost simultaneously the valiant O'Rourke departed in haste for the South.

Safely below the Mason and Dixon line, O'Rourke traveled

from place to place and earned considerable prestige and money by giving boxing exhibitions with two other Irish fighters, O'Connell and Gallagher. Eventually reaching New Orleans, he built up a big following among Irish longshoremen and members of crews of vessels that plied between England and the Gulf of Mexico.

Burke remained in New York, and while waiting for a fistic engagement, he earned his living by means of the same exhibitions that he had given on a tour of England and Wales just before he left for America: He appeared in representations of Greek and Roman statuary.

Down in New Orleans, O'Rourke opened a boxing club in the rear of his place and put on savage bare-fist encounters in which rivermen and smugglers figured. This tavern prospered. All through the winter of 1835 O'Rourke conducted boxing matches at his club, and as his personal reputation grew, he augmented it by publishing cards in the papers to the effect that in the following spring he proposed to go to England to fight the best men there—"preferably Burke, who murdered Byrne." Swollen with success, he published, in February, 1836, a sweeping challenge to the world in the New Orleans newspapers. Styling himself champion of America and Ireland, he offered to fight any man in the world for a side bet of one thousand dollars.

Deaf Burke, still in New York, had just filled a theatrical engagement at Conklin's Hall when he read O'Rourke's challenge, which had been reprinted in one of the local papers. He conferred with William Fuller, the English boxing instructor, who agreed to back Burke for five hundred dollars against O'Rourke. Burke immediately started off on the long and uncomfortable journey to New Orleans.

On the day of the fight, according to the New Orleans *Item,* "from an early hour swarms of men—fashionable Creoles, French gamblers, halfbreeds, Yankee sharps, Irish toughs, and smugglers and picaroons from the Barataria swamps and lakes—began to leave New Orleans for the field of battle. A regulation twenty-four foot ring, with outer ropes after the English fashion, was erected. The heterogeneous mob closed thick around the enclosure, reflecting the belligerent mood which was natural in the gathering of so many and varied nationalities. Hardly a man was there who had not ruffian stamped on his face save the few English gentlemen and Creole aristocrats, and there was a free and ostentatious display of pistols, bowie knives, bludgeons, and sling shots. The rough element—in a heavy majority—was the O'Rourke contingent, and Caldwell whispered to his English friend, Brandham, the cotton buyer, that Burke wouldn't have a chance with that gang."

With the first call of time, it was evident that the roughs would allow Burke not even a semblance of fair play. Breaking the outer barrier of ropes, they surged around the inner ring shouting insults at the Englishman and calling on O'Rourke to pulverize Simon Byrne's assassin.

The first round ended with Burke throwing O'Rourke heavily with a cross-buttock. Then in the second, the rowdies began their open interference with the British champion. Mickey Carson, one of O'Rourke's seconds, sprang into the ring and violently shoved the Deaf 'Un into the arms of his opponent. Burke was taken off his guard and O'Rourke easily hurled him to the ground.

Burke, assisted to his feet by his seconds, turned on Mickey Carson and swore he'd bash his face in if he tried it again. Carson responded by drawing from under his loose blouse a bowie knife. With a vile oath he replied that if Burke came near him he'd rip him from the navel to the chin.

At the opening of the third round, Burke landed two powerful blows near O'Rourke's right eye and had his opponent clearly in distress. Mickey Carson again attempted his interference. Burke turned on him in fury, and with a straight left he caught Carson full on the nose and sent him crashing to the ground. The ruffians, with cries of rage, cut the ropes and swarmed into the ring. Burke stood his ground for a moment and bowled over several of his assailants, including O'Rourke's other second, a levee tough named McSweeney. Jim Phelan, one of Burke's seconds, did his best to stay the mob, but seeing that the toughs were intent on killing the British champion, he cried to Burke, "Run for your life!"

Burke broke through the thinnest part of the crowd and gained the fringe of the nearby wood. There Mr. Caldwell, a theater proprietor, who had stood by him and attempted to hold back the would-be murderers, provided him with a horse ready saddled for such an emergency, placed a bowie knife in his hand, and bade him ride as fast as the nag would carry him.

Burke, naked save for his muddy fighting trunks and spiked shoes, his brawny torso all stained and streaked with blood, his face bruised and swollen, holding the bridle of the horse in one hand and waving the bowie knife in the other like a Comanche, galloped madly toward the distant city. He frightened fashionable Creole ladies out for an afternoon drive and threw people along the way into panic with the thought that a maniac had escaped from the high-walled insane asylum out on the city commons.

Burke did not spare the horse. He urged the failing animal over the newly laid cobblestone of Chartres Street, crossed Canal Street into the recently opened American section of the Gravier plantation, known as Camp Street, and pulled up in front of Mr. Caldwell's St. Charles Theater. Leaping from his panting, foam-flecked steed, he ran through the narrow alley, pushed aside the startled watchman at the players' entrance, and rushed upon the open stage, where Junius Brutus Booth, the great tragedian, was rehearsing Macbeth with the stock company. In his strange St. Giles dialect, worse than the most involved Cockney, Burke explained his predicament to the astonished tragedian, and Booth volunteered to hide him in his dressing room until the gendarmes could be summoned from the Cabildo.

Four days after the fight, the English master of fisticuffs boarded a Mississippi steamboat bound for St. Louis and made his way back to New York. Lucky to be alive, he remained in America long enough to fight and defeat Paddy O'Connell in ten rounds at Hart's Island. In the summer of 1838 the man who was champion of England returned to his native land. The United States had no recognized champion at that time, but it would be a matter of simple justice to recognize Burke now as the fighter most deserving of the title in 1838.

A MICHIGAN MASTODON IN ENGLAND

Although Burke's visit to the United States did much to stimulate boxing on this side of the Atlantic, from the British point of view the tour was merely a provincial junket. It passed almost unnoticed in London, and Burke himself passed into oblivion in 1839, when he lost the English championship to William Thompson, whose *nom de guerre* was Bendigo.

Perhaps the most interesting feature of that bout was the new set of rules under which it was conducted. Broughton's Rules, in use for nearly a hundred years, were replaced in 1838 by the London Prize Ring Rules, and the Burke-Bendigo set-to was the first title match to employ the revised code.

Many of the refinements specified in the new rules had for some time been in use, but uniformity had hitherto been lacking. Codification assured that all fights would be conducted under the same general conditions. The size of the ring was standardized. The "square of a yard" in the center was replaced by a "scratch." Contestants were forbidden to kick, gouge, and butt with their heads. If either fighter deliberately went down without having been struck or thrown, his disqualification was made automatic. Seconds were obliged to remain outside the ring except between rounds. These and other changes did much to clean up the sport, and they had the double advantage of making boxing safer for the fighters and lifting its tempo for the paying customers.

After winning the championship, Bendigo suffered an injury to his knee, and he was forced to stop fighting. Early in 1841 Nick Ward, younger brother of Jem, met "Big Ben" Caunt and defeated him. In a return match lasting only thirty-five minutes, Ward lost. Caunt claimed the championship and shortly thereafter left on a tour of the United States. Interest in boxing had increased tremendously in America, and the English titleholder profited handsomely by giving exhibitions in various parts of the country.

While on tour, Caunt was challenged by an unknown gentleman from Michigan named Charles Freeman. It was said that his backers were ready to post ten thousand dollars, an un-heard-of sum in those days, and Caunt eagerly hurried to New York, where the fight was to be held. There he experienced the nastiest shock of his life. Freeman turned out to be a giant, towering six feet, ten inches, magnificently muscled and propor-tioned. Although Caunt was a big man himself, he wanted no part of the challenger—at least not in the ring. Instead he offered

BEN CAUNT

to take Freeman under his wing, promising to make his fortune if he would accompany him to England. The big boy from the Wolverine State quickly agreed, and in March, 1842, Caunt and his protégé began their tour of the British Isles.

Nothing like Freeman had ever been seen, and the money poured in everywhere he was billed to give exhibitions. The Primo Carnera of the nineteenth century was a competent boxer, very agile for his weight and size, and his fame increased. So great was his reputation that for months no fighter could be persuaded to meet him in a match to the finish. It was not until late in the

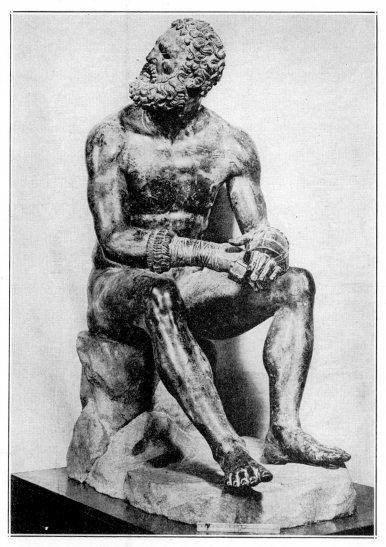

Ancient Greek boxer, complete with cauliflower ears. This bronze statue is in the Museo delle Terme in Rome.

Jack Broughton and Jack Slack as they squared off for their championship bout in 1750.

Daniel Mendoza (left), who revolutionized
ring science, and Richard Humphries. They
met four times, Mendoza winning the last
two fights.

Bendigo (William Thompson), who won the title from Deaf Burke in 1839.

Henry Pearce, the "Game Chicken," champion of England, 1805.

Gentleman John Jackson, who won the championship from Mendoza in 1795. Although he at once resigned the title, Jackson remained the most celebrated figure in British boxing for another twenty-five years.

Typical prize fight of the early nineteenth century. While the artist may have burlesqued his drawing slightly, the seconds and bottleholders closely attended their principals all through a fight.

Tom Molineaux, American Negro, as he faced the English champion, Tom Cribb, in 1810. Cribb won.

Jem Ward, champion of England,
1825.

Tom Cribb, champion of England,
1809.

A sparring exhibition at the Fives Court in London, from the painting by T. Blake, about 1820.

Tom Sayers, champion of England, 1857.

Jem Mace, champion of England, who won the world bareknuckle title in 1870 by defeating Tom Allen at Kennerville, Louisiana.

Tom Hyer, first recognized holder of the American championship, 1841.

1858: John Morrissey (left) successfully defending the American title against John C. Heenan, the "Benicia Boy." Challenged to a return bout. Morrissey resigned the championship to Heenan.

year that Bill Perry, who was known professionally as the Tipton Slasher, issued a challenge.

On the afternoon of December 6, 1842, the battle began. From the start the American forced the fighting, Perry frequently falling to avoid punishment. At the end of seventy rounds the referee called a halt on account of darkness and ordered the bout continued the following day. Perry, however, was in no hurry to resume a contest in which he had suffered so severely, and he succeeded in having the battle put off for two weeks. When the contestants resumed, Perry did little but drop to the ground every time they came to close quarters. He was so plainly outclassed and unwilling to fight that the referee disqualified him in the thirty-seventh round.

This was Freeman's last fight. A little later the first American who might have claimed the championship of the world was struck down by tuberculosis. In spite of his vast bulk, he gradually wasted away, and on October 18, 1845, he died.

Shortly after the beginning of Freeman's illness, Ben Caunt returned to the ring and once more claimed the crown. Several years passed before a satisfactory opponent could be found, but in 1845 he was matched against the old war horse Bendigo, whose injured knee had forced him to retire half a dozen years earlier. Caunt was awarded the decision after seventy-five bitterly contested rounds, when the referee disqualified his opponent, who had lost his footing, for going down without having been struck. Bendigo fought once more, this time winning from Tom Paddock on a foul. He then permanently retired and, having been moved by the fervor of an itinerant evangelist, became a preacher himself.

When Caunt retired from active competition, Perry, the Tipton Slasher, once more came forward. He fought the best men available and vindicated himself for his poor showing against Freeman in 1842. In 1850 he became champion, winning from Tom Paddock in twenty-seven rounds on a foul.

On September 29, 1851, Perry dropped the title the same way he had won it, losing on a foul to Harry Broome. By a curious turn of the wheel of fortune, Tom Paddock, who had three times contested for the championship, was the man to wrest the title from Broome, on May 19, 1856, after one hour and three minutes. Two years later, on June 16, 1858, Tom Sayers, one of the gamest fighters in ring history, defeated Paddock for the heavyweight title in a battle lasting one hour and twenty minutes.*

By this time, although the change was hardly visible, the focal point of pugilism had shifted from England to the United States. The history of boxing was destined hereafter to be concerned largely with action in the American ring.

FIRST AMERICAN CHAMPION

The visits of Deaf Burke and Ben Caunt to these shores did much for American prize fighting, but the game was so sternly frowned upon and repressed by the authorities that it had to be largely conducted on a bootleg basis. Needless to say, the unfavorable conditions hindered the development of native talent.

The first authentic battle fought here under regulation rules was the contest between Jacob Hyer and Tom Beasley in 1816. But for a quarter of a century afterward, although impromptu bouts took place in various sections of the country, there was no recognized American heavyweight champion. Then Tom Hyer, son of Jacob, beat Country McClusky (or McClosky) at Caldwell's Landing on the Hudson. This first unmistakable fight for the championship was held September 9, 1841. It went 101 rounds and lasted two hours and fifty-five minutes.

Pugilism in Tom Hyer's day was curiously mixed up with politics. In New York, Tammany Hall had in its train a dangerous band of picked fighting men. The Native Americans, a party which broke away from Tammany as a gesture of defiance to foreign domination, and adopted as its slogan, "No Irish need apply," was likewise equipped with a pugilistic brigade which numbered such eminent leaders as Tom Hyer and Bill

---

* After Paddock beat Broome for the title, May 19, 1856, illness compelled him to retire, and Perry reclaimed the championship. On June 16, 1857, Sayers beat Perry, but when Paddock recovered his health he reclaimed the crown. Exactly one year later, Sayers beat Paddock, thus establishing himself as the unquestioned champion of England.

YANKEE SULLIVAN

Poole. On the Tammany side John Morrissey, Yankee Sullivan, Lew Baker, and James Turner were the big names. Many encounters took place between the opposing factions. A beating Hyer gave Yankee Sullivan led to the murder of Hyer's colleague, Poole, an event which created no little excitement at the time.

Poole, famed as a rough-and-tumble fighter, never sought distinction in the ring. It was enough for him that he was considered invincible outside the ropes; he was perfectly content that his pal Hyer should hold the ring honors. Huge, long armed, broad shouldered, a human grizzly bear Bill Poole was a man who never met his equal in a go-as-you-please encounter.

On one occasion, Yankee Sullivan, whose dislike of Hyer amounted to a mania, flew into a rage when some joker slyly insinuated that he was afraid of the Native American favorite. He went hunting for Hyer. Sullivan's quest ended at a saloon at Park Place and Broadway, where he assaulted Tom. There he speedily discovered that he had undertaken a task beyond his powers. In less than three minutes Hyer beat Yankee to a pulp.

The upshot of this impromptu mill was a formal challenge from Sullivan to Hyer for a ring battle involving the American championship, and a match was arranged for a stake of ten thousand dollars. Meanwhile Poole was murdered. It was clear that the fight for the heavyweight title would be a savage affair.

Of the two men, Sullivan possessed by far the more impressive record. He had battled with considerable success in Australia, Ireland, and England, had never been defeated, and could boast of ten clean-cut victories under London rules, whereas Hyer's principal achievement was his victory over Country McClusky.

Tom Hyer was a singularly handsome man, six feet, two and a half inches tall, beautifully proportioned, modest, and well-behaved, but a tiger when his temper was aroused. Sullivan, four inches shorter and thirty pounds lighter than Hyer, of stocky, compact build, was a turbulent spirit. Yankee was ever ready to fight in the street, a saloon, or the ring. Any location was a good one for this son of Erin, who was born near the city of Cork, April 12, 1813.

The place selected for the battleground was Pool's Island, on the border of the state of Maryland. There, on the night of February 6, 1849, both pugilists were temporarily domiciled in the only two houses standing on that lonely stretch of land. In the offing hovered two steamers, aboard which were several hundred eager sportsmen.

Meanwhile, a force of police officers had set sail from Balti-

more, intent on preserving the peace. Upon landing, the police
surrounded the house where Hyer lay sleeping. Awakened by
the sound of tramping feet, Hyer realized his danger. Hastily
putting his trainer, George Thompson, in his bed, Tom crept
downstairs and concealed himself on the ground floor. A little
later, he fled to the beach and boarded a waiting boat.

The officers proceeded to the bedroom vacated by Hyer. Seeing big George Thompson lying snugly under the covers, they
took it for granted that he was the man for whom they were
searching. Thompson meekly submitted to arrest. The police
next proceeded to Sullivan's resting place. Yankee, suddenly
confronted by the minions of the law, turned to his sparring
partner, Tom O'Donnell, pushed him toward the door, and exclaimed, "Run, Sullivan, run like hell!"

The constables, completely deceived, held O'Donnell, who
put up a convincing struggle. While the officers were engaged
in subduing him, the real Sullivan quietly slipped away and
soon found himself on board the craft designed for his reception. The constables' steamer, attempting to pursue the fugi-
tives, ran upon a rock and stuck there hard and fast, while the
merry lawbreakers sailed triumphantly away.

Thus the gladiators escaped from the guardians of the law,
and with their backers and followers they started up Chesapeake
Bay to find a new location to set the stakes. The motley crowd,
eager for the battle, gave word to the captain to halt at the first
convenient spot, no matter in what state. When a suitable landing place was located, they found the ground covered with
snow. After it was removed, fresh earth was sprinkled on the
battle site, a ring was staked off, and by four o'clock all was
ready. Snow was falling and a cold wind whistled through the
ropes.

As the fighters shaped up for the fray, Yankee weighed only
155, to 185 for Tom. Both looked in the pink, but Hyer, a
great jumper and oarsman as well as a skilled boxer, was far
more imposing.

Sullivan made a rushing fight of it. During the first three
rounds he was repeatedly thrown with stunning force. Hyer,
with his long reach, also staggered Sullivan with a succession

of blows, while Yankee's leads frequently fell short of the target. Sullivan was soon in dire distress. Yet he fought on desperately until near the close of the sixteenth round. Then, as he reeled against the ropes, his second, Country McClusky, stepped forward, took hold of his man, and removed him from the ring without waiting for the call of time. Hyer was officially declared the winner in sixteen rounds. The time was seventeen minutes, eighteen seconds.

The victor was not at once acclaimed in a manner suitable to a person of his achievement. Instead, on his way back to New York he was arrested by the Philadelphia police and turned over to Maryland authorities, who charged him with rioting. Political influence brought about his release before trial, and Hyer then returned to New York, where his friends greeted him like the conquering hero he was. Yankee Sullivan, his victim, was removed to a hospital after the battle, and it was discovered that he was suffering from what was reported with due restraint as a "slightly fractured skull."

Hyer, after a suitable period of celebration, issued a challenge to Bill Perry, the Tipton Slasher, to fight him for the heavyweight championship of the world. He offered to meet the Slasher for ten thousand dollars a side, plus five thousand dollars, give or take, to cover traveling expenses. Whether it was the amount of the bet or Hyer's readiness to go abroad that discouraged Perry cannot be reported with certainty. Whatever Perry's reason may have been, he disregarded the challenge.

CHAPTER 5

THE SECOND TROJAN WAR

AMERICAN ring history from the middle of the
nineteenth century through the early part of the twentieth is
primarily the history of Irish supremacy. In every division, the
headliners were with few exceptions either immigrants from the
land of Erin or native sons of Hibernian parents who had come
to these shores to seek their fortune.

Shortly after the great battle between Tom Hyer and Yankee
Sullivan another great pugilist appeared with the championship
as his goal. His name was John Morrissey. Among the noted
fistic heroes who flourished in both sporting and political worlds
in America during the past hundred years, none was more
spectacular than he. A politician, a leader in Irish-American
affairs, a powerful figure in Tammany Hall, he was always ready
for a drag-out or an up-and-down scrimmage with any person
who stood in his path.

Morrissey was born in Templemore, County Tipperary, on
February 11, 1831, and his parents, like thousands of their
compatriots, were "poor but honest." They emigrated to this
country by way of Canada when John was only three years old
and settled at Troy, New York. Morrissey's father was a day
laborer who had a difficult time making both ends meet, and
with the arrival of other children, all daughters, his task was
lightened only when John became old enough to lend a helping
hand.

John had little schooling, and it was not until he was eighteen that he had learned to read and write. From then on,
although he was entirely self-taught, he acquired not only
sufficient ring science to make himself heavyweight champion

but also the kind of knowledge that brought him election to the Congress of the United States.

Morrissey at fifteen had already gained quite a reputation as a slugger. In 1847, when he was sixteen, he had developed into a fine muscular specimen, a fist fighter extraordinary. He was now ready to face the world on his own. With a robust

JOHN MORRISSEY

frame, two iron fists, and ample endurance, he began to look for the sort of job where such assets could be turned into cash. He found one as bartender in the Troy saloon owned by Aleck Hamilton, a sports promoter.

At this time, by a remarkable coincidence, another embryo heavyweight champion was growing up in Troy. Two years younger than Morrissey, his name was John C. Heenan. He was the leader of the "West Troys," a gang of tough lads in constant conflict with an equally tough crew headed by Morrissey. One night four of Heenan's followers entered Hamilton's saloon and, after a number of drinks, refused to pay. Morrissey swung into action, gave a thorough drubbing to the most truculent member of the quartet, and collected the reckoning. Hamilton was delighted. When Morrissey on another occasion sent Malachi Brennan, a celebrated bully from Albany, home on a stretcher, Hamilton urged his accomplished bartender to take up fighting professionally.

A little later, during the 1848 political campaign, Hamilton visited New York City. In conversation with "Dutch Charley" Duane, a friend of Tom Hyer and a noted rough-and-tumble fighter himself, Hamilton jokingly told him that he had a barkeep up in Troy who could take his measure. Enraged at this gratuitous insult, Duane proceeded to beat the tar out of his taunter.

When Morrissey's boss told him about the beating, John silently rolled down his sleeves, took off his apron, went directly to the steamboat landing, and left for New York. Next day at the Empire Club, Duane's hangout, he briskly demanded to see the villain, and when he was informed that Mr. Duane was at the races he announced that he was Irish and would be delighted to fight anyone else in the place. At once Morrissey was attacked by half a dozen men, and only the intercession of Captain Isaiah Rynders, leader of the club, saved him from a frightful thrashing.

Captain Rynders, pleased with the lad's courage, offered him shelter in a room on the upper floor and told him he could remain as long as he wished. Morrissey became extremely friendly with his benefactor and through him obtained a position as a runner for an immigrant boarding house along the water front. Again Morrissey found his fists handy in deterring his tough rivals from stealing his patrons. One of these ruffians was Tom McCann, a man renowned for his dirty fighting tactics. Hearing that Morrissey not only had worked in on his trade along the water front but was also making passes at his girl, McCann sailed into him one night in the barroom of the St. Charles Hotel on Broadway.

McCann was a powerful fellow, and for a time he had all the better of the milling. He maneuvered Morrissey around the room until he got him close to the cannonball stove in the center. Then he suddenly upset the stove, scattering the glowing coals over the floor and forcing Morrissey's back against them. Though burned severely, Morrissey refused to yield. Despite the pain, he rolled and tossed until he got on top. He then pounded McCann into insensibility. For the rest of his life Morrissey was known to his intimates as "Old Smoke."

After the California gold rush had got under way, Morrissey, like thousands of other adventurers, caught the fever and went to the Pacific Coast. When he arrived in San Francisco, he and a crony named Cunningham decided they could get the gold more easily by opening a gambling house than by digging for it, and with a bankroll furnished them by some friends they went into business and cleaned up a small fortune.

Tom Hyer, who had by then retired as champion, had also gone to the Coast; when he returned to New York, his training partner, George Thompson, remained to try his hand as both prospector and fighter. When Thompson whipped a fellow named Willis at Sacramento for a side wager of two thousand dollars, Morrissey's friends dared Thompson to take on their young Irishman. Thompson agreed, and a match was made for Mare's Island, August 31, 1852, for two thousand dollars a side.

By far the cleverer and harder hitter, Thompson had the better of the first eleven rounds, fought in sixteen minutes. Then, fearing that the crowd, almost wholly a Morrissey following, would kill him if he won, he deliberately fouled to lose the battle. By accepting defeat, Thompson got out of a tight hole and the Morrissey gamblers benefited handsomely.

Morrissey now returned to New York. After an unsuccessful attempt to get Hyer into a match, he accepted a challenge from Yankee Sullivan, who was then forty years old and weighed, as he had when he lost to Hyer, only 155 pounds. Morrissey scaled 175 and had just passed his twenty-second birthday.

Although he battled in his customary vigorous fashion, Yankee was unable to keep up the pace set by his more youthful opponent. In the thirty-seventh round a free-for-all fight started among the spectators, and Sullivan, becoming involved with a couple of outsiders who had broken through the ropes, left the ring and refused to answer the call of time for the next round.

John Morrissey was consequently proclaimed winner and champion of America. The date was October 12, 1853.

The disgrace of losing to his Tammany rival embittered Yankee to such a degree that he resolved to leave New York forever. The gold fields beckoned him as they had Hyer and Morrissey, and he set forth for California. But San Francisco offered enticements that the gold camps could not match, and Sullivan became a figure in the underworld. Crooked gamblers were then in control of the tumultuous city of the Golden Gate, but in the spring of 1856 the respectable citizens formed a vigilance committee to clean out the evil element. Judge Lynch reigned, and his sentences were mercilessly carried out. Among many others, Yankee Sullivan was thrown into jail, and on May 31 he was found dead in his cell. Whether he was a suicide or the victim of a vigilante's hand has never been satisfactorily determined.

Shortly before Sullivan's violent end, John C. Heenan, Morrissey's boyhood enemy from Troy, appeared in New York. He too had been lured by California's gold fields and had lived for a time in the town of Benicia, across the bay from San Francisco. There he built a formidable reputation as a fighter and gained the picturesque sobriquet of Benicia Boy. When he returned to the East, he was famous. Heenan wanted the heavyweight title —and he particularly wanted to take it away from his ancient rival, John Morrissey.

Thus a family feud reached its culmination when the implacable enemies confronted each other in a ring at Long Point, Canada, on October 20, 1858.

The physical advantages rested with Heenan, who weighed 195 pounds against Morrissey's 175 and was superior in height and reach. During the opening rounds, the hopes of the Benicia Boy's backers mounted high. But John Morrissey was never so dangerous as when hard pressed. He repeatedly attacked the body, causing Heenan to give ground under a bombardment of stomach punches.

Heenan rallied and drove his opponent to the ropes. Then came the decisive break of the battle. Morrissey neatly ducked a straight right, and Heenan's hand smashed into the wooden stake in a neutral corner. It was noticeable from then to the eleventh and final round that the Benicia Boy got little use out of his right. From that moment Morrissey had the fight well in hand, and Heenan went down to defeat.

JOHN C. HEENAN

Challenged to a return engagement, Morrissey resigned the title to the Benicia Boy.

When Morrissey retired from the ring, he succeeded in gaining the friendship of Commodore Vanderbilt, who was beginning his great career as a railroad king. Through Vanderbilt, Morrissey had access to valuable information on the stock market, and he made a tidy profit, which he used to open a gambling house in Saratoga. In 1863 he and John Hunter and

JOHN C. HEENAN TRAINING FOR HIS BOUT WITH MORRISSEY. PACE WAS GOVERNED
BY A SPEEDOMETER IN THE TRAINER'S CART.

William R. Travers organized a race meeting at Saratoga, and the following year he helped to found a jockey club which today still flourishes.

Morrissey gave up prize fighting entirely and devoted himself primarily to politics. In 1870 he received a nomination for Congress, won the election, and served two terms in Washington. After that he was chosen to run for the New York state senate on a reform ticket. Supported by Republicans as well as by anti-Tammany Democrats, the former stanch Tammany-ite gave everything he had to the fight against the corrupt and discredited organization and won. In 1877 he was again sent to Albany, but the campaign completely exhausted him, and he was unable to take his seat. He died in Florida in the spring of 1878 at the early age of forty-seven.

Tom Sayers and the Benicia Boy

Of all the names of champion heavyweights who brought glory to the British ring none is more glorious than that of Tom Sayers. His great battle in 1860 with John C. Heenan, the Benicia Boy, holder of the American championship, was the first international combat that stirred public interest to fever heat on both sides of the Atlantic.

But long before that famous affair Sayers had been the pet of the Fancy. Little Tom's fighting weight in the early years was only 140 pounds—less than the welter limit of these days. Later, he seldom scaled over 152. Frequently conceding fifty or sixty pounds, he lost only a single fight in his entire career. Sayers was truly a marvel of the ring. He was idolized by the English sports enthusiasts, and pugilism rose to great heights during his reign.

Sayers was born near Brighton on May 25, 1828, the son of a poor shoemaker. When he was only seven, his father put him to work helping push hog boats off the beach. Later Tom was apprenticed to a bricklayer, and while thus employed he engaged in many fist fights. So skillful was he that he was induced to enter a novice tourney, which he won. Thereafter he became an ardent follower of the sport, and when he reached his twenty-second year he decided to give up his employment and become a professional fighter.

In his first genuine ring encounter he whipped Aby Couch (or Crouch) in thirteen minutes. That bout, arranged for March 19, 1849, was a strange battle. It started at Edenbridge in Kent, but the police stopped it. The fighters and their followers then adjourned to Redhill, where the pair fought until darkness set in. After a postponement of two weeks they resumed, and from this third meeting Sayers emerged triumphant.

Still another such bout began the following year on October 22, when Sayers clashed with Dan Collins. Police interference halted the contest after the ninth round. A new field was speedily found, and the rivals battled savagely for an hour and fifty-two minutes, when darkness descended. A draw was declared, and it was not until the following spring that they fought to a finish, with Sayers knocking out Collins in forty-four rounds. Then in rapid succession he beat Jack Grant and Jack Martin. Encouraged by these triumphs, Sayers, although scaling only 140 pounds, challenged the middleweight champion, Nat Langham.

Langham accepted, and they met on October 18, 1853. Owing to an illness that had interrupted training, Sayers was not in good physical condition. Even so, he battled magnificently for more than twenty rounds. Then Langham landed a left which closed one of his opponent's eyes, and thereafter he centered his attack on Sayers' optics, with the result that Sayers was practically blind in the fifty-ninth round. Still the little gamecock came to scratch with unflinching courage. Groping vainly to find his adversary, refusing to quit despite his battered, blinded condition, Sayers maintained the unequal contest for ten more rounds, when his seconds mercifully threw in the sponge.

This was Tom's first defeat, and it was destined to be his last. Langham won only after two hours and two minutes, in the most desperate encounter he ever had waged. Sayers lost no time in rechallenging his conqueror. But Nat Langham had had enough of Tom. The middleweight champion retired, preferring to rest on his laurels.

On February 2, 1854, Sayers knocked out George Sims, another middleweight, in an encounter lasting only five minutes. No more opponents of the middleweight class being willing to take on the terrible Sayers, he invaded the heavyweight division.

In a fight with Harry Poulson, lasting three hours and eight minutes, Sayers won by a knockout in the hundred and nine-tieth round. Darkness halted a battle between Sayers and Aaron Jones after three hours of fighting; a continuation of the mill several weeks later resulted in victory for Sayers in eighty-five rounds. On June 16, 1857, Sayers clashed with William Perry, the celebrated Tipton Slasher, in a match for the heavyweight championship, a belt and one thousand dollars a side. The Slasher, over six feet tall and scaling two hundred pounds, was a heavy favorite in the betting, but in the tenth round his sec-onds threw in the sponge in token of surrender. Tom Sayers had taken the heavyweight title from the best man in England, a pugilist who outweighed him by forty-eight pounds. In the year following, he further clinched his right to the crown by whipping Tom Paddock and Bob Brettle, and by twice defeat-ing Bill Bainge.

Meanwhile in America, John Morrissey, having beaten Heenan, retired permanently. Heenan, unable to get a return match with his conqueror, claimed the championship of the United States and at once made overtures for a match with Sayers for the world championship. Sayers was willing, and arrangements were concluded whereby the two titleholders would fight in England for the belt and twenty-five hundred dollars a side.

Other British and American pugilists of prominence had faced each other in the ring, but this was the first time that the recognized heavyweight champions from opposite sides of the Atlantic were matched to battle for the world crown. No other contest in fistic history had ever created interest to compare with this one—the first international boxing match to excite people who normally paid little attention to the sport.

Not only was the British press represented at the scene of battle by special writers, but the New York *Spirit of the Times* and Frank Leslie's *Illustrated Weekly* assigned their best reporters and artists to cover the story. Among the artists was Tom Nast, the man whose vigorous cartoons helped so largely some ten years later to break up the corrupt Tweed gang that had dominated New York politics and looted the municipal treasury of many millions.

Never before had a prize fight drawn together such a huge and varied gathering. Men in all grades of society, from lords to laborers, from merchants to crossing sweepers, from bankers to pickpockets, flocked in thousands to the field near the town of Farnborough where the ring was pitched.

Literary lights of the age were present in abundance. In fact, one London newspaper referred somewhat scornfully to "the many knights of the pen" who lowered the dignity of their profession by attending a low squabble between two "knights of the fist." Notwithstanding this censorious attitude on the part of one journal, the event was given great prominence by the English press as well as the American. It is not too much to say that the Heenan-Sayers combat was the first prize fight to rank as real news on both sides of the ocean. (In New York a young news vendor named Brentano, who later opened a book store that still prospers, had the foresight to order a large consignment of London papers containing detailed accounts of the fight. So hungry for the story were his customers that Brentano quickly disposed of the lot at two dollars a copy.)

It was about half past seven on the morning of April 17, 1860, when Heenan and Sayers answered the call of time. Notwithstanding the great physical disparity—Heenan stood six feet, two inches, and weighed 195 pounds; Sayers stood five feet, eight, and weighed 149—the little Briton was freely backed by his countrymen to win. The bets of the few Americans in attendance were eagerly taken. There were also many Englishmen who did not allow sentiment to influence their judgment, and these practical gamblers laid heavy wagers on Heenan's chances.

Sayers drew first blood in the opening round with a straight left to the face, and in a sharp close-quarters rally that followed, he had somewhat the better of the milling. But the big American, using his weight and strength to good advantage, floored Sayers in the second, third, fourth, and fifth rounds.

In the sixth, Sayers blocked a terrific swing with his right forearm. So great was the force of the blow that it snapped a bone in the guarding arm, and for the balance of the fight it was practically useless. Though in great pain as a result of this injury, Sayers, always a competent ring general, saw clearly that his one hope of victory lay in an attack on Heenan's eyes. He proceeded to follow this plan of campaign with considerable success, closing his opponent's right eye in the seventh round. Heenan, continuing his slugging assaults, again sent Tom to the ground.

The eighth round saw Heenan's left hand rendered nearly as useless as Sayers' damaged right when the Benicia Boy broke a bone against his opponent's hard head. Still Heenan forced the pace, with Sayers playing incessantly for his eyes. They fought for twenty minutes without a pause.

Heenan scored a number of clean knockdowns between the ninth and the thirty-fourth round, but by now the American was nearly blind. The betting at this point centered chiefly on whether Sayers, exhausted and with a broken right arm, could survive until blindness and a broken hand would compel the American to surrender.

In the thirty-seventh round the police arrived and entered into hostilities with the surging, yelling crowd, which, contrary to all British precedents, resisted their attempts to force a passage through to the inner ring. At this moment, Heenan, having rushed Sayers to the ropes, was holding his adversary in a grip of iron, and it seemed as if the game little Briton was about to collapse. An unknown hand now cut the ropes, and the crowd invaded the ring.

Still the rivals kept on fighting although the referee had ordered the battle stopped as soon as it became a free-for-all in the thirty-seventh round; the chief official then left the ring himself. According to London rules, with every fall or knockdown terminating a round, Heenan and Sayers fought five more rounds before they were stopped. Officially the battle ended in the thirty-seventh, after two hours and twenty minutes of fighting, and was scored as a draw.

Heretofore it had been customary when a draw was declared

to fight the battle over again. But Sayers' extraordinary courage in the face of heavy odds and Heenan's aggressiveness had made heroes of both, and even the most violent partisans were satisfied to allow the question of supremacy to remain unanswered. Accordingly, an agreement was reached whereby a silver championship belt was given to each man.

AFTER THE ROPES HAD BEEN CUT DURING THE HEENAN-SAYERS FIGHT.

In America it was the universal opinion that Heenan would have won the fight if the ropes had not been cut. The action of the referee in leaving the scene and the rule of the mob that broke into the ring in that historic thirty-seventh round came in for severe condemnation. Magazines that had always shunned fight items now found it convenient for circulation purposes to come to the aid of Heenan and attack the British for their failure to observe fair play. Even from the pulpit the action was denounced. British writers and orators were equally vehement, insisting that Sayers would surely have won if the ropes had not been cut.

It was on July 14, 1860, that Heenan returned to New York.

The greatest gathering that had ever paid homage to a sports-man was present at Jones Woods, in the Yorkville section of the city, at a festival given in his honor. Fifty thousand tickets were sold for the occasion, and the hero received a king's greet-ing. Even John Morrissey was present. He not only made up

TOM KING

with his Troy rival but contributed to the ten-thousand-dollar testimonial fund that was subscribed.

After Tom Sayers' retirement Heenan was universally ac-knowledged to be champion of the world, and he decided to return to Europe. On December 10, 1863, with Sayers as his second, the Benicia Boy met Tom King. This time the gods were unkind to the American, for he was beaten in the twenty-fourth round, after thirty-five minutes of milling.

This was Heenan's last fight. He died at the age of forty, on October 28, 1873.

CHAPTER 6

JEM MACE AND HIS CONTEMPORARIES

IN THE three years between the Sayers-Heenan and Heenan-King bouts, three other men had claimed the English heavyweight crown. One was Tom Paddock, the first claimant after Sayers' retirement. The second was Sam Hurst, a 210-pounder known at the Stalybridge Infant, who took away Paddock's dubious title in nine and a half minutes. The third was Jem Mace, whose name has gone down in ring history as one of the cleverest men who ever climbed inside the ropes.

Although Mace, who was born on April 8, 1831, denied having any Romany blood in his veins, he was popularly believed to have and was constantly referred to as the Gypsy. Perhaps his nickname derived from the fact that he had at one time been an itinerant fiddler. But though his origins may be obscure, there is no uncertainty whatever about his boxing career and the tremendous place he still occupies in the annals of the sport.

It was through the loss of his violin that Mace turned to the prize ring. He was at Yarmouth standing outside a tavern when a drunken fisherman, riled at young Mace, who was tuning up his fiddle, smashed the instrument. Jem went into action and soon had his man helpless on the ground. A passerby who watched the fight pressed a sovereign into Mace's hand and remarked, "You ought to be a prize fighter."

"Those words of encouragement," says Mace in the story of his life, "started me on a professional fighting career."

His first pro battle was against Slasher Tom Slack on October 2, 1855, a mill in which he was returned the winner in nine rounds. Next, he decisively whipped Bill Thorne, a clever middleweight, who had twenty-three pounds advantage over the victor. Then, after dropping a two-round fight to Bob Brettle, on September 21, 1858, he faced Posh Price, whom he whipped in eleven rounds. After Price, he took on Bob Travers, American Negro middleweight. This battle, fought on February 21, 1860, was stopped by the police in the sixth round. On the following day they fought fifty-seven more rounds before Mace was declared the winner.

Jem now took on Brettle, who had beaten him in 1858, and the unwelcome arrival of the police was all that saved Bob from defeat. The two clashed once more the next morning, and Jem gave his opponent a sound beating in just twelve minutes.

By this time Mace had grown heavier, and although he never tipped the scales above 160 pounds, he resolved to try for heavyweight honors. A match with Sam Hurst was arranged, with the British title at stake.

Like Sayers, Mace made up what he lacked in size by bringing science to bear. Hurst stormed ponderously against his lighter opponent, only to be swiftly countered with straight lefts, bewildered by rapid footwork, and pounded to a standstill. The referee stopped the contest and declared Jem victor after fifty minutes had elapsed.

Mace won the British crown on June 18, 1861. On January 28 of the following year he defended it against Tom King. Although the latter outweighed Mace by thirty pounds, their battle, fought in a whirl of snow and rain, resulted in victory for the champion in fifty-three rounds. In a second encounter, on November 26, 1862, King, when on the verge of exhaustion, landed a wild swing on Mace's temple. So deadly effective was the blow that Mace suddenly collapsed two rounds later. A new champion was crowned, and Mace went into temporary eclipse.

Tom King at once announced his retirement. But British sportsmen were unanimous in their insistence that King should fight Heenan, who was eager to defend the world-championship title he had justly assumed upon Sayers' retirement after their drawn battle of 1860.*

* In 1862, more than a year before arrangements had been concluded with King, Heenan announced his own retirement. By the time Heenan had revoked this decision, Joe Coburn was claiming the American championship—which he

King and the Benicia Boy met at Wadhurst, December 10, 1863, and, as already related, the Englishman won. Having gratified his countrymen's fondest desire, Tom King declared he had fought for the last time. (True to his word, he remained in retirement so far as the ring was concerned. But he did not abandon his interest or activity in athletics, and a little later he became a champion oarsman. He was also a familiar and successful figure on the English turf. King died on October 3, 1888.)

With King definitely out of the fistic picture, Mace was universally recognized as world heavyweight champion. In a battle with Joe Goss on September 1, 1863, won by Mace in one hour, forty-five minutes, thirty seconds, the man who had both beaten and lost to Tom King proved that his brain had not lost its cunning, nor his capable fists their punishing power. As a master of ring science, Mace stood head and shoulders above all his contemporaries.

Meanwhile in the United States Joe Coburn had stepped into Heenan's shoes. After the Benicia Boy retired, Joe clinched his claim to the American championship by defeating Mike McCoole at Charlestown, Maryland, on May 5, 1863. Born in Ireland, July 20, 1835, Coburn had come to the United States as a child. The lad grew to manhood on New York's East Side, where he became known as a competent rough-and-tumble scrapper. After engaging in a number of bare-knuckle bouts with minor lights of the ring, young Joe was matched with Ned Price, a sturdy and undefeated veteran. By holding Price to a draw in a bitterly contested engagement lasting three hours and twenty minutes, Coburn found himself with a real reputation.

In 1864 Coburn went to England for the express purpose of fighting Mace. Jem accepted the challenge, and a match was arranged for October 4, 1864. But since Coburn insisted that one of his personal friends be named as referee, the bout was called off and Coburn returned home.

Mace remained idle until May 24, 1866, when he again

———

successfully defended against Mike McCoole before Heenan, still "world champion," fought King in England!

clashed with his former foeman, Joe Goss. The bout was a list-less affair in which neither contestant tried to accomplish any-thing, and after an hour and five minutes a draw was declared. Jem took prompt steps to sustain his reputation as a real fighter. Rematched with Goss on August 6, 1866, he gave Joe a terrific beating, stopping him in twenty-one rounds.

Ned O'Baldwin, Irish heavyweight champion, now challenged for the world's title. Mace accepted, but the Celt was arrested while preparing for the battle, charged with conspiracy to break the peace, and placed under bond to insure his good behavior.

At this time the good people of England, following the ex-ample of their blessed Queen Victoria, were in a state of almost orgiastic virtue. A reform wave swept the country. The clergy preached sulphurous sermons against the "ruffians of the ring." Prize fighting was becoming daily a more perilous pastime as the magistrates, falling in line with the popular trend, imposed heavier and heavier jail sentences on persons brought before them who were in any way associated with the ring.

A great exodus followed. O'Baldwin, Tom Allen, Joe Wor-mald, Joe Goss, and a host of lesser lights sailed for the United States. In a sense, they were jumping out of the frying pan into the fire, for the transatlantic brand of Victorianism differed only in detail from the native variety. The fistic tide, neverthe-less, set strongly toward the United States.

With no opponents left at home, Mace departed on a tour of the Antipodes. He was given a cordial reception in Australia, and his boxing exhibitions netted him a neat profit.

In the meantime Ned O'Baldwin and Joe Wormald met in battle at Lynnfield, Massachusetts. Police interfered, Wormald declined to resume later, and O'Baldwin was declared the win-ner. There was no title involved in this affair of October, 1868, even though it had been billed by the promoters as a contest to decide the world's championship. Mace was still the accepted monarch of the heavies.

By this time Mace had decided that his proper base of opera-tions was North America. Soon after his arrival he was matched with Tom Allen. The latter, born in Birmingham, England, had beaten a number of fairly good men and fought a thirty-four-round draw with Goss.

The Mace-Allen battle took place at Kennerville, Louisiana, on May 10, 1870. Mace won in ten rounds, after forty-four minutes of desperate action, thus reinforcing his title to the world's heavyweight championship. Joe Coburn then challenged Mace. Jem, now in his fortieth year, was eager to retire, but he had gained a great deal of popularity in the United States and did not like to risk losing it by refusing to give Coburn his chance. He therefore agreed to a match, and they met at Bay Saint Louis, Missouri, November 30, 1871. It was a hard-fought combat, with Mace displaying the science that had made his name famous. Coburn did most of the forcing but found it difficult to get through the champion's magnificent defense. Both men were extremely weary when a draw was declared at the close of the twelfth round.

Mace retired immediately after the Coburn engagement. Next to Tom Sayers, he was esteemed by his countrymen above all the bare-knuckle clan. His willingness to sacrifice weight to opponents, his affability, his good behavior, and the fact that he kept the world's title safe for England all contributed to his popularity. He did more to foster the pure science of boxing than any other man of his era, and it was due to him that the use of gloves in ring competition became more and more common as time went on. Great as Mace was when fighting under London Rules, it was as a glove artist that he appeared at his best.

Mace returned to England after his retirement. He died in Liverpool, November 30, 1910, in his eightieth year.

Another Boy from Troy

The decade of 1860–1870, unsettled by the Civil War and the following period of reconstruction, provided just three fighters with clear title to the championship of the United States. But in addition to these three—Heenan, Coburn, Mace—there were several others whose pretensions to the heavyweight crown cannot be entirely dismissed. Whether or not any of them is now entitled to recognition as a pre-1870 champion, it is only fair to record the names of such front-rank contenders as Mike McCoole, Joe Wormald, Ned O'Baldwin, and Tom Allen as worthy of consideration. Of these, Allen is particularly deserving of mention, for after he lost to Mace, as recounted in the preceding section, he continued to fight, and three years later, on September 23, 1873, he beat McCoole in a recognized championship bout. He held the American title until 1876, when Joe Goss, former champion of England, won a very dubious decision based on a foul.*

The next four years formed a dreary period in American boxing history. But a young Irish-American fighter was coming along in Troy, New York, a city which had already produced two heavyweight champions, Morrissey and Heenan. He, too, was destined to win the championship. His name was Paddy Ryan.

The Trojan Giant, as he was dubbed, was born in the town of Thurles, County Tipperary, Ireland, March 15, 1853. He was six feet, one-half inch tall and weighed 222 pounds. Literally and figuratively, Ryan stood head and shoulders above most of the competitors of his time, for even though Paddy had little ability as a boxer, he appeared at a time when ring science was almost unknown to members of the fistic fraternity. What he lacked as a puncher he largely made up with his ability to toss his opponents. By the time he was nineteen, he had proved himself the best grappler in Troy, and local sporting figures were convinced that in Ryan they had the next heavyweight champion.

During the next few months Ryan engaged in several rough-and-tumble frays that increased the enthusiasm of his followers, and they planned to have their idol matched with Johnny Dwyer, who had vague claims to the championship. But before

---

* In the Introduction it is stated that Jem Mace was the last Englishman to win the American title. It should be explained that Allen, though born in England, was a naturalized citizen of the United States when he won the American championship in 1873. As for Goss, also an Englishman, who asserted his right to the championship after the 1876 fiasco with Allen, the best that can be said is that his "win" vacated the title.

the match could be arranged, Dwyer announced his retirement, and Ryan, eager to wear the crown, offered to fight any man in the world for one thousand dollars a side and the title. The ancient Joe Goss accepted, and a championship match was scheduled.

It was first agreed that the battle should be fought at Long Point, Canada, and the pugilists and a large number of sportsmen journeyed to Erie, Pennsylvania, which was designated as the starting point. With everything in readiness and the fans ready to cross to the Canadian battleground, a hitch arose, and Goss refused to go through with the program. After a lengthy conference, Charley Johnston, a Brooklyn sportsman who acted as stake holder, rearranged matters, and the fighters agreed to settle their differences on May 30, 1880, at Collier's Station, West Virginia.

In this bout, Ryan did what no other fighter in American ring history has ever accomplished—he won the championship in his first professional battle! He not only had never climbed inside ropes before but had actually not even laid eyes on a squared circle.

Ryan had the advantage in height, weight, reach, and youth. But Goss proved vastly superior in ring generalship and cleverness. He gave Paddy enough of a beating to have satisfied two ordinary men, but though the Trojan was ludicrously lacking in skill, he was plucky and able to withstand the punishment.

Goss took care to avoid Paddy's badly timed punches, frequently going down to do so when they were at close quarters. On the other hand, though Goss landed frequently, his punches lacked steam, his judgment of distance was poor, and he wasted much energy with blows that were often short of their mark. Ryan had all the better of it when he got a chance to grapple with his opponent.

Round after round they kept at each other. Goss was wearing himself down pounding his young opponent, who, while superficially battered, had small trouble keeping the battle alive. As time went on, it became clearer and clearer that little short of a miracle could save the old warrior.

In the eighty-sixth round a severe right-hand cross counter

felled Goss; his seconds claimed a foul, but it was disallowed. Joe was carried to his corner, and when time was called for the start of the eighty-seventh session, he was unable to come to scratch. Paddy Ryan thus became champion of the United States, and it is safe to say that he was the least experienced heavyweight who has ever held the title in this or any other country.

In some respects it is less extraordinary that Ryan should have become champion than that he ever had a chance to try for the crown that fitted him so badly. For a truly great man— the greatest ring personality, if not the greatest fighter, in history—was already on his way to glory when Ryan won from Goss. The great man was, of course, John L. Sullivan, the pride of Boston, the United States, and the world.

CHAPTER 7

ENTER JOHN THE GREAT

JOHN LAWRENCE SULLIVAN was born October 15, 1858, on Concord Street, Roxbury, Massachusetts, a suburb of Boston. He came of hardy Irish stock, his father, Michael, hailing from Tralee, County Kerry, and his mother from Athlone, County Roscommon. His paternal grandfather had been a noted wrestler and a champion performer with the shillelagh.

Sullivan received his early education in the public schools. Bright and alert, he had no more interest than the average boy in classroom work, but he took to athletics as a cat takes to cream. His specialties were baseball and boxing. So good a ballplayer was he that for a time he played professionally, and after he became famous he frequently donned a uniform to appear with the Boston team or with local clubs when he was on the road giving boxing exhibitions.

After leaving high school, John L. attended Boston College for a time, for his devout and devoted mother hoped that her husky offspring would enter the priesthood. He endeavored to comply with his mother's wishes, but a life of sacrifice and renunciation was not suited to his ebullient temperament. At the end of sixteen months, he resigned both his priestly ambitions and his academic career. In that time, however, he had derived considerable benefit from two subjects, the drama and elocution. Both of them were to prove useful to him in the future, on the stage and the lecture platform.

For several months after leaving college John L. was at loose ends. He entered four amateur boxing tournaments, coming out ahead in each instance and winning some repute as a heavy puncher. But amateur boxing was merely his relaxation. By way of providing himself with bread and butter, Sullivan proceeded to learn the plumbing trade.

As a plumber he seems to have fared well until he had an argument with his foreman. That gentleman, a bulky person who fancied himself as a scrapper, forced a fight upon the youth. At least, that was how John L. described the situation to the head of the firm next day when the foreman was regretting his recklessness in bed with a broken jaw. John's plumbing career ended with the fracture.

Sullivan next turned tinsmith. For eighteen months he stuck to his new trade, but by that time he was thoroughly bored. He threw down his tools and took to baseball. Signed as a semipro, John sometimes drew down as much as a hundred a week. Playing and getting paid for it was more to his taste.

One night Sullivan attended a boxing benefit performance at the Dudley Street Opera House, Boston Highlands. Tom Scannel, a boxer of local reputation, swaggered to the edge of the platform and proclaimed loudly that he would take on anyone in the house and stop him in three rounds. He made it quite clear to his audience that he was addressing Sullivan, who occupied a seat in the front row.

The sports knew John by this time, and yells of "Sullivan!" were heard from all parts of the house. The big boy was willing. He removed his collar and tie, pulled off his coat, rolled up his sleeves, mounted the stage, and declared himself ready for action.

Scannel, wearing green tights and a confident smile, pranced lightly up to Sullivan, with his guard up. Sullivan, thinking that his opponent would first shake hands, as was the custom in the amateur tourneys, extended his right glove. Instead of acknowledging the courtesy, Scannel let go a left swing that landed on Sully's cheek and staggered him.

Scannel laughed aloud at his own cleverness. But his merriment was short lived. John L., infuriated by what he considered an act of treachery, charged like a bull, smashed through Scannel's defense, and slammed a right to the jaw that knocked Scannel clean off the platform. He crashed into the orchestra circle and lay senseless.

It did not really take the kayo of Scannel to convince Sullivan that his forte was fighting. He had known that for some time. But at nineteen he was still an unknown except among his own personal followers, and it was difficult for him to obtain a professional match. Now, however, he got his chance. He was signed to fight Johnny "Cocky" Woods in Boston. Woods, a tall, well-built fellow, was so highly thought of by the experts that he had at one time been matched with John C. Heenan, then the champion; in consequence of interference by the authorities, this battle did not come off.

Woods was a good two-handed fighter, equipped with a heavy punch. A tried veteran, he was established by the gamblers as a favorite over the novice. But John L.'s friends were present in force and backed their man generously to win. They were not disappointed. Sullivan, after sizing up his man, lost no time in preliminary feinting. Disregarding Woods's attempt to counter his rush with a straight left, John closed in and caught his opponent with a terrific clubbing right on the jaw. Woods dropped. He was out cold.

This quick victory launched the youth definitely on the pugilistic ocean. He was now in heavy demand for exhibition engagements, and the following year, 1879, he won easily over Dan Dwyer in Revere Hall, Boston. Since Dan was the recognized champion of Massachusetts, Sullivan's fame increased. It further expanded when he whipped Tommy Chandler, a well-known and formidable heavyweight.

Fight fans talked more and more about the young New England sensation. He particularly attracted the attention of two famous Boston sports, Tom Farley and Jim Keenan. They became his backers.

Sullivan's big chance came when "Professor" Mike Donovan, world middleweight champion, came to Boston to give an exhibition in the latter part of 1879. The professor, who later held the post of boxing instructor at the New York Athletic Club, was deservedly rated as one of the most scientific boxers of the day.

Sullivan pleaded to be allowed to go on with Donovan, who, aware that the youth had had little experience, at first refused.

Donovan, always conscientious where his public was concerned, did not want to inflict a novice upon the spectators. But John persisted, and at last Donovan gave in, after having been assured by William Muldoon, the champion wrestler, who had seen Sullivan in action, that the Bostonian was not easy picking.

As if to prove Muldoon right, Sullivan bored in at the start and never let up. He rushed Donovan all over the ring, and the only thing that saved the veteran from being knocked out was his generalship.

"You're the goods, young fellow, and I'm betting you'll go far in this game!" said Donovan after the set-to.

Besides William Muldoon, his friend Billy Madden had seen Sullivan fight. The two were staging a variety show in Boston, and they agreed to put on John for an exhibition. Joe Goss, a claimant of the heavyweight title, was to appear in a benefit arranged for him, and Madden induced him to take on Sullivan for three rounds.

Goss was clever and tricky, but despite all his cleverness he was clearly outclassed. Sullivan dropped him with a right on the mouth in the second round. Joe was so badly dazed that he refused to continue unless Sullivan promised to let up on him. Sullivan agreed, and the bout went the limit. Said Goss at its conclusion, "I didn't think anyone could do that to me. You've got the kick of a mule in your fists, and you're going right to the top, son. I'd hate to tackle you in earnest!"

Following the Goss affair, Sullivan earned further prestige by giving the experienced George Rooke a terrific beating. Rooke was knocked down seven times in quick succession, and the bout was stopped to save him from further punishment.

By now Sullivan's fame had spread to other American sporting centers. The Boston Strong Boy was much in demand. Picking up all he had learned about boxing in hard fights, he had thrust himself into the spotlight by force of will and heavy punches.

Overnight, John had become a sensation, and they were talking about him everywhere.

Macon McCormick, America's ace reporter, then editor of the *Cincinnati Enquirer,* was an ardent fight patron, and he made up his mind that this new knockout artist must show his wares in the Middle West. Macon made a special trip to Boston to offer Sullivan a match in Cincinnati with Ohio's leading heavyweight, "Professor" John Donaldson. Sullivan accepted with alacrity.

Donaldson was a veteran of many battles and had no fear of Sullivan. With perfect confidence he answered the call of time and smiled at the scowling youth from the East. Sullivan, always intent on his work, opened the proceedings with a rush. Donaldson was hurled from one post to another and soon went down under a shattering volley of punches that seemed to come from all directions. The bout at once degenerated into a farce, and in the third round Donaldson decided that he had had enough and quit. But since the crowd threatened him with worse things outside the ropes if he didn't continue, the beaten man ruefully consented to resume. After taking another series of blows, he threw up his hands and quit again. He addressed the crowd, pleading that he was not in condition to do himself justice with such a battler as Sullivan; he promised that he would fight the Easterner in a return match when fully prepared.

Two months after the Cincinnati affair, they again faced each other in a back room of the Atlantic Garden in the Ohio city. Donaldson brought every trick in his fistic repertoire into play to avoid mixing matters with his slugging adversary. He side-stepped, ducked, clinched, and frequently avoided punishment by dropping to the floor or sprinting around the ring. But always the Boston terror pursued, and in the tenth round he cornered his elusive opponent and knocked him out cold with a right on the jaw.

The fight made so much talk around Cincinnati that the indignant authorities swung into action. The following day Sullivan was arrested and charged with engaging in a prize fight. He was brought into the court over which a Judge Moriarty presided. It happened that His Honor was an ardent fight fan and had been one of the most interested spectators at the ringside on the preceding day.

The courtroom was packed when the trial started. The first witness was called. He was one of several spectators of the contest who had been caught in the police net.

"What is your name?" asked the judge.

"Johnny Moran, Your Honor."

"Were you present when this alleged prize fight took place last night at the Atlantic Garden?"

"I was."

"Do you recognize any persons in this room, besides the defendants, who were among those present at the Atlantic?"

"Faith, I do, Your Honor. But I'm afraid if I answer, you may hold me for contempt of court!"

This answer provoked general laughter. The judge indulged in an elaborate judicial cough.

"Did you see a prize fight?" he continued.

"Oh, no, Your Honor. I saw a foot race."

"Very interesting," commented the magistrate. "Who was ahead in that race, Mr. Moran?"

"Well, Donaldson is a fine sprinter. He was mostly in the lead by a quarter of a mile, but Sullivan was hot on his trail."

"Did Mr. Sullivan catch him?"

"He did just that, Your Honor. Sullivan got right on his heels, and then he barely touched him, just to let him know that he had caught up!"

"What happened then?"

"Oh, that was the finish, Judge. Donaldson was tripped up, and couldn't continue. He hit the boards with an awful thud that took all the speed out of him. So he had to stop running and call it a day!"

"A very clear, lucid account of this athletic pastime," commented the judge. "You possess powers of observation and description, Mr. Moran!"

Then addressing the court in dignified fashion, Judge Moriarty delivered his verdict:

"The excellent testimony of this keen-eyed witness, who apparently saw everything that happened, convinces me that no prize fight took place, and consequently no breach of law occurred. No doubt remains in my mind, therefore, as to the legality of the entertainment. It is plain that these men merely engaged in a foot race, which cannot be listed as a violation of the law. The defendants are discharged."

By now Sullivan had proved to the entire satisfaction of the experts that he could fight like a tiger, was almost as fast as one, and could strike with the same effectiveness. He was well started along the road toward national and international fame.

Back in Boston, he gave several glove exhibitions with Joe Goss that drew capacity crowds. Billy Madden, one of the most capable members of the pugilistic managerial brigade, past or present, now took John in tow in real earnest. Billy had projected a cross-country tour for Sullivan, which he rightly figured would prove that the Strong Boy was entitled to a shot at the heavyweight title, lately won by Paddy Ryan.

Madden's first move in his campaign was to visit New York City with Sullivan. For John's debut, he selected Harry Hill's famous dance hall and boxing emporium on Bleecker Street, near the Bowery, the acknowledged rendezvous of America's most prominent habitués of the world of sport. Billy created a terrific sensation at Hill's one night by making an offer of fifty dollars to anyone in the house who would undertake to stand up four rounds against Sullivan. The challenge was directed particularly toward Paddy Ryan, who was present, but the champion ignored it.

Madden's offer was accepted by Steve Taylor, a bare-knuckle artist of considerable repute. But Taylor was outclassed, even as Joe Goss, George Rooke, and Donaldson had been. He lasted only two rounds. Sullivan made a splendid impression on Harry Hill's customers. He looked every inch the true fighter, a modern Hercules whose strength was apparently inexhaustible.

In Billy Madden, Sullivan had a perfect master of ballyhoo and an adviser of phenomenal shrewdness. It was Billy who made Sullivan's name virtually a household word in America. His standing offer of fifty dollars to any man who could stay four rounds with Sullivan sounded an entirely new note in fistic advertising. Madden knew well the value of waking up the public with something that had never been known before. The story of the fifty-bucks reward was published everywhere, and the fact that nobody ever earned it by remaining four rounds with the Boston biffer made it increasingly effective.

Sullivan's first important professional fight outside the metro-

politan area in New York State took place on a barge anchored
in the Hudson River, near Hastings. John Flood, known as the
Bull's Head Terror, was his opponent. Five hundred sports paid
ten dollars each to see the battle. The combatants fought with
skintight gloves, under London Prize Ring rules, for a stake of
1,000 dollars, of which 750 dollars went to the winner and 250
dollars to the loser. The fight lasted sixteen minutes, with Flood
knocked down or thrown in every round. The victim's seconds
threw in the sponge in the eighth, acknowledging defeat.

Madden then took John L. to Philadelphia and Chicago. In
both cities he gave boxing exhibitions and made good his manager's defiance to all comers. The Quaker City fans saw him
knock out Fred Crossley in one round, and he whipped two well-
known sluggers for the edification of Chicago ring patrons.

These latter victims of the Strong Boy's punch were Captain
James Dalton, a tugboat skipper who, besides having won many
ring battles, had defeated every man along the river front who
dared tackle him in rough-and-tumble style, and Jack Burns, an
enormous, strapping fellow, known as the Michigan Giant.
Dalton survived three rounds, but was nailed with Sully's pile-
driving right in the fourth. Burns was pounded silly and took the
full count before two minutes of the first frame had elapsed.

When Sullivan and Madden returned to the East, negotiations
were well under way for John's shot at Ryan's crown. These were
concluded on October 5, 1881, when articles were signed for a
fight to a finish with bare knuckles, to take place the following
February, for twenty-five hundred dollars a side.

This battle for the heavyweight championship was held at
Mississippi City on February 7, 1882, thirty-three years to the
day after Tom Hyer had beaten Yankee Sullivan for the title.
Public interest was very great. Thousands of enthusiasts from all
parts of the country, anticipating a real pugilistic treat, had journeyed south to the battleground. Every hangout of fight fans in
the United States was the scene of rabid bickerings over the
gladiators' merits. Throughout the land, as never before, people
in all walks of life were discussing a prize fight. The names Ryan
and Sullivan were on everybody's lips. For the first time in
American journalistic history, the newspapers hired famous nov-

elists and dramatists, and even members of the clergy, to write their impressions of a prize fight. Among those so employed were Henry Ward Beecher and T. De Witt Talmadge, the most celebrated divines of the day; Nat Goodwin represented the dramatic brotherhood, and Oscar Wilde, then on a lecture tour of the United States, accepted an assignment to write a story for a British publication.

The battle, though exciting, was a one-sided affair. Sullivan, standing five feet, ten and one-half inches, and weighing 196 pounds was much the smaller man. But he was far stronger than Ryan, and even in Paddy's own specialty, wrestling, he was notably superior.

John was awarded "first blood" by the referee, a decision that elated the Sullivan followers, who had wagered heavily on it. In the fourth round, Ryan was bleeding profusely and was badly winded. When time was called for the fifth, Paddy had to be helped out to toe the scratch. He was puffing like a grampus, although still full of fight. But Sullivan sprang upon the champion and allowed him no rest.

The eighth round was the beginning of the end. In a final rally, Ryan summoned all his strength and courage and went into a furious, give-and-take mix-up. They slugged away madly, their bodies glistening with sweat in the bright sun, their jaws grimly set.

Then came the crucial moment. Sullivan's terrible right crashed against Ryan's jaw. Paddy staggered back and toppled to the ground as stiff as a dead man. He was carried to his corner, where his seconds worked frantically to bring their man to scratch for the ninth round. But when time was called, Ryan could scarcely move. He staggered out gallantly to meet his inevitable doom.

Sullivan wasted no time. He tore in like a battering ram. His first blow struck Ryan's temple. Then his sledge-hammer right crashed home behind the left ear. Ryan crumpled up. His face turned gray. His legs and arms were outstretched. He lay completely motionless.

It was all over for Paddy. The man who had won the championship in his first professional fight had lost it in his second.

As for the new champion, at the age of twenty-three he stood like Alexander of Macedon after his destruction of the Persian cavalry at the Granicus. The world lay before him to be conquered.

Like Alexander, John was destined to prevail against all antagonists for ten years. And like Alexander, he was to bear the proud cognomen of the Great.

CHAPTER 8

LAST BARE-KNUCKLE
TITLE FIGHT

$\mathbb{S}$ULLIVAN loved fighting. After winning the title, he at once sought further action, and in the same year he stopped John McDermott at Rochester in three rounds, knocked out Jimmy Elliott in three rounds, and went through a four-round session in New York with Tug Wilson, a British heavyweight. Sullivan had agreed to stop the Englishman within four rounds,* but the artful Tug managed to go the limit by continually clinching, holding, and slipping to the floor. Since he was on his feet at the finish, Wilson was awarded the thousand-dollar reward that had been promised him if he accomplished the presumably impossible task.

Great was the wrath of the champion. But his reputation suffered little, for Wilson made no secret of the fact that he had gone into the ring determined to make a hugging match of it. Tug went home with his money, turning a deaf ear to all entreaties to try his hand at earning another purse. He became an innkeeper in the old English tradition, prospered, and never fought again.

On May 14, 1883, Sullivan met Charlie Mitchell of England in a glove bout staged in New York City. Tales of Mitchell's uncanny skill had preceded him to these shores, and in the opening round he demonstrated his cleverness by side-stepping the champion's rushes. Once, catching Sullivan partly off balance, he landed a short jolt to the head and knocked him down.

---

* A new set of rules, issued in 1867 by the Marquis of Queensberry, was gradually superseding the London Prize Ring code. Under the new rules, a round consisted of three minutes of fighting; between rounds there was a one-minute rest period.

Sullivan, unhurt, but wild with rage, charged Mitchell like an infuriated bull. Though the little Englishman gave a striking exhibition of defensive tactics, Sullivan's strength and crashing punches were too much for him. In the third round Police Captain Williams interfered and stopped the battle. Mitchell was almost out on the ropes.

Herbert A. Slade, the Maori, was Sullivan's next opponent. Slade, whose ability had been vouched for by no less a master of the game than Jem Mace, retired world champion, made his American debut before a New York gathering of fight enthusiasts who looked for great things from the much-touted Australian giant.

The big man towered above Sullivan as they faced each other, but neither superiority of height nor weight availed him. Sullivan's rushes carried Slade clean off his feet. The Maori was assailed with body punches that bent him in half. Early in the third round the man from the Antipodes was hurled across the ring by the impact of a clubbing right to his jaw and was unable to continue.

These victories over foreign invaders naturally added fresh luster to Sullivan's shield. But what finally raised John to the pinnacle of popularity was a tour of the United States, during which he offered the sum of one thousand dollars to any man who could stand up to him for four rounds. He prescribed gloves for these encounters, and it was this tour that popularized their use all over the country.

Across the continent he went, never evading a challenger. No complete record was kept of the men he knocked out, but it has been roughly estimated that no less than fifty opponents went down to defeat before the champion's irresistible blows. While other pugilists had in the past filled limited engagements of this kind, Sullivan's stunt of taking on all challengers for a period extending over nine months was without precedent.

Between January, 1884, and December, 1886, Sullivan added fourteen important victories to his record. The closest he came to losing was in his battle with Patsy Cardiff, at Minneapolis on January 18, 1887. In spite of breaking his left arm, he succeeded in getting a draw in six rounds.

During his reign, Sullivan mingled world tours, formal and informal exhibitions, meeting-all-comers stunts, and vaudeville appearances with his regular professional career. After Sullivan had made his name a household word in every city, town, and hamlet in the United States he decided to try a European junket for a change. On October 27, 1887, he sailed for Liverpool accompanied by his trainer and sparring mate, Jack Ashton, and his manager, Harry S. Phillips.

Queried by a reporter as to the object of this cruise, John answered, "I'm going for money, glory, and revenge, particularly the last. I've been abused in the papers, I've been lied about and condemned by men who, for commercial reasons, wanted to see a true American, a son of the Stars and Stripes, whipped by some foreigner. So now, I'm intending to get even by unfurling Uncle Sam's victorious flag in the land from which my enemies brought men they hoped would conquer me. If there are any fighters abroad who think they can whip me, I guess I'll give them a chance. That goes especially for Charlie Mitchell and Jem Smith!"

It is a matter of record that no prominent American athlete ever received such an enthusiastic welcome from British sportsmen as did Sullivan. During the journey from Liverpool to London, he was given one ovation after another in the intermediate towns. At the station in London, the crush of eager spectators was so great that Sullivan's party had to fight its way toward the cab rank.

John himself, in an effort to avoid the mob, leaped into the first cab he reached, and then the real fun began. Everyone was crazy to shake his hand, and seven persons, among whom were two leading heavyweight boxers, rushed the vehicle. Some got inside, others clung to the sides. The load was too great for the cab. Its floor caved in, and Sullivan, along with several of his impulsive admirers, hit the cobblestones in a heap. The Boston Strong Boy roared a deep-chested laugh as thousands cheered. The incident increased John's popularity.

That night he appeared in a sparring exhibition where he made the acquaintance of Jem Smith, claimant of the British heavyweight title. Smith, in turn, introduced him to the audience.

"I consider it a high honor," said Smith, "to be the means of introducing this great American fighter. I now understand why his countrymen idolize him. His popularity has been transferred to England, and it is a pleasure I'll never forget to present to you the Champion of Champions—John L. Sullivan!"

Jem Smith's eloquence stirred his hearers to a tempest of applause. As Sullivan came forward to respond to the generous welcome, the tempest increased.

The Great One was never distinguished for his diplomacy. All his life he had been accustomed to speak his mind, without caring in the least whether he stepped on anyone's toes. He spoke as he fought, aggressively, when he thought the occasion so demanded, and the compliments paid him by Smith hadn't softened his belligerent disposition in the least.

"Gentlemen," said the champion, "I am more than grateful for the fine reception you have given me, but I must state that I have come all the way from my native land for the sole purpose of licking Jem Smith and Charlie Mitchell, the men who have repeatedly challenged me—but at a safe distance of three thousand miles. Now I'm here, right on their own camping ground, and I'll give 'em a chance to make good their boasts!"

He paused and pointed successively to Smith and Mitchell. Cheers and laughter greeted his gestures.

Then John turned to Smith and, looking him squarely in the eyes, roared in his window-rattling bass, "Yes, Mr. Smith, that's what I'm here for. I want to lick you—just as much as you want to lick me!"

Several days after his arrival in London, Sullivan issued a statement: "In America it is customary to put up the money first and do the talking afterwards. My forfeit money is posted for a fight with Jem Smith, but he hasn't covered it. Either he must put up or shut up. But I'm afraid that neither Smith nor Mitchell want to meet me between the ropes."

Sullivan was right about Smith, but before he left London on a tour of the British Isles he and Mitchell had signed articles for a fight to decide the championship of the world. Then he began a series of exhibitions that took him through Birmingham, Liverpool, Manchester, Newcastle-on-Tyne, Leicester, Nottingham, Derby, Sheffield, Preston, Oldham, and many other boxing centers. Crossing to the land of his parents' birth, he was given a hero's welcome by the enraptured Irish. Next the champion and his party visited the Scottish cities of Glasgow, Edinburgh, Aberdeen, and Dundee. The triumphal tour ended in Wales.

On returning to London, Sullivan was invited to breakfast in the regimental mess of the Scots Guards. His nominal host was Captain Cliff, but the real host was the Prince of Wales (later King Edward VII), who had expressed a desire to meet the champion.

When John was presented, he delighted his royal host by remarking, "Well, Prince, next to Jem Smith, your champion, who I'm so anxious to whip, the Prince of Wales is the man I most wanted to see when I came to England."

That evening Sullivan obliged the Prince by giving a boxing exhibition at the Pelican Club with his sparring partner, Jack Ashton. After leading the applause, the Prince shook Sullivan's hand and congratulated him on his skill, splendid figure, and fighting qualities. (That particular handshake gave birth to a wisecrack that went the rounds for years—"Let me shake the hand that shook the hand of the Prince of Wales!" It also formed the basis of a song that was sung in vaudeville all over the United States.)

On March 10, 1888, came the Mitchell fight. The site chosen was Baron Rothschild's estate at Chantilly, France. Most of the spectators were British, and since secrecy had to be maintained in order to avoid interference by the authorities, the crowd was strictly limited in number.

The ring was set up behind a stable, on ground utilized as training quarters for the Baron's race horses. For thirty-six hours a heavy rain had been falling. It had stopped by the time the fighters were squared off, but the ground was so soggy that they were ankle deep in mud. During the battle, fought under London rules, there were intermittent showers.

The muddy condition of the ring favored Mitchell, for Sullivan's greater weight was a handicap on such heavy footing. Mitchell was tricky and knew how to make use of every inch of the big ring. John knocked him down fifteen times, but Charlie came back to scratch gamely after each fall, apparently little the worse for the buffeting he took.

The principals were frequently compelled to stand against the ropes and rest. But they carried on desperately, in spite of growing fatigue and darkness. The thirty-eighth round ended with both Sullivan and his opponent falling from weariness. The officials then prevailed upon the pair to agree to a draw in the thirty-ninth session, after they had fought for three hours and eleven minutes. Sullivan at that time, according to the late Arthur Brisbane, had had much the better of the engagement.

Upon returning to the United States, Sullivan was given a great ovation by the fans even though the fight had ended so unsatisfactorily. Their confidence in the champion was unshaken, and they attested the esteem in which they held him by giving banquets in many cities.

It was during one of those testimonial dinners in Boston that Sullivan was informed that Richard K. Fox, publisher of *The Police Gazette* and his enemy for years, had awarded a belt to Jake Kilrain, designating him as world champion. Of course, Fox had not the slightest right to bestow such a title on Jake, but the crafty publisher attained two objectives: he enraged the Great One and lured him into a match with Jake.

Before that battle could take place, however, John had to overcome another antagonist. Always a terrific man with the bottle, he had for months after the Mitchell draw been drinking even harder than usual. Even his iron constitution was bound to break under the strain of protracted alcoholic orgies, and he finally collapsed. He was confined to a sick bed from August to November, 1888, and the news of his debauchery and breakdown was freely circulated. Sullivan was always good copy for the newspapers. Whatever he did—fighting, drinking, wenching, or just walking down the street—was good for a story. When the news came out that the champion's gigantic spree had thrown him the pious readers pointed to the "horrible example," the sporting fraternity laughed at what they regarded as a great joke, and his real friends grieved to see so great a fighter the victim of his own uncurbed appetites.

When John recovered, he accepted Kilrain's long-standing challenge and went into training under William Muldoon's supervision. Sullivan was practically a physical wreck when Muldoon took him in hand, but the gifted trainer, an iron disciplinarian, put John L. in the pink of fighting condition after six months of strenuous work.

The starting point for the fight fans was New Orleans. Nobody was told just where the ring would be pitched because, no matter where the battlers went, they were likely to run into governors, sheriffs, state militia, and other representatives of the law. But a special train had been engaged, and on Sunday morning, July 7, 1889, it pulled out of the New Orleans station, bearing Sullivan, Kilrain, their handlers, and hundreds of followers. The destination was still "unknown."

The fighters had special cars. They also had empty mail cars in which to limber up. The fight fans crowded all the other cars and even climbed onto the roofs, where they defied the trainmen, and rode fare free. When the train reached Richburg, Mississippi, the "secret" site of the battle, Kilrain went to the home of a local lumber magnate, named Fisk, who was one of the promoters. Sullivan was provided with rooms in another private residence.

In a clearing in the woods, about a quarter of a mile from the center of Richburg, Fisk had built a wooden arena where the fight was to be staged. When the principals arrived, they found a shouting mob waiting. Spectators even roosted in the trees surrounding the theater of war.

The ring was pitched on the turf. Kilrain was first to climb through the ropes, and then John entered, accompanied by Bill Muldoon and Mike Cleary. Although Sullivan held the championship and was regarded, in spite of his recent illness, as the greatest fighter of all time, the betting was at even money. And there was plenty of cash in evidence.

John Fitzpatrick, later mayor of New Orleans, was the referee, Bat Masterson, once sheriff of Dodge City and in later years the boxing expert of the *Morning Telegraph* of New York, was timekeeper for Jake, while Tom Costello held the watch for John.

It was high noon and the sun was blazing when the gong clanged and the battlers began their long struggle for the heavyweight championship of America. After a lively start, Sullivan shot a left to the jaw that missed. Kilrain parried neatly and back-heeled his man, getting a clean fall. The crowd roared. Sullivan was fit to be tied. Jake had won the first round.

Sullivan picked himself up and went to his corner. He said to Kilrain, "So you want to wrestle, do you? Well, Jake, I am going to give you more than enough of that."

From then on Sullivan forced matters, but for more than forty rounds the battle was kept nearly even by Jake's great gallantry and spirit. After the forty-fifth round the tide turned definitely in Sullivan's favor. Only Kilrain's gameness kept him in action. When he was too weak to stand erect, after seventy-five rounds that had lasted two hours and sixteen minutes, his seconds threw in the sponge.

The Sullivan-Kilrain encounter was the last heavyweight championship fight held under London Prize Ring Rules. Thereafter the gloves were to decide the arguments of title claimants. The bare-knuckle man had had his day.

It is hard to reconstruct the impact of a battle that was fought so long ago, and the task is one for a poet rather than for a reporter who had been born only two years before. A great American writer and singer of verse has recounted his distant impressions. It seems appropriate to quote from Vachel Lindsay's *John L. Sullivan, the Strong Boy of Boston:*

When I was nine years old, in 1889,

. . . . . .

I heard a battle trumpet sound.
Nigh New Orleans
Upon an emerald plain
John L. Sullivan
The strong boy
Of Boston
Fought seventy-five rounds with Jake Kilrain.

. . . . . .

In mystic, ancient 1889,
Wilson with pure learning was allied.
Roosevelt gave forth a chirping sound.
Stanley found old Emin and his train.
Stout explorers sought the pole in vain.
To dream of flying proved a man insane.
The newly rich were bathing in champagne.
Van Bibber Davis, at a single bound
Displayed himself, and simpering glory found.
John J. Ingalls, like a lonely crane
Swore and swore, and stalked the Kansas plain.
The Cronin murder was the ages' stain.
Johnstown was flooded, and the whole world cried.
We heard not of Louvain nor of Lorraine,
Or of a million heroes for their freedom slain.
Of Armageddon and the world's birth-pain—
The League of Nations, and the world one posy.
We *thought* the world would loaf and sprawl and mosey.
The gods of Yap and Swat were sweetly dozy.
We *thought* the far-off gods of Chow had died.
The mocking bird was singing in the lane. . . .
Yet . . .
"East side, west side, all around the town
The tots sang: 'Ring a rosie'
'LONDON BRIDGE IS FALLING DOWN.' "
And . . .
John L. Sullivan knocked out Jake Kilrain.*

---

* From the *Golden Whales of California*, by Vachel Lindsay. Copyright, 1920, by The Macmillan Company and used with their permission.

CHAPTER 9

EXIT JOHN THE GREAT

JOHN L. SULLIVAN was now as much an American institution as strawberry shortcake, fireworks on the Fourth of July, and the high-wheeled bicycle. Everywhere he went people paid him homage. They paid him cash, too, and it didn't matter what kind of entertainment he had to offer. In the ring or out, John the Great was the biggest drawing card of the day. As the hero of a melodrama entitled *Honest Hearts and Willing Hands,* he toured the country and hauled in the shekels. The fact that he spent his money as fast as it came in—sometimes he spent it even faster—did not lessen his popularity. Nor did his habit of walking into a saloon, ordering a round of drinks for all, and announcing that he could lick any blankety-blank son-of-a-so-and-so in the place. Everybody knew it was true. At least nearly everybody.

One of the handful of doubters in 1891 was a twenty-five-year-old San Franciscan named Jim Corbett who had learned to fight as a kid in the tough Hayes Valley section of his native city. After he became a bank clerk, Corbett kept on boxing; he won the championship of the Olympic Club and later became the club instructor. In 1889, after having turned professional, he beat another San Franciscan, Joe Choynski, in a grudge fight held on a barge in Carquinez Strait, and the following year he took on Jake Kilrain. Most people weren't greatly impressed when Corbett won a six-round decision from Jake. Even after Corbett fought sixty-one rounds to a draw with Peter Jackson, the talented Australian Negro (whom Sullivan refused to meet because of his color), he was thought of simply as a "pretty good" heavyweight. There was, as everybody knew, only one real fighter in the world. His name was John L. Sullivan, and he was invincible.

In the late spring of 1891, Sullivan arrived in San Francisco preparatory to sailing for Australia, where he was booked to give a number of boxing exhibitions and, with his company, to present *Honest Hearts and Willing Hands*. Corbett had just fought Jackson, and since he had been deprived of the purse because the referee declared the bout a draw, his friends decided to give him a benefit. When Sullivan was offered half the gate —it amounted to at least five thousand dollars—he consented to go four rounds with the ex-bank clerk. John specified that evening clothes should be worn instead of the customary tights and that he and his opponent should spar with heavy gloves.

As a boxing match, the bout held on the stage of the Grand Opera House, June 26, 1891, was a farce. Sullivan, who was out of training, did not exert himself. As for Corbett, he contented himself with feinting and side-stepping. Neither man landed a real punch. The spectators hooted in disgust.

But Corbett was well pleased. Getting into a clean shirt after the exhibition, he remarked to Billy Delaney, his second, "I can beat this fellow! He's a sucker for a feint."

The youthful William A. Brady, then at the start of his long career as a theatrical impresario, took Corbett under his wing. Importing Jim to New York and presenting him on the stage— the handsome boxer was even at that time a box-office success— he built up his reputation to such an extent that Sullivan agreed to meet him for the championship. On March 10, 1892, articles were signed for a fight with five-ounce gloves before the Olympic Club of New Orleans for a twenty-five-thousand-dollar purse and a twenty-thousand-dollar stake, the bout to take place on September 7 of the same year.

More than three years had elapsed since Sullivan had beaten Kilrain. During that period John L. had not donned a glove except for exhibitions. Idleness, the enervating life of the stage, long nights of carousal with boon companions, all had taken toll of his vitality, shortened his breath, and increased his girth. He was no longer the iron-sinewed youth who had demolished Steve Taylor at Harry Hill's eleven years before. It is doubtful if even Muldoon, who practically rebuilt Sullivan for the Kilrain combat, could have done much toward improving his physical condition at this time.

OLYMPIC CLUB, NEW ORLEANS

Sullivan totally underestimated Corbett, believing firmly that, in or out of condition, he could defeat the Californian easily. John L. had reached that stage in a fighter's career where training was a dismal grind. At his best, the Boston Strong Boy heartily disliked the task of conditioning himself. At his worst, with no Muldoon to drive him and discipline him, he went through daily exercises in desultory fashion.

What did it matter? He was sure to win anyway.

There is a mixture of tragedy and comedy in the picture of this bulky, self-confident gladiator intoning a popular ballad as, surrounded by admiring satellites, he rode magnificently in an open carriage from his hotel to the arena. In reality his carriage was a tumbril, and the guillotine awaited him at the top of the hill. Ignorant of his fate, he sang right lustily as he rolled along. Always a merry soul except when actually waging warfare, John the Great never felt merrier than when a fight and victory were in prospect.

The Corbett-Sullivan battle for the heavyweight championship was a red-letter day in ring history. Besides witnessing the fall of the premier pugilistic idol, it definitely set the seal of public approval on the use of gloves in heavyweight championship contests as opposed to the bare knuckles and rough, mauling tactics under London Prize Ring Rules. The Queensberry era of boxing came triumphantly into its own with the successful staging of the battle in New Orleans. It was not the first important fight to be waged under the new rules. Corbett had defeated Jake Kilrain at Crescent City on February 8, 1890, with what the old-timers were wont to call "the mufflers." Corbett's sensational sixty-one-round draw with Peter Jackson on May 21, 1891, was also fought with gloves, and there had been other such matches promoted among leading boxers in all classes. But this was the first in which a heavyweight title was at stake.

Corbett had faith in himself. He did not underestimate Sullivan's punching powers. But he knew his opponent's weaknesses. Jim figured that he could make the slugger miss often, fool him with quick footwork, and gradually wear him down. That was the strategy he successfully followed in their fight.

Trainloads of visitors from far and near poured into New Orleans to attend that memorable battle. Each carried its quota of straight sports, gunmen, pickpockets, and gamblers. But so keen was the public interest that the more shady spectators were themselves overshadowed by respectable citizens.

The Olympic Club was dressed in gala style for the big night.

The wide tarpaulins that formed the roof had been removed to provide ample ventilation for contestants and spectators. Shortly before the scheduled hour a sudden heavy downpour of rain drenched the crowd and the tarpaulins were hurriedly replaced —but not in time to prevent the turf on which the battle was to be fought from becoming wet and soggy. To remedy this condition and protect the fighters' footing, a heavy layer of sawdust was spread over the earth.

There isn't much to the story of that battle. Corbett, young, lithe, active, and brainy, stepped jauntily around the massive hulk of what had once been a great fighting man. He evaded Sullivan's sweeping leads, hooked, countered on the retreat, cut and jarred John L. incessantly. Sullivan rushed in vain. His formidable right hand which had won for him so often was useless against a flitting shadow.

The end came in the twenty-first round, when Sullivan dropped from sheer exhaustion. For the first time in his career, he heard a referee count the fatal ten over his prostrate body.

When the Boston Strong Boy came to, he arose, faced the crowd, and said, "I fought once too often. But I'm glad that it was an American who beat me and that the championship stays in this country."

They cried over John L. on that September day in New Orleans. For Sullivan's downfall was something far more to the millions who adored him than the present generation can easily understand. Their hero had become a symbol of national glory, a manifestation of America's greatness. The Bostonian occupied an altogether unique position in the emotional structure of America's working millions. They swore by him, condoned his faults, admired his very human frailties, loved him.

Corbett was the complete antithesis of John L. He was quiet spoken, conservative in dress, fastidious in his tastes, and a born diplomat. He was no prig, but the flowing bowl had no lure for him and tavern brawls were not included in his hours of relaxation. It was eminently fitting that the sports writers should tag him Gentleman Jim.

There was no denying Jim's good influence upon boxing. The times were changing rapidly and the breed of sportsman was changing with them. Corbett appeared at precisely the right moment. It was a fortunate thing for the prize ring that the Queensberry code, which was designed to favor the scientific boxer, should receive its first important test in a match that was won by the greatest master of ring science up to that time.

But the immediate popular reaction was unfavorable. A long period elapsed before Gentleman Jim overcame the prejudice engendered because he had dared to hurl Sullivan down from the heights. Oddly enough, it was the Irish sports, then all-powerful in ring affairs, who were most bitter. They couldn't forgive this interloper for the sin of defeating the pride of their race. The anti-Corbett campaign was all the more ludicrous because the new champion and the old had the same essential qualities—both had first-crop Irish parents, both had been born in the United States.

Eventually Corbett lived down the awful "crime" he had committed at New Orleans. By degrees he won the affections of his own generation of young athletes who admired his fine science and emulated the pattern of his decent behavior. With Gentleman Jim boxing may be said to have come of age. Henceforth the sport was to be an increasingly respected member of the entertainment community.

As for the fallen champion, the legend of invincibility woven around him persisted long after his defeat. Thousands of his worshipers attributed his loss of the title entirely to lack of condition and insisted that were Muldoon to take John in hand again the ex-champion would regain his crown. But Sullivan was through as a fighter and knew it. He never attempted to come back.

Now that time has in some measure dispelled the glamour that surrounded the heroic figure of the Strong Boy, one can gain a fair estimate of his real ability by considering the solid facts in connection with his rise and fall. When he won the championship from Ryan, stopped Mitchell in their glove combat, knocked out Maori Slade, and made his triumphal tour through the country, meeting and whipping all comers in four-round bouts, John L. Sullivan was a supreme fighting man. He was still a great fighter when, after his collapse and subsequent revamping by Muldoon, he came back and outslugged Jake Kilrain. From then on, however, his retrogression was rapid. Whether Sullivan ever realized how far back he had gone is doubtful. He may have known that something of his former strength and quickness was lacking, but his egotism was so great that he probably believed himself capable of beating anybody in the world even if his physical powers had dropped 50 per cent.

Yet, in his latter days, he displayed symptoms of caution to which the young, roaring, brawling, tempestuous Sullivan had been a stranger. He evaded a match with Peter Jackson by drawing the color line—which was just as well for him, since Jackson would probably have beaten him as decisively as did Corbett a little later. During his tour of Australia, John L. was formally challenged by Joe Goddard, the "Barrier Champion," and a big purse was offered for the match by Sydney sportsmen. Sullivan refused, sending instead his sparring partner, Jack Ashton, against Goddard. The latter knocked out Ashton in eight rounds, and John returned to the United States without taking on the winner.

But when all is said and done, John the Great deserved his title. Even today, though the ring has known more skillful wearers of the heavyweight crown, many people call him the Champion of Champions.

After his retirement he made another fortune on the stage. Not that he was anything of an actor, quite the contrary. He was just himself (though now grown monstrously fat), good-humoredly aggressive, bellowing forth stale jests, telling ancient yarns, going stolidly through his monologue, and—always—getting a big hand from all parts of the house.

In vaudeville and on the lecture platform, he was uniformly successful. Those of a later generation flocked to hear and see him even as their fathers had done, and they cheered him to the echo. Long before his death, Sullivan had sworn off drinking and become a lecturer on temperance. He was verging on sixty when he died at Abington, Massachusetts, on February 2, 1918.

CHAPTER 10

GENTLEMAN JIM AND
THE NEW ERA

You may talk about your champions in the good old days of yore,
   The heroes of the prize ring in savage mills galore,
The gallant gladiators who battled doggedly
   As brave as jungle lions, and game right to the core;
But for splendid speed and science none of them could compare
   With him who holds the title now, a true American,
Jim Corbett of the Irish breed, the wizard boxing lad
   Who took the fighting crown away from John L. Sullivan!

IN THE Golden Nineties, the vaudeville stage—they called it "variety" then—was paying tribute to the new champion with the ballad from which these lines were taken. He may not have been a great popular hero. He may never have enjoyed the unrestrained affection that Sullivan had earned. But Corbett was nonetheless admired, and he had one thing very few professional fighters ever won. That was universal respect.

James J. Corbett was born in San Francisco on September 1, 1866. His father, Patrick J. Corbett, had sailed from Ireland for New Orleans in 1854. He soon left the Crescent City for the Golden Gate. There the sturdy son of Erin found the climate to his liking, and his lively Celtic temperament buoyed him through the early struggles for a livelihood. He married in 1857, and to him and his wife were born twelve children, with the future heavyweight champion fourth on the list.

Those were the days when San Francisco was divided in two by the Market Street cable-car line, which ran from the bay to the foot of Twin Peaks. The part below Market was (and still is) known as "south of the slot," because of its cable slot. That was where the fighters came from.

Tad Dorgan, famous cartoonist, came from that section. So did David Belasco and David Warfield, celebrated in the theatrical world. It produced many pugilists, including Jimmy Britt, his brother Willus, who fought for the mere joy of fighting, Abe Attell, who won the featherweight title, and Willie Ritchie, who took the lightweight championship from Ad Wolgast and lost it to Freddy Welsh in London. The San Francisco Athletic Club, run by Alec Greggains, once a prominent middleweight, was located "south of the slot," and that club brought various fighters under the spotlight. It was a turbulent locality. A boy born in that part just had to fight. It was in the air.

When Jim Corbett was a small boy, the entire family migrated across the slot. The day of the hegira was a bitter memory for James J. Corbett. He had to head the migration, leading the family cow, and he felt so humiliated by the job he had been given that he wept his way across Market Street.

After this move Corbett's dad established an institution of much importance to San Francisco—a livery stable and undertaking parlor. The place figured prominently in the lives and deaths of the city's residents in that period. Many of them rode to christenings, weddings, and funerals in the Corbett hacks.

Corbett senior built up a thriving business and had no difficulty in bringing up his children decently. Like the parents of John L. Sullivan, he had set his heart on having Jim study for the priesthood. But that hope never materialized, for James J.'s ideas did not run in a religious groove.

Jim Corbett gave early evidence of his fistic prowess. He indulged in all kinds of athletic competition as a lad. He was a fast sprinter, an excellent baseball player, a good gymnast, and was noted for the skilled manner in which he handled his "dukes." Had he not taken up professional boxing he would probably have adopted baseball as a career.

After leaving school Corbett went into a mercantile establishment, where he became a clerk with a reputation for being unusually quick at figures. When he grew to young manhood he quit that position for the post of teller in a branch of the Nevada National Bank of San Francisco. That rise in the social scale for his son warmed the cockles of Corbett senior's heart. Next to having Jim enter the priesthood, his becoming a bank employee was the grandest thing that could have happened to him. So thought Corbett's dad, who would have been properly horrified if at this juncture anyone had even hinted that James J. would shed the mantle of conventional respectability for the trunks of prize fighter!

Jim's real boxing education began when he became a member of the Olympic Club and gained the attention of the instructor, "Professor" Watson. A middle-aged Briton brought from England by the Olympic executives, Watson was a painstaking teacher with genuine ability for imparting scientific knowledge to his pupils and with a keen eye for fighting merit.

Corbett was as anxious to learn as Watson was to teach him the finer points of the game. The pupil progressed so rapidly that the Briton matched him for a bout with the club's amateur middleweight champion, Dave Eiseman. Dave was a good slugger, and most of his fellow members expected him to dispose of Corbett quickly. The canny Watson had kept Corbett under cover, and only a few individuals realized how good the new pupil really was.

Though the bout was an exhibition, Eiseman went in for a knockout from the first call of time. The first round ended amid storms of applause for the novice who had stood up to the middleweight star. In the second frame, after a furious exchange at close quarters, a straight right to the chin sent Eiseman sprawling through the ropes and clean out of the ring. The battle ended with Jim Corbett the winner.

From that victory, Corbett progressed to heavyweight, as well as to middleweight, champion of the club. He was soon recognized as the most amazing amateur boxer on the Pacific Coast. Whenever a prominent professional heavyweight came to San Francisco, Corbett made a point of boxing with the visitor in private. He quietly became an expert.

For several years after he turned professional, Corbett had a fame that was purely local, but his brother Californians swore by him as a coming champion. His greatest rival was Joe Choynski, also a "native son" with a strong following. Joe was a shrewd ring general, a scientific boxer, and a terrific puncher. The two first met on May 30, 1889, in battle near Fairfax, California, with two-ounce gloves, but police interfered and stopped the bout in the fourth round. Following the custom of the old-timers of the London ring, the principals determined to continue hostilities at the earliest possible time. On June 5, the battle was resumed on a barge anchored in Carquinez Strait near Benicia. On this occasion Corbett kept the two-ounce gloves with which the argument had started, but Choynski selected skintights—in this case a pair of leather driving mitts with corded backs capable of inflicting a nasty cut when a blow was landed.

Twenty-seven rounds were fought at top speed before Choynski, choking from the blood that was flowing from his nostrils back into his throat, was compelled to strike his colors. They were a fairly evenly matched pair, with just enough advantage in Corbett's favor to turn the balance.

Corbett's defeat of Jake Kilrain in nine rounds before a New Orleans club on February 18, 1890, brought the young Californian into national prominence. Though less than eight months had elapsed since Kilrain had given John L. Sullivan the toughest battle of his career, young Corbett, outweighed by eighteen pounds, won from the veteran with ease.

On May 21 of the following year, Corbett astonished the boxing world by holding Peter Jackson to a draw. Corbett's sixty-one round bout with Jackson, one of the truly great Negro heavyweights, stamped the Californian as the man to watch in the future. At this time he weighed no more than 165.

A few weeks later came the sparring exhibition with Sullivan at the Grand Opera House in San Francisco. The Boston Strong Boy disliked Corbett and referred to him contemptuously as "that California dude." He conceived the monstrous joke of sparring in full dress, and he and Corbett actually boxed in starched linen and white ties, with only their coats removed. But Jim was unperturbed by the attempt to humiliate him. He discovered that the Great One was made to order for him in a contest which called for speed and science, and when the two met for the championship in 1892, the "dude" applied the knowledge he had acquired in the Grand Opera House and ground his beefy opponent into hamburger.

Following his defeat of Sullivan, Corbett made his stage debut, under the management of Billy Brady, as the hero of a melodrama entitled *Gentleman Jack*. The engagement was a highly successful one, and more than a year passed before Corbett began to think of defending his title. Then an opponent appeared in the person of Charlie Mitchell, claimant to the championship of England, who had come to the United States for the express purpose of fighting the American titleholder.*

The Englishman and Corbett first encountered each other in the lobby of the Hoffman House in New York, and Mitchell immediately set about insulting Corbett. Mitchell had a spectacular command of billingsgate, and he cursed Corbett with such vehemence that the American would have sailed into him on the spot if friends had not interfered. Corbett, usually so cool and balanced, insisted that Brady (who managed him in the ring as well as on the stage) arrange for a fight with as little delay as possible.

The fight took place in Jacksonville, Florida, January 25, 1894, for a twenty-thousand-dollar purse and five thousand dollars a side.

Corbett, at twenty-eight, in the full flush of his physical powers, outweighed his opponent by twenty-four pounds. He stood six feet, one inch, in his socks, as against Mitchell's five feet, nine inches. Mitchell, at thirty-three, had long since seen his best days. He had lived hard and fast, engaged in many grueling fights with bare knuckles as well as gloves, and the pace had told on him. Indeed, Mitchell himself knew very well that unless he could manage a knockout at an early stage he had scant chance of victory. His plan of campaign was to enrage Corbett to a point where the California lad would lose his head and rush him and perhaps leave an opening for a decisive blow.

When the men walked to the center of the ring to receive instructions from "Honest John" Kelly, the referee, Mitchell, in a voice clearly heard by the press-stand occupants, poured out a stream of filthy insults at Corbett. He wound up with one un-

* Jem Smith, though much inferior to Mitchell as a fighter, was at this time recognized as champion of England.

printable reference to Jim's domestic relations, and Corbett turned pale with rage.

The echo of the first bell had not died away before Corbett was on top of his antagonist, slugging away with both hands. Nobody had ever seen the champion perform in such reckless style. He was, as Mitchell had hoped, beside himself with fury. Charlie saw the opening he had been watching for and shot through a left to the nose, drawing first blood. But that was as close as he came to triumph. Jim, transformed from the polished boxer to the savage fighter, was bent on a knockout. The first round was a Mitchell massacre, the second a repetition, and early in the third the end came when Mitchell went down for the last time under a hurricane of blows.

Corbett's rage had not yet spent itself. As Mitchell fell to his knees, the champion followed with a right to the jaw which brought forth a yell of "Foul!" from Pony Moore, Mitchell's father-in-law, who was in the Englishman's corner. Referee Kelly paid no attention to the claim and counted Mitchell out.

The majority of the spectators were almost petrified with astonishment when they saw the clever, scientific Corbett switch to wild, rushing tactics. But the men in the press stand understood—they had heard Mitchell's remarks before the bout started —and the consensus of opinion was that Corbett couldn't have been blamed if he had killed the Englishman.

One would scarcely suppose that whipping their best heavyweight would have been Corbett's ideal preparation for endearing himself to the English people, but a few weeks after the Jacksonville affair Corbett sailed for Mitchell's native land with his *Gentleman Jack* company. But either Mitchell's compatriots didn't regret his downfall to any great extent, or a natural curiosity to see the man who had whipped not only their own Charlie but the celebrated John L. proved stronger than national pride. In any case, Corbett played to crowded houses all through his tour.

Jim was given an unusual tribute when he played in Islington. Old Jem Mace appeared on the stage and presented him with a gold-headed cane. The veteran then complimented Corbett as the most scientific boxer he had ever been privileged to gaze upon and concluded with the wish that "Mr. Corbett may hold the world's championship until the stick I have given him wears out!" *

Jim Corbett now stood alone upon an eminence. No heavyweight of real ability was in sight, and after taking on a mediocre fighter named Peter Courtney, in a bout arranged for the benefit of Thomas Edison's Kinetoscope, the champion announced his retirement and named as his successor Peter Maher, an Irishman.

But if there was no top-flight heavyweight to do battle with Corbett, there was the very formidable Bob Fitzsimmons, who had beaten Jack Dempsey, known as the Nonpareil, for the middleweight title a few years earlier. Fitzsimmons showed his contempt for Corbett's nomination of Maher by knocking the Irishman senseless in one round. Thereupon Corbett decided to return to active service, and a match with Fitzsimmons was arranged.

The battle between Corbett and Fitz on March 17, 1897, in Carson City, Nevada, struck a new and vigorous note in pugilistic ballyhoo. It was the first fight to be staged in a specially built open-air arena in American fistic history. And it was notable for being the first ring contest of which motion pictures were filmed.

Jut before the fight got under way, Corbett walked over to Fitz and extended his hand. Fitz ignored the gesture, and the bell rang.

The men sparred cautiously for an opening. Corbett was the first to land, with a light jab. Fitz moved forward. Corbett feinted, then like a flash he sent a left hook to the stomach, evading Fitz's counter. Jim speeded up, and his famous left jab landed several times on Fitz's face. The crowd could see that Fitzsimmons, while intent on forcing matters, was completely outclassed at long-range sparring.

Soon Fitzsimmons was bleeding profusely from the nose and mouth. In the sixth session, Corbett dropped him with a beauti-

---

* Though some sports authorities denied that Corbett was world champion, many critics, Mace included, contended that Corbett's victory over Mitchell entitled him to the crown.

fully timed cross on the jaw for a count of nine. Fitz looked shaky when he went to his corner at the end of the round and the gamblers were offering ten to four on Corbett.

But Fitz possessed marvelous powers of recuperation. He appeared surprisingly fresh and confident when he came up for the seventh. He cut loose at once with several right swings for the jaw.

In the middle of a fast rally in the eighth round, Fitz suddenly stepped back, shifted, and planted a solid left on Corbett's midsection. It was a stiff punch, and it hurt. Corbett covered up and boxed rapidly in an attempt to conceal the effects of the blow, but those close by the ringside knew that it had taken a lot out of the swift-moving Californian.

"I found the right spot that time," remarked Fitz to his seconds as he sat in his corner after the round was over.

That stomach punch marked the beginning of the end for Corbett. He was slowed up considerably, and as his speed faded, his attack weakened. In contrast, Fitzsimmons began moving faster, forcing the pace relentlessly. Thanks to his wonderful skill, Corbett still outboxed him, but the snap had gone out of his blows. He was fighting automatically and was so obviously tired that by the close of the tenth round the betting odds had shrunk to even.

In the early stages of the combat Fitz had been jabbed so persistently that the blood continued to leak profusely from his mouth and nostrils. His face was a crimson mask, and Corbett was spattered with his opponent's gore. A good many of the spectators thought that Jim was handing Bob an awful lacing, but the knowing ones observed that the champion was going to pieces, slowly but surely.

Fitz kept on shooting his right for the jaw, but without hitting that mark. He thus lured Corbett into raising his guard higher and higher. When the fourteenth round got under way, Bob was ready for the kill.

After the champion had shot several lefts to the face, Bob feinted for the jaw with his right. As Corbett raised his arm to protect his jaw, Fitz executed his famous shift, bringing his right foot forward. Then in went a right to the heart, followed

1860: The famous match for the world championship between Sayers, the English titleholder, and Heenan, champion of the United States. The battle, fought in England, ended in a draw when spectators cut the ropes and invaded the ring in the thirty-seventh round.

1889: John L. Sullivan (left) and Jake Kilrain in the last bare-knuckle championship fight, staged at Richburg, Mississippi.

1892: Sullivan and James J. Corbett in their championship match in New Orleans. Corbett won by a knockout in the twenty-first round.

Sullivan in his prime, 1885.

Charlie Mitchell, claimant of
the English title, who made
several unsuccessful attempts
to win the American cham-
pionship.

Paddy Ryan, last of the
heavyweight monarchs to lose
his crown in a bare-knuckle
fight.

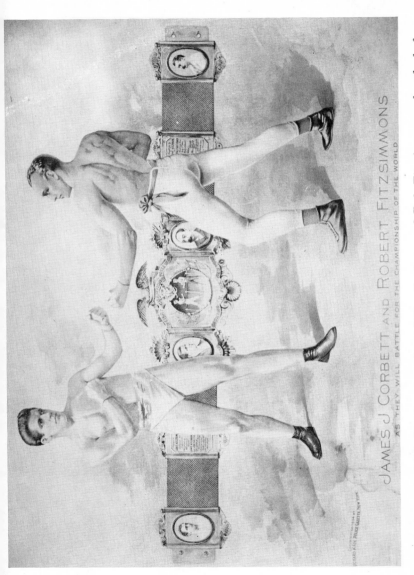

JAMES J. CORBETT AND ROBERT FITZSIMMONS
AS THEY WILL BATTLE FOR THE CHAMPIONSHIP OF THE WORLD

1897: An artist's idealized conception of Jim Corbett and Bob Fitzsimmons shortly before their bout for the championship at Carson City, Nevada. The famous Richard K. Fox belt appears in the background.

A clinch before Fitzsimmons delivered his "solar plexus" punch in the fourteenth round to end the fight.

One of the earliest fight photographs: Corbett deflects Fitzsimmons' right in the eleventh round.

1902: Jim Jeffries and Fitzsimmons before the start of their second fight. On this occasion, Jeffries, who had won the championship from Fitz in 1899, successfully defended his crown.

1908: Tommy Burns attempts a left hook as Jack Johnson toys with him before knocking him out to win the heavyweight title.

1910: Johnson successfully defends his title against veteran Jim Jeffries. Here, in the fifteenth round, Jeffries' chief second tosses in the sponge.

1915: Jess Willard knocks out Johnson in the twenty-sixth round of their championship fight in Havana.

by a left that landed with terrific force in the pit of Corbett's stomach.

Almost paralyzed by the punch, the champion went down. As the referee reached the count of eight, Jim blindly groped for the rope beside him, missed it and fell on his face. Referee Siler tolled off the fatal ten, and Bob Fitzsimmons was the new world champion.

With that knockout was born the much publicized "solar plexus" punch. In reality, as Fitzsimmons freely acknowledged, it was nothing but the old-time wallop in what bare-knuckle fighters referred to as "the mark." The real novelty was Fitz's lightning shift that put him in position to drive into the stomach at close range. But Bob Davis, who reported the battle for the *New York Journal,* overheard two San Francisco physicians discussing the punch. They remarked that it had landed on the solar plexus, which is the scientific designation of the great nerve center in the diaphragm. Davis liked the sound of the phrase and played it up in his account of the fight. Then other sports writers took up solar plexus, and soon it became a part of pugilistic history.

Corbett's ring career did not end with his loss of the title. He was still a great boxer and fighter.

In a bout with Tom Sharkey before the Lenox Club of New York on November 22, 1898, Corbett was declared loser on a foul in the ninth when Con McVey, one of his seconds, jumped. into the ring while the fight was in progress. The referee had no choice but to disqualify Jim.

On May 11, 1900, Corbett put up the greatest battle of his life against Jim Jeffries (who had won the championship from Fitz in 1899) at the Seaside Athletic Club of Coney Island, New York. For twenty-two rounds the ex-champion bewildered Jeffries with his fast footwork and spectacular two-handed attack.

The fans who had expected to see in Jeff's opponent a broken-down gladiator received the surprise of their lives when Corbett fought in that ring by the sea. Corbett did not overlook a single point, however small, that might aid him in his quest for new honors. Round after round he threw his punishing left into

Jeff's somber face, and Jeff was totally unable to block the blows. When Jeffries crouched, Corbett would straighten him up with a left feint for the head, followed by a right hook or uppercut to the chin.

In the sixth round, Corbett landed seven lefts in rapid succession on the champion's nose and mouth and escaped without a return blow. The fight then looked so one-sided that the champion's adherents were badly worried.

In the ninth, Corbett suddenly switched from a jab to a hook and put two very hard lefts on the chin that staggered Jeff and almost put him down. The champion went back on his heels and Corbett rushed him, having the better of the mix that followed.

Coming out for the tenth, Corbett resumed his jabbing tactics. He landed with almost monotonous regularity, and the blood flowed freely from the champion's nose and mouth. Whenever Jeffries rushed in, trying for a one-punch knockout, the agile challenger either blocked the punches or slid smoothly out of range.

Round after round this sort of thing went on, with Jeffries determinedly chasing Corbett but unable to corner him. Only once, in the fifteenth frame, did Jeff get home a solid wallop. It was a hard right that caught Gentleman Jim on the jaw and almost floored him. The titleholder was completely outclassed, and there was every indication that victory would go to the challenger who was out to regain the heavyweight crown.

At the conclusion of the nineteenth round Billy Brady, now manager of Jeffries, commanded the champion to go in and fight. "Your only chance of winning is to knock him out," said Brady. "He'll grab the title sure if you don't mix with him."

Jeffries obeyed his orders. From then on he waded into Corbett, never giving him an opportunity to get set. The ex-champion was beginning to tire, and Jeff succeeded in landing some hefty punches. Jim still outwitted Jeffries, but in the twenty-second round the champion cornered his opponent. As they broke from a clinch, Jeff swung a hard right, and though it only landed on the shoulder, it still had force enough to floor the recipient. Corbett jumped up quickly and mixed it, but he was badly hurt by a vicious right jolt that caught him on the ribs just as the bell rang.

When they came up for the twenty-third session, Jeffries cut loose, full steam ahead. He crashed his famous left hook into Corbett's stomach. The challenger staggered back against the ropes. Jeff followed the attack with a right swing to the jaw that beat Corbett down. He lay with his head resting on the lower rope and was in this position as Referee White counted him out.

Though Corbett failed in his quest to regain the championship, he gave a magnificent demonstration of skill and courage. Together, the two fighters produced one of the finest exhibitions of science versus brute strength that the ring has ever known.

In August, 1900, Corbett and Kid McCoy engaged in a match that ended with McCoy taking the full count in the fifth round. Then followed three years of idleness for Corbett. It was not until August 14, 1903, that he met Jeffries for the second time. San Francisco, the home town of both fighters, was the site. Gentleman Jim was now thirty-seven years old, and Jeffries experienced comparatively little difficulty in knocking him out in the tenth round.

The ring was to know Jim Corbett no more as a contestant. His retirement after the second fight with Jeffries was for all time. Henceforth, Corbett devoted his chief attention to the theater, where his popularity was to survive for the rest of his life.

Jim Corbett, master scientist of the ring, died at Bayside, Long Island, on February 18, 1933, in his sixty-seventh year.

CHAPTER 11

RUBY ROBERT, THE
LANKY MARVEL

ROBERT FITZSIMMONS was another of those extraordinary athletes in the same category with Tom Sayers and Jem Mace who apparently never heard of the ancient proverb that "a good big man can always beat a good little man." If he was familiar with the saying, he, like Sayers, ignored it. Or perhaps he took delight in proving that he was the exception to the rule. In any case, this spindle-shanked, freckle-faced, red-headed middleweight who succeeded in becoming heavyweight champion of the world was one of the most spectacular heroes in the history of boxing.

Fitzsimmons was born on June 4, 1862, at Elston, Cornwall, England. When he was nine years old his family moved to Lyttleton, New Zealand, where Fitz went to school and distinguished himself as an athlete, specializing in sprinting and football. Boxing was then taboo as a school sport, but in spite of rules the youngster learned to spar, and he at once discovered that he had a remarkable skill with the gloves.

Fitzsimmons seemed to possess a sort of sixth sense when in action. Outside the ropes he was just an average person of no exceptional mental endowment, but in the ring he was a brilliant thinker, capable of making instant decisions.

His first ring battle was with a huge blacksmith named Tom Baines, but better known as the Timaru Terror. The youngster tamed the Terror by knocking him out in less than a round, and the feat caused a tremendous sensation in local sportdom—so much so that Fitz was immediately selected to represent Timaru in a boxing tourney promoted by Jem Mace, world's champion then touring the Antipodes.

At the time Fitz weighed only 140 pounds, but he was large

of frame and loose-jointed. Mace figured him as a lightweight and warned him against entering a competition where he would be opposed by heavyweights. The young aspirant replied that nothing worse than a licking could befall him, and his entry was accepted.

Mace changed his mind about Fitzsimmons' chances when he saw him stripped and noted his sinewy arms and back muscles, developed by hard labor at the blacksmith's forge. Yet the veteran champion did not fully realize what a fighting phenomenal freak he had unearthed in this out-of-the-way corner of the globe until he had watched young Robert knock out four men in succession to win the amateur championship of New Zealand.

A year later, Mace again made his appearance with a show of fistic stars, and Fitzsimmons immediately offered to box any one of them. Mace at that time was grooming Herbert Slade, the Maori heavyweight who, he fancied, had the making of a champion. (It was this same Slade, still piloted by Mace, who was knocked out by John L. Sullivan in New York, August 6, 1883.) Jem decided that Fitz would provide a good test for his protégé.

From the start Fitzsimmons took the aggressive and pounded the Maori so fast and viciously that Mace stopped the battle in the second round to keep the leading light of his galaxy of pugilists from being extinguished. Fitzsimmons didn't like this, and in the course of the argument that followed, he offered to box the champion. Jem was prompt to accept, doubtless intending to teach the brash young man a lesson. But the New Zealanders objected to the matching of a mere novice with the world titleholder and raised such protest that Mace, fearing trouble, excused himself.

Fitzsimmons now proceeded to take up fighting "in a serious way." His opening campaign was not conducted with gloves, but with naked fists and under the tough old London rules. With his pipestem underpinning, it might be expected that Robert was altogether unsuited to a game in which wrestling was so important. Nevertheless he made a fine beginning, knocking out Arthur Cooper in three rounds, Jack Murphy in eight, and Jim Crawford in three.

There was little money to be made in Timaru, and Fitzsimmons decided to go to New South Wales. Since the proceeds of his first professional bouts added up to less than the price of his passage, the future world champion shipped as a stowaway aboard the two-masted schooner, *Botany Bay.* Upon landing, he went to work as a horseshoer. Assured of eating regularly, he began to look for a match.

On December 17, 1889, under Queensberry rules, he whipped Dick Ellis in three rounds before a Sydney club. His next fight was with Jem Hall, on February 10 of the following year. Fitz was counted out in the fourth round.

From time to time numerous statements appeared in print to the effect that the Hall tilt was prearranged. Hall was a first-class man, however, and his knockout of Fitzsimmons did not surprise his admirers. But after Fitzsimmons had built up an American reputation he repeatedly stated that he deliberately "lay down" in accordance with an agreement with gamblers who were betting on Hall to win in the fourth round.

Whether Fitzsimmons was guilty of double-dealing or not, the result of the Sydney bout with Hall provided him with the funds he required for an American invasion, and in due course he arrived in San Francisco.

Those were the days of the old California Athletic Club, an organization backed by such men as General Miles, Senator Fair, M. H. De Young, John D. Spreckels, and other prominent citizens who loved the boxing game. The club was not run to make money but solely for the entertainment of its members. Purses were distributed—not large ones compared with the financial rewards garnered by modern pugilists, but sufficiently generous to attract the best talent, and the men went in and fought their best.

There was no stalling allowed. Either the principals performed satisfactorily, or they were ordered out of the ring and received no pay. Unless a fighter was well known, he could not obtain a match before the California Athletic Club without a tryout at the hands of some reliable pugilist selected by one of the executives.

Though Fitzsimmons exhibited clippings from the home journals attesting to his ability, the club officials were not impressed.

He didn't look like a fighting man. In fact, no one ever looked less like a pugilist. His head was rather small and quite bald, except for a flaming red fringe over his ears. His eyes were narrow and without much expression. His mouth was wide and vague, and his lower lip drooped considerably. Standing up, Bob appeared to be all legs—legs that suggested nothing so much as a knock-kneed crane.

A careful observer would have noted in addition that his shoulders were of extraordinary breadth. His chest was deep. His arms were long and sinewy. His hands were huge, bony, and covered with long white hair. Freckles covered his entire body. By any standard, Fitz presented an appearance that was, to say the least, unusual. As a figure of fighting manhood, he was grotesque, fantastic, incredible.

And so it is not surprising that Fitzsimmons was given the laugh and told that he would have to demonstrate his wares in the club gymnasium before his application to fight in public could even be considered. The lanky gladiator did not hesitate; in fact, he jumped at the notion of showing his wares for nothing. Frank Allen, a husky middleweight noted for his punching powers, was given the assignment of investigating Fitz's worthiness.

Several members of the board of directors witnessed Fitz's American debut. They were detained from their other affairs for precisely two minutes. In that short period they saw sad things happen to Mr. Allen. The freckled freak first jabbed him silly, then crossed him with a short right that sent Allen revolving in somersaults across the floor.

When they picked up and revived the investigator, it was discovered that his right wrist was fractured by the fall, also that Fitzsimmons' right cross had shattered beyond repair a gold bridge in Allen's left jaw. The directors were now convinced that Fitz was a genuine fighting article. So was Allen, who in later years was wont to testify to the force of Fitz's punch by saying, "He broke my wrist with a wallop on the chin!"

Twelve days after the tryout, Fitzsimmons met Australian Billy McCarthy in a bout with five-ounce gloves for a 1,250-dollar purse, which was good money for any fighter and a treasure trove for Fitz, whose earnings theretofore had been very meager.

McCarthy was a stocky, hard-hitting chap with a formidable record. Three months before he had traveled twenty rounds with the middleweight champion, Jack Dempsey.* Though defeated, Billy had given the titleholder such a hard argument that the critics rated him second-best man of his weight in the country.

McCarthy, who fancied himself as a humorist, started the crowd laughing when, surveying his knock-kneed antagonist as they stood together in the ring center, he made a loud remark about a "bald-headed kangaroo." But after the gong rang, the comedy changed abruptly to black tragedy so far as he was concerned. First Fitz knocked him into his own corner with a straight left. As soon as he rose, Fitz floored him with a short right.

Fitz's style was all his own, but it was deadly effective. From the second round to the ninth, when McCarthy, battered and helpless, was declared loser, the issue was never in doubt. The "bald-headed kangaroo" was on his way to glory.

On June 28, 1890, Fitzsimmons stopped Arthur Upham in five rounds before the Audubon Club of New Orleans in a mill fought with five-ounce gloves for a thousand-dollar purse. Freckled Bob's ability was now sufficiently established to warrant a match with the middleweight champion. Jack Dempsey, the celebrated Nonpareil, agreed to meet the challenger at New Orleans, January 14, 1891, for the middleweight crown, a purse of twelve thousand dollars, and a side bet of two thousand dollars.

The bout took place in the amphitheater of the Olympic Club before nearly four thousand fans who paid ten dollars each for the privilege of seeing it. The purse of twelve thousand dollars was the largest ever offered up to that time, and the receipts set a new high mark for a glove contest.

In the first round Dempsey clinched repeatedly. Fitz scored heavily and was roundly cheered for his great work.

* A generation later, a promising young heavyweight christened William Harrison Dempsey discarded his first two names in favor of "Jack." The two fighters were not related to each other.

The second and third rounds found Fitz piling up more points as he punched his opponent from one side of the ring to the other. The Nonpareil clinched repeatedly to avoid punishment.

The fourth and fifth rounds found Dempsey engaged in a running race, with Fitz always after him. Dempsey received a terrific right to the heart just before the end of the fifth, and in trying to get away, he slipped and fell.

In the sixth, the champion was badly punished, and in the seventh he staggered all over the ring. He was bleeding profusely. Fitz got Dempsey against the ropes and pummeled his body. When the men broke, Fitz uppercut his opponent, sending him to the floor. After Dempsey arose he was met with staggering blows to the jaw.

In the eighth and ninth, Dempsey took further punishment. He was very groggy, and Fitz hit him at will.

In the tenth, Fitz charged into Dempsey's corner and landed a blow on Jack's neck. Dempsey attempted to close to avoid punishment and received a heavy right-hander on the jaw. He then was knocked to his knees by an uppercut. He got up and clinched, but another uppercut brought him to the ground, with Fitz falling on top of him. The Cornishman again sent Dempsey to the ground with an uppercut just before the round ended. Only the ringing of the gong saved Dempsey from a knockout.

In the eleventh Dempsey was knocked through the ropes, and when he returned to the ring, he was floored three times more. After the third knockdown, with Fitz still as fresh as if he were just boxing a three-round exhibition, Dempsey's seconds had to carry their man to his chair. Again only the bell saved the champion.

In the following round Dempsey was floored three times. When Jack hit the canvas the third time, Fitz thought the fight was over and walked to his corner to the cheers of the crowd. Then to Bob's amazement, Dempsey got to his feet. Fitz leaped up and was straightening to land a knockout when the gong once more saved Dempsey.

Dempsey answered the call of time in the thirteenth, but he

was thoroughly groggy. Fitz sent the Nonpareil down with a right-hander to the mouth and then followed with a vicious dig to the right side that hurled Dempsey panting to the ropes. Fitz rushed in and caught Dempsey on the jaw with a felling blow. Jack tried to regain his feet but could not. His seconds, realizing his helpless condition, threw in the sponge.

Winning the world middleweight title brought Fitzsimmons international recognition. But it did not bring him universal popularity, for he had committed the same sin that Corbett was to commit a little later when he destroyed the myth of Sullivan's invincibility. People do not like to have their idols shattered, and Jack Dempsey was an idol.

Dempsey, of course, was simply overmatched against Fitz. He had earned the title of Nonpareil by beating the best men in his division—but the best were not particularly good. When he met the great Cornishman, his long string of victories was of no avail. Both he and his reputation went down under the attack of a better man.

Nor is there any justice in the complaints of Dempsey's admirers that their hero was the victim of unfairness. Overmatched he was, but not because Fitzsimmons was any bigger than he. The official weights were 150¼ for Bob, 147½ for Jack.

During the next two years Fitzsimmons, who literally fought himself out of opponents in the middleweight division, began taking on the big boys. Among them was Peter Maher, Irish heavyweight champion, whom he stopped in New Orleans in twelve rounds. He also scored a signal revenge over his old rival and former conqueror, Jem Hall, by knocking him out in four rounds before the Crescent City Club of New Orleans.

A bout between Joe Choynski and Fitzsimmons, at catch-weights, on June 17, 1894, was stopped by the Boston police in the fifth round, after Choynski, repeatedly floored, was about to be counted out.

The following September Fitz fought his last battle as a middleweight, knocking out his fellow countryman, Dan Creedon, in two rounds. He now determined to go after the heavyweight title, and on February 21, 1896, he took on Peter Maher, whom he had beaten once before. By this time Maher had been given the blessing of Jim Corbett, who had decided to retire, and Peter thus held vague claims to the championship.

The Fitzsimmons-Maher encounter was, to say the least, a bizarre affair. It involved, among other persons, the famous—some called him infamous—Judge Roy Bean, who was spoken of as "the law west of the Pecos," and who owned the famous Jersey Lily Saloon in Langtry, Texas, chosen site of the battle.

Dan Stuart, promoter of the fight, and some two hundred prize-fight enthusiasts, arrived at Langtry on the afternoon of February 21. When the party detrained, it found twenty-six Texas Rangers lined up at one end of the station. Also present were United States marshals, soldiers, and other representatives of law and order, who had been assembled to prevent the fight.

Bean, who represented the promoter, had a polite conversation with the leaders of the posse. There was nothing wrong, Roy insisted. Just a nice lot of peaceful Americans were "touring" that part of the country. They did not even want to stop at Langtry. All they wanted was to be allowed to cross the Rio Grande into Mexico.

The arguments of the persuasive Judge Bean were duly considered. It seemed reasonable enough to let these pleasant people move across the border. While arrangements were being made, everybody adjourned to the Jersey Lily, where Bean had thoughtfully placed his choicest liquors on sale.

It was not long before permission was given to cross the Rio Grande. Bean led the way across the prairie, down a straggling, rocky road to the river. Cut by brambles, scraped by jagged rocks, the sports moved on. They waded through silt for seventy-five yards to a pontoon bridge that had been thrown across the river and walked over into Mexico.

On the Mexican side, a canvas enclosure had been put up and a ring erected inside. At the entrance stood Bat Masterson, Dodge City marshal, gun in hand, ready for trouble. Bat, later fight expert for the *Morning Telegraph* in New York, was a pal of Stuart's. With Bat was Joe Vendig, Stuart's money man, who took tickets. The price was twenty dollars. There were no gate crashers—at least there were none in the strictly legal sense.

To the west of the canvas enclosure, however, was a precipitous bluff, and on the American side, though at a greater distance, was a similar high point. From these vantage points hundreds of Mexicans and Americans got an unobstructed view of the ring free of charge.

The referee was the famous George Siler, who was the standout of his time and worked in most of the big fights around New York. He got out two pairs of five-ounce gloves, tossed them to the handlers, and told the battlers to get ready. After a short delay brought on by a dispute about the stakes had been settled, the gong sounded.

Fitz ambled to the center of the ring and feinted. He dodged one blow, but Maher clipped him with a right to the jaw. They went into a clinch, and Maher let Fitz have it with a right. They had agreed to have no hitting in the clinches, and Siler warned Peter that if he did it again he would be tossed out of the ring.

As they broke, Fitz shot a left. Then he found the body with a right and followed with a left. Fitz loosed another right but was short. Maher landed a right and a left on the side of the head. Once again they clinched.

Fitz backed away, and Maher swung a left to the head. Bob sidestepped, then smashed his right to Maher's jaw. Maher measured his length on the white canvas cover of the ring. He tried to get up, fell back, and was counted out by Siler. It was all over in half a round.

After Siler had formally proclaimed Fitzsimmons the winner, Martin Julian, whose sister Rose had married Fitzsimmons, stood up.

"Gentlemen," said he, "Mr. Fitzsimmons has worked himself up from the bottom of the ladder and by the decision of the referee is now champion of the world. He is ready to defend the title against all comers, at any time or place. No man is barred, and all comers will receive recognition."

Before Julian could proceed any further with his windy oration, the attention of his audience was distracted by a much louder noise outside. A cry had gone up that the rushing current was sweeping the pontoon bridge away. Everybody made a dash for the floating bridge, and all got back to the Langtry side without mishap.

Bob did not fight again until December 2, when he lost to Tom Sharkey on a questionable foul * in the eighth round in San Francisco. Then came the fight, described in the preceding chapter, in which Fitzsimmons won the heavyweight championship from Corbett at Carson City, Nevada. Fitzsimmons' weight was officially given as 167 pounds, Corbett's as 183.

For more than two years after winning the crown, Fitz toured the country with a theatrical troupe. He drew large houses and made money, but the life was a wearing one and not conducive either to good health or to the preservation of fighting form. When on June 9, 1899, he faced Jim Jeffries at Coney Island, he had passed his thirty-seventh birthday and was used to a free and easy existence. He was no longer the high-geared, splendidly accurate fighting machine that had finished Corbett in 1897.

Fitz selected Jeffries as a good practice target to begin with after his long layoff because he had always found big men easy to handle. Jeffries, in his opinion, was merely a mountain of inexperience. So little did the champion think of the prowess of his prospective foe that on the very night before the battle Ruby Robert was the life of the party at a convivial gathering where all the guests, himself included, drank vigorously and held high revel until dawn.

When Jeffries knocked out his overconfident opponent in the eleventh round, his victory came as a stunning surprise to all but a few wise gentlemen who had had inside information on Fitzsimmons' real condition. Fitz himself was by no means convinced that his day was done and immediately began a vigorous comeback crusade. In the following October he knocked out Jeff Thorne of England in less than a round before a Chicago club, and in 1900 he scored four clean knockouts in succession over Jim Daly, Ed Dunkhorst, Gus Ruhlin, and his old-time enemy, Tom Sharkey.

These victories qualified him for a second chance with Jef-

---

* Actually, Fitz knocked out Sharkey with a fair punch. But the gamblers had bribed the referee, and Fitz knew it would be futile to protest. His reputation was undamaged, for the true facts were soon disclosed to all.

ries, and they clashed on July 25, 1902, at San Francisco. Fitzsimmons, his lean, forty-year-old frame trained to perfection, gave Jeffries the worst thrashing ever administered to him. For nearly eight rounds he hammered the giant mercilessly with both hands, breaking his nose, cutting both cheeks to the bone, and opening gashes over each eye. It seemed certain that the big fellow would be compelled to surrender.

But Jeffries, a tremendous man, all solid bone and sinew, a miracle of endurance, kept pressing doggedly forward. Suddenly he sank a terrific right to the stomach and followed with a crashing left hook to the jaw. Fitz fell heavily and was counted out. Both of Jeffries' eyes were closed, and the champion was so blind that he had to be led from the ring to his dressing room—but he was still the champion.

By now Fitzsimmons had definitely seen his best days, but he refused to retire. In 1903 he defeated George Gardiner in twenty rounds at Mechanics Pavilion, San Francisco, winning the title of light heavyweight champion, a newly constituted class that had only recently been recognized by boxing authorities. This was the third crown he had gained. He held it until 1905.

On December 20 of that year, Philadelphia Jack O'Brien, one of the fastest and most scientific fighters of his day, stopped Fitzsimmons in thirteen rounds. Fitzsimmons did not fall to the floor while the fighting was in progress. He reeled feebly to his corner at the end of the thirteenth round. During the rest period he twice slipped from his chair, and Referee Eddie Graney called a halt.

Two years later Jack Johnson knocked out the sturdy old veteran in two rounds. Revisiting Australia, the ex-champion engaged in battle with Bill Lang, then champion of the Antipodes, and was defeated in twelve rounds. His final ring appearance was at Williamsport, Pennsylvania, with Dan Sweeney in a no-decision bout of six rounds on January 29, 1917. Ruby Robert was nearly fifty-five, an age that made him the Methuselah of modern heavyweights.

After his retirement Fitzsimmons made a fair living on the vaudeville stage but never approached the big-money mark reached by Jim Corbett. Ruby Robert was filling a Chicago stage engagement in 1918 when an attack of influenza developed into double pneumonia and caused his death in his fifty-sixth year.

The veteran of more than three hundred ring battles died a poor man. One of the great pugilists of all time, he was born too early to profit from the million-dollar gates that brought financial independence to many a lesser fighter.

CHAPTER 12

BOILERMAKER FROM THE
GOLDEN GATE

JAMES J. JEFFRIES, although born in Carroll, Ohio, on April 15, 1875, early became a California resident, and his youthful ring triumphs identified him so closely with San Francisco that the sporting world regarded him as a native son.

He first attracted outside attention when Jim Corbett was training, in March, 1897, at Carson City for his battle with Fitzsimmons. Newspapermen in daily attendance at Corbett's camp were favorably impressed by the massive youth who was employed as one of the champion's sparring partners.

Jeffries, who had hardened himself at his trade of boilermaking, was remarkably active for his size. His job at Carson City was to provide the champion with a target, but he didn't seem to mind his daily beating, and he was such a magnificent specimen of athletic manhood that speculation was rife about what he could accomplish if he possessed but a tithe of Corbett's science. It was said that Jeffries could run one hundred yards in eleven seconds, and he was quite candid in telling the newspaper scribes that he hoped to couple his speed with what he could learn about glove work from Corbett and then develop his own pugilistic career.

It was a sound idea, and Jeffries benefited greatly thereby. No boxer of average intelligence could have sparred daily with Corbett without picking up useful knowledge. Jeffries made good use of his opportunities although he never became a flashy or even clever boxer. But those Carson City experiences served to file down his rough edges and taught him a lot about defense and attack that proved of immense value in his later career.

After his sparring engagement ended, Jeffries went back to San Francisco. The long spell of training had put him in rare condition, and within eight months he knocked out T. Van Buskirk in two rounds, Henry Baker in nine, and fought twenty-round draws with Gus Ruhlin and Joe Choynski. Ruhlin and Choynski were numbered among the first-flight heavies of the day. Both were veterans compared with Jeffries, and the fact that he held them even spoke well for his future.

In 1898 Jeff knocked out Joe Goddard, Peter Jackson, and Pete Everett in quick succession and won a decision over Tom Sharkey in twenty rounds. All of his fights had so far taken place on the Pacific Coast, but now his manager deemed him ripe for conquests in the eastern field, and they invaded New York. Since the metropolis was a hard place for a young boxer to obtain recognition unless he possessed political influence or had accomplished something of such a sensational nature that he could not be disregarded, Jeffries' mentor made a bold publicity bid by matching him to meet two men on the same night.

This gesture earned Jeffries considerable space in the Gotham newspapers. Steve O'Donnell of Australia, Peter Jackson's favorite pupil, and Bob Armstrong, a Negro heavyweight, were chosen to test the ability of the big boy from the Golden Gate. Jeff was billed to fight ten rounds with each man before the Lenox Athletic Club.

Fortune was against Jeffries on this occasion. He had not quite mastered the art of accurate delivery. In his anxiety to make good by stopping Armstrong quickly, he missed frequently; when he did land, it was all too often on the back of the Negro's hard skull. The latter was an old, experienced ringster, wise in defensive tactics. Armstrong made little attempt to fight back; his object was simply to stay the ten rounds, and that he succeeded in doing.

The decision was awarded to Jeffries, but the victory was a costly one. Both hands were so badly bruised and swollen from contact with Armstrong's iron head that it was impossible for him to don the gloves for the second engagement, and the bout with O'Donnell had to be canceled.

The sporting writers treated Jeffries with good-humored contempt in their accounts of his eastern debut, rating him as a

strong, willing, but hopelessly clumsy performer. Deeply morti-
fied, Jeff returned to the Coast.

Yet this fiasco was the very thing that gave the California
boilermaker his chance. For Bob Fitzsimmons, having finished
for the nonce his theatrical engagements, was ready for active
service. Two years had passed since he won the title from
Corbett. After such a long period of fistic idleness, Fitz was determined to make a cautious start, and Jeffries was selected as
his first opponent because the champion had watched him box
Armstrong! He figured the big, slow fellow would be easier
game than any of the lighter, more experienced aspirants for
top-notch honors.

Fitzsimmons was naturally a heavy betting favorite, and great
was the astonishment when the champion went down to defeat
in eleven rounds at Coney Island on June 9, 1899.

The story of what happened before that fight is even more
interesting than the account of the battle itself. William Brady,
a master manager and strategist, was handling the affairs of
Jeffries at the time, and he was a firm believer in getting the
mental edge on an opponent. Brady figured that in Jeffries he
had the next heavyweight champion if only the ex-boilermaker
could be made to believe so himself.

Jeffries was not much of an egotist, and on the day of the
contest with Fitzsimmons he was shaky, sullen, and nervous.
Brady feared for his fighter. Words could not change Jeffries'
demeanor, hence action was necessary.

With Bill Delaney, his chief trainer, and Jack Jeffries, Tommy
Ryan, and Ed Dunkhorst, all of whom had helped train the
husky Californian, Brady took a stroll to the clubhouse to in-
spect the dressing rooms which Jeff and Fitz would occupy.
Brady moved the couch in Jeff's room so that it would be the
first thing to strike the eye as one entered. Then with Delaney
to aid him, Brady went to the hotel to talk matters over with
Jeffries.

"Jim," he said, "Fitzsimmons thinks you are a big dub who
has nothing but weight and heft. The papers say that Fitz in an
interview declares he'll knock you out with the first good punch
he lands. He will, if you don't perk up and realize that you are

much stronger than he is and can hit as hard and take it better than he can.

"I had to give Fitz the idea that you were easy when we first arranged the match. He refused to sign, so I had to play a ruse on him. I told him what trouble I always had in getting you to train. I conveyed the impression that you were flabby, had no confidence in yourself, and that all I wanted was to be given a chance to get some money out of the match. Now he thinks all you have is size and bulk and he'll knock you out whenever he wants to.

"It's going to be the other way around, Jim," continued Brady. "You'll do the knocking out if only you'll do what I ask of you."

With that Brady outlined his plan to break Fitz's self-confidence and morale and to make Jeff more sure of himself. He decided to place fear in the heart of Fitz and here was his plan:

Martin Julian, Fitz's brother-in-law, was to supervise the weighing in of Jeff, and Brady figured that if he could start an argument with Julian, he could get Fitz out of his quarters to see what was up, and thus, for the first time, have Ruby Robert get a close look at the brawny, hairy-chested, powerfully built man whom he was to meet for the title that evening.

His plan developed. Brady started to discuss the meaning of a clean break in a manner that compelled Julian to disagree.

"Well," shouted Brady, "if you don't know what a clean break is, then get Fitzsimmons out and let him and Jeff settle the disputed point." Fitz overheard the argument and rushed out into the hall.

"What's up?" he demanded.

That was all that Brady had wanted. He had coached Jeff on this situation.

Fitz threw open the door of Jeffries' room, and the first thing he saw was a mountain of solid muscle reposing on the couch. He had expected to find his opponent flabby and out of condition, and he was visibly shaken by the presence of the naked giant lying there trained to perfection.

Brady didn't give Fitz much chance to think. He tossed a pair of pajamas to Jeff, and the challenger, following instructions, looked at the champion without flickering an eyelash.

"What are you doing here?" growled Jeff.

Brady started to explain, whereupon Jeff, following the plan of campaign, roared, "You talk too much, Brady. I can settle this in a jiffy."

With that, Jeff grabbed Fitz and gave him his own interpretation of the rule on a clean break. Fitz, unprepared, found himself pushed around the room like a baby. Jeff wound up by giving Bob a shove against the wall that made his jaw sag.

"Shucks," Jeff remarked comfortably after the visitors had left his dressing room, "why, he ain't half as strong as Tom Sharkey. I licked Tom and I can lick him!"

That night Fitz lasted through eleven rounds of terrific fighting, but Jeff had more than his physical advantage of thirty-eight pounds. He had the will to win and the confidence that he would win. The combination was irresistible, and a new champion was crowned.

But even the combination of superior size, youth, and the mental edge might well have been insufficient if Jeffries had not also been under the tutelage of Tommy Ryan, the middleweight champion. Tommy was one of the cleverest boxers and best ring generals of the Queensberry era. He took Jeffries in hand, boxed with him constantly, and, among other things, taught him to assume a crouching pose that, combined with the big fellow's tremendous reach, made it almost impossible for an opponent to penetrate his guard. In later years, this fighting position became known as the "Jeffries crouch" and was adopted by many other boxers.

Jeffries did not rest long on his laurels. Five months later, on November 3, 1899, he faced Tom Sharkey at Coney Island in a title bout. The ex-sailor challenger, who had previously lost a close twenty-round decision to Jeffries, was a much improved fighter, and many enthusiastic admirers backed him to defeat the champion.

The bout was scheduled for twenty-five rounds, and during the early stages Sharkey forced the pace. Jeffries, assuming the crouching posture that had stood him in such good stead against Fitzsimmons, remained mostly on the defensive, paying strict attention to the instructions of his chief second, Tommy Ryan, and disregarding the screaming demands of the crowd to "go in, fight, and stop stalling." Sharkey, greatly overmatched in height, weight, and reach, was constantly cheered for his aggressiveness, while Jeffries came in for a considerable amount of acid criticism. Jeff scaled 215 to 183 for his adversary, and the sympathies of the crowd were overwhelmingly with the smaller man.

The Coney scrap was one of the most brutal, most grueling in the history of the ring, in which both men took terrific punishment. Game and tough as Sharkey was, his furious assaults gradually slackened. Jeffries was countering him fiercely with left hooks to the jaw and straight right jolting smashes over the heart. But it was not until the last five rounds that the bigger man took the offensive in grim earnest. When he did, Sharkey was compelled to back, and by then much of the sting had gone out of Tom's punches.

Before the gong clanged for the final round, Tommy Ryan gave his charge a drink of champagne. Braced by this stimulant, Jeffries charged from his corner like a wild bull and made a whirlwind finish. Sharkey was overwhelmed, and though he fought back gallantly to the last bell, Referee George Siler pronounced the champion victor.

After the battle, it was found that two of Sharkey's ribs had been fractured. Jeffries was uninjured.

On April 6, 1900, Jeffries knocked out a mediocre boxer named Jack Finnegan at Detroit. The following month he stopped ex-champion Jim Corbett in the twenty-third round of a very close engagement at Coney Island. Then the following year Jeff clashed with Hank Griffin, Negro heavyweight, who managed to survive the four rounds in which the champion had agreed to stop him. Later in 1901, Joe Kennedy and Gus Ruhlin fell before the champion's knockout blows.

On July 25, 1902, Fitzsimmons tried conclusions for the second time with the man who had deprived him of his title, and again he went down to defeat, this time in eight rounds. In a return engagement with Corbett, in August 1903, Jeff knocked out the polished veteran in ten rounds.

During the latter part of 1903, Jeffries and Fitzsimmons joined forces and toured the West, giving sparring exhibitions and meeting all comers. At Butte, Montana, Jack Munroe, a miner and former football player, agreed to engage in an exhibition of four rounds with Jeffries. Fat and out of condition, Jim boxed lazily until the third round. Then Munroe, catching him off balance, drove a left to the body and Jeffries went down. He was up in an instant and rushed savagely, but Munroe backed away and resorted to clinching tactics to save himself. There were no more sensations, but the story of how Jeffries was floored by an unknown was immediately telegraphed all over the country, and the exaggerated details made it appear that the champion had barely escaped a knockout.

Munroe was at once taken in hand by Harry Pollak, a cagey manager, who realized that there was money in the idea of advertising him as a potent challenger for Jeffries' title. Jack was really a third-rate proposition. But Pollak knew his business too well to allow the truth about the miner to become public property.

Munroe got plenty of theatrical booking and fought a few six-round bouts with carefully selected pushovers. He was accorded a tremendous amount of publicity by sporting writers who should have known better. Perhaps they did, but many went to absurd limits in booming the Munroe stock.

So great was the praise of the miner that Jeffries was forced to recognize it by accepting his challenge for a title bout. The champion agreed to take on Munroe at Jim Coffroth's Mechanics Pavilion in San Francisco in the latter part of July, 1904. But while training, Jeffries suffered an outbreak of a virulent blood disorder with which he had been afflicted in the past, and the affair was postponed until August 26. As might have been expected, the match was a howling farce.

Whatever Munroe's shortcomings as a gladiator may have been, he had never seemed to lack courage. Yet when facing Jeffries, he acted like a rabbit in a hungry python's cage. The first round ended with Munroe prostrate on the canvas. The second again saw him reposing supine. This time the bell did not save him, and the referee counted him out. (But Munroe was far from being a coward. During World War I, he went to the front with the Princess Pats, a famous Canadian regiment that underwent such fiery ordeals that it had to be recruited to full war strength three times before the struggle ended. In that contingent of hard-bitten warriors, brawny Jack Munroe, armed with his favorite weapon, a woodsman's ax, was a holy terror whenever he went over the top and mixed in free-for-alls with bayonets and trench knives at close quarters. Once, during a night attack, he was badly wounded but crawled back to rescue a crippled officer and dragged him to safety. His heroism was duly recognized by the Canadian government.)

On May 13, 1905, Jeffries announced his retirement. There was such a scarcity of fitting opponents for the huge champion that no match in sight offered a sufficiently large reward. Also, he probably realized that he was no longer able to get into first-class condition. Training had become a wearisome grind for the big fellow, as it does sooner or later for every fighter.

With Jeff out of the running, Marvin Hart, of Louisville, set up a claim for the championship on the strength of a decision he had gained over Jack Johnson. Hart was then matched with Jack Root of Chicago, and the battle, billed as being for the world heavyweight title, took place at Reno, Nevada, on July 3, 1905. With Jeffries officiating as referee, Hart won by a knockout in the twelfth round. Jeffries, having agreed to name the winner as his successor, accordingly proclaimed Hart as the new titleholder.*

Hart was never an impressive performer. He had won his victory over Johnson in a dubious twenty-round affair at San Francisco in which the referee plainly favored the white man at the clever Negro's expense. In any case, the uncertain honors bestowed on him by Jeffries were of short duration, for on February 23, 1906, he lost a decision to Tommy Burns in twenty rounds. After that, Hart was never again given serious consideration.

* In February, 1949, Jeffries declared to a representative of mine who interviewed him in California that he had not agreed to pass his title on to Hart, but that a fight promoter had done so, using Jeffries' name without his permission.

CHAPTER 13

THE "UNDERSIZED" CHAMPION

IT IS THE fashion nowadays to look upon Tommy Burns as an undersized heavyweight who became champion largely on his own say-so and who, by losing the crown to Jack Johnson, precipitated a period of unrest and discontent that ended only with the defeat of Johnson by Jess Willard at Havana. The appraisal is harsh, narrow, and unjust.

Burns missed greatness by a wide margin, but he was a very good fighter, and the claim he laid to the championship had real merit and was recognized by fistic authorities the world over. It also may interest present-day fighters to know that they are his debtors, for he was the first to catch a glint of pugilism's "golden gate." The day he drew thirty thousand dollars for his *losing* fight with Johnson he put the game in the big-money class. His successors have far exceeded the mark he set for them, but he was the one who pointed the way.

In addition to the measure of skill and punching power with which he was endowed, Burns had two other good qualities that enabled him to win the championship and a snug fortune. These were his imagination and his self-reliance.

Burns, whose real name was Noah Brusso, was born at Hanover, Canada, June 17, 1881. Though at the best he scaled 175 to 180 pounds and was only five feet, seven inches tall, he had a remarkable reach * of 74½ inches and was a model of compact development. Until his meeting with Johnson, he had participated in fifty-three contests of which he lost only three, drew eight, and won forty-two.

Burns presented a curious contrast to Jim Jeffries and John-

* See "Reach" under Glossary in Appendix.

son, his predecessor and successor, respectively, as titleholder. There was a general disposition to view Tommy as a sort of synthetic champion, yet despite his physical handicaps, he showed to good advantage against the bigger men. He was fast, clever, and the owner of a dangerous punch, as he proved when he stopped the veteran Jim Flynn and Bill Squires, the Australian heavyweight king.

Entering the ring in 1900, he rose to the title in six years by the simple process of first visualizing his opportunities and then making the most of them. Tommy never had a manager. He didn't need one.

Tommy began to fight as a welterweight, and it was not until 1905, when he weighed 171, that he started to campaign in California as a heavyweight. After watching him in action, Promoter Tom McCarey wanted him to fight Marvin Hart, who had just beaten Jack Root and was claiming the heavyweight title vacated by Jeffries.

"He's a big, tough fellow," demurred Burns.

"I'll give you fifteen thousand dollars to fight him," tempted McCarey, knowing Tommy had never received anywhere near that much before.

"I'll take it," said Burns. "Send for him."

He fought Hart, beat him in twenty rounds, collected his fifteen thousand, and proclaimed himself champion of the world. Then he proceeded to prove his right to the crown.

Lacking a unanimous following, the self-named king of the Queensberry realm had no choice but to prove it the hard way. So, a little more than a month after he had defeated Hart, the Canadian stepped into the ring with Jim O'Brien at San Diego, March 28, 1906, and knocked him out in the very first round. On the same night he accommodated Jim Walker in the same way.

Fireman Jim Flynn, who had proved his worth as a contender, met Burns at Los Angeles on October 2 and was knocked out in fifteen rounds.

Tommy's next bout was with Philadelphia Jack O'Brien. They fought a twenty-round draw on November 28, 1906, at the Pacific Athletic Club in Los Angeles. It was a tough battle, a fight full of action, but very even, and Referee Jeffries' decision of a draw met with popular favor. Burns scaled 172 for this bout.

After defeating Joe Grim, the India-rubber Baby, in three rounds in Philadelphia, January 10, 1907, Tommy again took on O'Brien and retrieved the favor he had lost in getting only a draw with the Philadelphian by defeating Jack in twenty rounds.

That bout took place at the Pacific Coast Athletic Club, Los Angeles, on May 8, 1907. Previously, O'Brien had laid claim to the title, basing his position on a draw with Burns and his fine all-around ring record, especially his knockout of Bob Fitzsimmons in thirteen rounds. To settle the matter of supremacy, it was agreed that the bout could not end in a draw; the third man in the ring was authorized to extend the contest beyond twenty rounds, if necessary, until a decision could be reached.

Burns's lead at the end of the twentieth round was so great that the referee, Jeffries, did not hesitate to declare Tommy the winner. That decision clinched the crown for him.

Burns's victory was a decisive one. With this triumph added to his string, Tommy then went out to conquer the world's best heavyweights, and for a year and a half he stopped eight opponents in international battles. With these victories he clinched world honors beyond doubt.

Bill Squires, an Australian boxer, was his first victim. Squires lasted just two minutes and eight seconds of the first round in their mill at San Francisco, on July 4, 1907.

Burns's first act following that quick victory was to sail for England and challenge Gunner Moir, the English champion. The Gunner accepted, and the fight was scheduled by the National Sporting Club for December 2, 1907. A fortnight before the fight, Burns sat incognito in the balcony of a small club where the Gunner was appearing at a benefit. One peek at the English champion sent Tommy tumbling out to bet four hundred pounds on himself with a bookmaker. His judgment was excellent. He carried Moir nine rounds to make it look good and knocked him out in the tenth.

Jack Palmer was Tommy's next foreign victim. Burns stopped him in four rounds on February 10, 1908, in London.

Burns next moved on to Ireland. In Dublin, on St. Patrick's Day, 1908, he knocked out big Jem Roche, the Irish champion, in the record time for a world heavyweight title bout of a minute and twenty-eight seconds. Then came a South African heavyweight named Jewey Smith, whom Tommy halted in the fifth round of a battle staged in Paris on April 18, 1908.

On June 13 he again encountered Bill Squires, this time in Paris, and put the Australian to sleep in the eighth round. With that accomplishment, Burns, who now was being hounded by Jack Johnson, decided to embark for other shores. Accompanied by Squires, he made his way to Australia. There, on August 24, 1908, they engaged in their third mill, and this time Squires lasted through part of the thirteenth round before hitting the canvas for keeps.

By now Burns had become a popular fighter in the Land of Kangaroo, and he decided to remain. Bill Lang, an Australian with a good record, got himself a match with Burns, and at Sydney, on September 2, he went the way of so many others. Lang was kayoed in the sixth round, and his fall maintained Burns's clean sweep of all foreign opposition and further supported his right to world honors.

So far the Canadian had triumphed and confounded his detractors. But Johnson, the huge Negro heavyweight, was now closing in on Burns's trail. He had voyaged to the Antipodes expressly for the purpose of forcing Burns into a match. The champion could no longer evade the issue. The Australian press and public opinion were too powerful for Burns to resist, and articles were signed for a championship match.

They met in Sydney in a bout promoted by Hugh McIntosh at his new Rushcutter's Bay Arena, on December 26, 1908— Boxing Day to the British—and McIntosh guaranteed Burns 30,000 dollars, a record sum. No boxing contest in Australia had ever created the intense excitement that prevailed on the day of the battle. The number of spectators exceeded sixteen thousand. The gate was 121,000 dollars. Like Burns's guarantee, this was also a record.

From the outset it was evident that, barring accidents, nothing could keep Johnson from winning. Burns, outranged and incessantly pounded by heavier artillery, gradually weakened. By the fourteenth round he had taken such a beating that the police interfered, and Jack Johnson was declared the victor. For the first time in ring history a Negro reigned as the undisputed heavyweight monarch.

Johnson had no love for Burns, both because of the chase Tommy had given him and of his oft-repeated statements that Jack had a yellow streak. He cut Burns to ribbons. He slashed him, he battered him—and the fans hooted him because they felt he could have finished Burns long before the fourteenth round.

Present at the fight was Jack London, then an enormously popular novelist and short-story writer, who was responsible for starting the movement that eventually brought Jim Jeffries out of retirement. He wrote a vivid, not to say lurid, account of the fight for the *New York Herald*, an account calculated to chill the blood of every member of the master race—that is to say, he appealed to the deep-rooted prejudices of the vast majority of white Americans:

> The fight, if fight it might be called, was like that between a colossus and a pigmy. It had all the seeming of a playful Ethiopian at loggerheads with a small white man—of a grown man cuffing a naughty child; of a monologue by Johnson, who made a noise with his fists like a lullaby, tucking Burns into his little crib; of a funeral, with Burns for the late deceased, Johnson for undertaker, gravedigger, and sexton.
>
> There was no fraction of a second in all the fourteen rounds that could be called Burns's. So far as damage is concerned, Burns never landed a blow. He never fazed the black man. It was not Burns's fault, however. He tried every moment throughout the fight, except when he was groggy. It was hopeless, preposterous, heroic. He was a glutton for punishment, and he bored in all the time, but a dew drop had more chance than he with the Giant Ethiopian.
>
> Johnson play-acted all the time, and he played with Burns

from the opening gong to the finish of the fight. Burns was a toy in his hands. For Johnson, it was a kindergarten romp.

"Hit here, Tahmy," he would say, exposing the right side of his unprotected stomach, and when Burns struck, Johnson would neither wince nor cover up. Instead he would receive the blow with a happy, careless smile directed at the spectators, turn the left side of his unprotected stomach and say, "Now there, Tahmy," and while Burns would hit as directed, Johnson would continue to grin and chuckle and smile his golden smile.

One criticism and only one can be passed on Johnson. In the thirteenth round he made the mistake of his life. He should have put Burns out. He could have put him out. It would have been child's play. Instead of which he smiled and deliberately let Burns live until the gong sounded, and in the opening of the fourteenth round the police stopped the fight and Johnson lost the credit for a knockout.

But one thing remains. Jeffries must emerge from his alfalfa farm and remove the golden smile from Johnson's face. Jeff, it's up to you!

Thus began the ballyhoo that brought Jeffries out of retirement two years later to face Johnson in that Reno ring where he was brutally beaten by the younger, faster, and more powerful black man.

Burns remained in Australia, where he again fought Bill Lang; he took a twenty-round decision from him on April 11, 1910, after having been out of the ring for nearly two years. Then he went to Canada, and at Saskatoon he defeated Bill Richard in six rounds on August 8, 1912.

From that time on, Burns took his fighting profession light-heartedly. But he never passed up a chance to rake in a purse when a good offer was made.

On April 2, 1913, he went six rounds, no decision, with Arthur Pelkey at Calgary, and the following year, on January 26, he met Battling Brant at Taft, California. Tommy showed much of his old style by knocking Brant out in four rounds. Four years later he clashed with Tex Foster in Prince Rupert, British

Columbia, and put him on the boards for good in the fourth round.

Tommy's last match followed the pattern of the one in which he dropped the title to Johnson—he lost the fight but got most of the money. In 1920 Tommy, now nearly forty years old, was in England. Joe Beckett was the British heavyweight champion, and Tommy, watching him in training one day, suddenly conceived the notion that he could lick him. He also conceived the notion of being his own promoter.

Burns challenged Beckett, who accepted. Tommy then engaged a newspaper friend to act as his front man and rented the Albert Hall. Time had taken its toll of Tommy's leg power and robbed his punches of their sting, and he succumbed to Beckett in seven rounds—but after paying Joe sixteen thousand dollars and settling all the bills incidental to the promotion of the fight, he cleared twenty thousand dollars for himself.

Burns may not have earned a place among the greatest heavyweights, but he did earn the plaudits of fight followers as a game, good fighter. He was the only champion who was forced to dispose of every title claimant in every land where boxing was followed before he received international recognition as possessor of the world heavyweight crown. Burns is now an ordained clergyman.

CHAPTER 14

FIRST NEGRO CHAMPION

JACK JOHNSON was born at Galveston, Texas, March 31, 1878. His first officially recorded battle took place on February 11, 1899, with Jim McCormick, known as the Galveston Giant, and resulted in a draw in seven rounds. One month later Jack again faced McCormick, and this time he won on a foul.

It was not until May 6 of the same year, in Chicago, that Johnson met an experienced professional for the first time. His opponent was another Negro, a fighter of substantial reputation in the Windy City whose name is recorded to posterity simply as Klondike. The Chicagoan stopped Johnson in five rounds. Jack, at that time a tall, gangling youth of generous frame, looked as if he needed a liberal course of feeding more than anything else.

Those were precarious days for the future heavyweight champion. Seldom knowing where his next meal was coming from, he watched hungrily for the chance of picking up a five-dollar bill by sparring three or four rounds before one of the many small clubs which provided entertainment for Chicago fight patrons. His defeat by Klondike relegated him temporarily to a back seat in fistic affairs. Matches were difficult to obtain unless a fighter had "shown something," and the year 1900 passed without Johnson appearing in a regular battle.

In 1901 he had better luck, winning six bouts with minor lights of the ring. He lost one fight, by a knockout in the third, to Joe Choynski, and fought a twenty-round draw in a return engagement with Klondike.

Johnson then did considerable fighting in the South, the Middle West, and the Pacific Coast, meeting the toughest opponents available and scoring victories. His early record shows fifteen- and twenty-round contests with such hardy ringmen as Frank Childs, Billy Stift, Hank Griffin, Pete Everett (one of the hardest-hitting Mexicans who ever put on a pair of gloves), George Gardiner, Sam McVey, Denver Ed Martin, Sandy Ferguson, Joe Butler, and Bob White, each one of whom was considered a good journeyman heavyweight. Johnson didn't lose a contest, though he drew in a number.

It was not until March 28, 1905, at the time Jim Jeffries was talking of retirement, that Johnson lost his first battle since Choynski beat him in 1901. His conqueror was Marvin Hart, then climbing toward the top of the heavyweight division. Since Johnson had also been making his way upward, Hart figured that a victory over the big Negro from Galveston would gain him recognition from Jeffries.

The Louisville fighter clashed with Johnson in San Francisco, and though Hart took the greater punishment of the two, Referee Alec Greggains gave the decision to Marvin on his greater gameness and aggressiveness. Johnson was always inclined to loaf.

From that defeat until the day when he lost the title to big Jess Willard in 1915, Johnson, although he dropped a few decisions, was never stopped. When he beat Burns he had a record of sixty-seven battles to his credit. Of those the toughest were with members of his own race. Hank Griffin, Denver Ed Martin, Sam McVey, Joe Jeanette, and Sam Langford all gave Johnson considerable trouble, especially the last two.

Langford, a short, squatty Hercules of terrific punching power, who was known as the Boston Tar Baby, met Johnson at the Lincoln A. C. of Chelsea, Massachusetts, on April 26, 1906, in a fifteen-round engagement. Langford floored Johnson for a count of eight in the seventh round, but the taller boxer had a larger margin of points to his credit at the finish and gained the verdict. Langford scaled a mere 158, to 185 for his opponent.

Although repeatedly challenged by Langford for a return match, Johnson persistently avoided him. The Tar Baby, a great fighter and skilled ring general, never had a chance to demonstrate his ability in a championship battle. After Jeffries' retirement the white heavies were a pretty poor lot, and none of them cared to mix with Langford unless the Negro fought under an agreement to let them stay the limit.

Johnson and Joe Jeanette were sworn enemies, and whenever they collided inside the ropes, the spectators were assured of a contest with no favors asked or given on either side. They crossed arms eight times. Four of these encounters were six-round no-decision bouts. Johnson lost another on a foul, still another was a ten-round draw. He took two decisions, one in fifteen rounds, the other in three.

After Johnson became champion he turned a deaf ear to challenges from both Langford and Jeanette. The white folks were easier game, and he had no intention of risking his hard-won title against such formidable adversaries.

Johnson was a cautious performer. After a boyhood of poverty, when fame and money came his way he was wise enough to evade unnecessary dangers. Six feet and a quarter inch in height, scaling 210 pounds in his prime, a smooth, slippery boxer who knew how to make every blow tell, the Galveston Giant seldom attempted to knock out an opponent unless he was so obviously helpless that no risk was involved. Jack was content to outpoint his antagonists, and the public in general grew to believe him deficient in punishing power. The men who fought him did not, however, share this mistaken idea. They were painfully aware that Johnson could hit with deadly effect when the spirit so moved him.

Following his victory over Burns, the champion won a six-round decision at Vancouver over Victor McLaglen, later a leading motion-picture actor. He also boxed no-decision bouts with Philadelphia Jack O'Brien, Tony Ross, and Al Kaufmann. In none of those affairs did Johnson exert himself to any great degree. He won as he pleased, and it satisfied him to loaf along, jabbing and picking his opponents to pieces.

Then came his battle with Stanley Ketchel at Colma, California, on October 16, 1909. Ketchel was middleweight champion and possessed a world-wide reputation as a knockout artist. But his challenge of the heavyweight leader was considered an example of astonishing boldness, for he normally scaled only

158 pounds * and stood only five feet, nine and three-quarter inches.

Johnson, knowing what a great drawing card the middleweight was, had agreed to let him stay the limit. Jack, who outweighed Stanley by forty-five pounds, was having a difficult time finding opponents just then, owing to the dearth of good material in the ranks of white heavyweights, and he judged correctly that a meeting with the middleweight king would react very favorably on his bank account.

Had Ketchel played fair with Johnson, the Negro would probably have kept faith with him—for by refraining from knocking out Stanley, he would subsequently have found it easier to secure matches with white heavies who might have been deluded into thinking that the once invincible Negro had struck the down grade. But Ketchel resolved to double-cross his partner in the game of cross they were playing with the public—a most unfortunate error on Stanley's part.

During the early rounds, Johnson, towering above his small opponent, boxed in indolent style, stopping Ketchel's repeated rushes with straight left jabs and seldom using his right except for blocking. Stanley could not land with effect on the big fellow, and it was rather a tame exhibition until the twelfth round. Then, during a close exchange, Ketchel put all his strength into a savage right that landed below Johnson's ear. The Negro fell heavily but bounced to his feet like a rubber ball.

Ketchel rushed and swung eagerly, but now Johnson, transformed for the moment into a black leopard thirsting for the kill, leaped to meet him. A right uppercut with all the weight of Jack's massive shoulders behind it caught Stanley square on the mouth and shocked him into instant unconsciousness as if he had been hit with a hammer.

Such was the fury of the blow that all of Ketchel's front teeth were broken off at the gums and he did not regain his senses for several minutes! Any doubts Ketchel or the Negro's critics may have entertained as to Johnson's ability to deliver a crushing wallop were effectually dissolved. Nor did Ketchel receive much sympathy when the story of the double-cross came out.

* Against Johnson, not being obliged to make this limit, he weighed 170.

Meanwhile the quest for a "white hope" was being vigorously conducted by big and little promoters. None of their finds proved of value, and nearly eleven months elapsed after John-son's victory over Ketchel before the champion was called upon to defend his title. His opponent was not a youthful graduate of the fistic university but the old war horse, Jim Jeffries, who had hung up his gloves "forever" more than five years earlier.

Independence Day, 1910, in Reno, Nevada, is one of the memorable days in the annals of pugilism. For three days prior to the fight, strangers had been pouring into the town by the thousands. Special after special pulled into the depot and disgorged sports from every point of the compass. The hotels and saloons were packed, and food could only be come by at a great expenditure of patience and money. Never had such a sight been seen before!

On the whole, it was an orderly crowd. Everyone was there to see the fight, and if the local jail suffered from a surplus population of pickpockets and other small fry of the criminal world, the traditional old-time gun-fighting fraternity was conspicuous by its absence.

The authorities, however, were not disposed to take chances, and everyone who presented himself for admission at the huge arena was searched for lethal weapons, whatever his rank or special status. Anyone armed with gun or knife had to deposit his weapon in the "cloakroom." He received a ticket in exchange that enabled him to recover his hardware as soon as the battle was over.

No fight in the American West would have been considered complete in those days without the presence of the veteran announcer, Billy Jordan, and the entry of the portly San Franciscan into the ring evoked a storm of applause. For the next hour Jordan was the busiest man in Reno, for upon him devolved the task of introducing more than a score of fistic celebrities to the public. How even his brazen throat withstood the tremendous strain is still a mystery. He presented, among others, Sullivan, Corbett, Fitzsimmons, Sharkey, Burns, Battling Nelson, and Abe Attell.

When the fighters stripped for the fray, it was quickly evident that the tales about Johnson having neglected his training were absolute canards. The Negro was trained to the hour, and he showed not the least sign of the nervousness that had been reported before he entered the ring. Jeffries, on the other hand, looked like anything but a man confident of his ability to make good his boast of putting the Negro away in ten rounds or less. Sunken cheeked and haggard eyed, he looked more than his thirty-five years, an impression which his prematurely bald pate did nothing to lessen. His eyes lacked fire, and his gaze was shifty. His flabbiness showed too plainly the result of his long layoff.

The fight was a one-sided exhibition in which the veteran went ingloriously down to defeat. The Negro completely outclassed him and handled California's former pride as if he had been a lumbering novice.

The battle inaugurated the era of huge purses in America, Johnson receiving 60 per cent—60,600 dollars, a bonus of 10,000 dollars, and 50,000 dollars for picture rights, a total of 120,600 dollars. The loser's share was 40 per cent—40,400 dollars, a 10,-000-dollar bonus, and 66,666 dollars for picture rights, a total of 117,066 dollars. The contest also was notable for the tremendous ballyhoo it was given by the press—something since painfully familiar to the public. No previous prize fight, waged with bare knuckles or gloves, had ever been so widely advertised.

The result of the mill was an awful blow to the prestige of the newspaper critics, who, almost to a man, had been carried away by enthusiasm for the white challenger and predicted victory for him. The late Tad Dorgan, of the *New York Journal,* was one of the few who refused to climb on board the Jeffries bandwagon; on the contrary, he boldly prophesied that the Negro would win.

The old trouble, lack of fitting opponents, kept Johnson idle for exactly two years after the Reno contest. Then another veteran was selected to meet him, in the person of Jim Flynn. Though a rough, tough heavyweight, he was completely outclassed by the champion in nine rounds on July 4, 1912, at Las Vegas, New Mexico. Police interfered and halted the unequal struggle.

In 1913 Johnson outpointed Frank Moran in twenty rounds,

knocked out a Russian wrestler named Spoul in two, and boxed an eight-round draw with Jim Johnson, another Negro warrior.

In the Jim Johnson fight, the champion broke his left hand and had to quit. The bout had been scheduled for ten rounds, and under present-day boxing rules Jack Johnson would have lost his crown on a technical knockout. Jack was tottering on the ropes, with his left arm hanging limp, when the club physician came to his rescue by declaring that the champion could not carry on further under the circumstances. Whereupon, in spite of screaming protests from the spectators, the referee declared the bout a draw.

The fights with Moran, Spoul, and Jim Johnson were staged in Paris. Jack Johnson had become a voluntary exile from his native land when, having been convicted and sentenced to a year in the penitentiary for violation of the Mann Act, he forfeited his bail and fled abroad. At that time Jack had been twice married, each time to a white woman, and it was an affair with another white woman that got him into a jam with the Federal authorities. He was merely another victim of the law that had been passed years before to prevent the wholesale transportation of prostitutes from one section of the United States to another.

While Johnson was a fugitive from justice, the hunt for a "white hope," so long unsuccessfully conducted, came to an end with the discovery of a man from the wide-open spaces named Jess Willard. Since Johnson could not enter the United States, the battle was fought in Havana on April 5, 1915.

Big as Jack Johnson was, Willard was bigger in every way. Cowboy Jess, six feet, six inches in height, scaling 240 pounds in the pink of condition, was the tallest heavyweight who ever competed under Queensberry rules. He was remarkably well proportioned, too, and against such a colossus the science and generalship of Johnson, now thirty-seven and well past his prime, were not enough. Willard won by a knockout in the twenty-sixth round.

The Negro was not knocked senseless but failed to rise after being floored in the final round. He lay on his back, one arm thrown across his face as though to shield his eyes from the flaming Cuban sun.

Johnson's position while he was being counted out gave rise to rumors that he had thrown the fight. It was argued that a man in a state of genuine grogginess would not have stretched himself in such a comfortable posture. Additional evidence was produced for this theory some years later when the defeated man permitted a statement to be printed under his signature to the effect that he deliberately "lay down." According to this story, Jack was broke, had to have money, and was in addition promised by the promoters that they would procure him a pardon for his offense against the law, provided he lost to Willard.

Johnson, of course, got money for his statement. That circumstance does not automatically discredit the man, even though he was never precisely a model of high ethics. But I am in a position to state flatly that Johnson was not being truthful. In the first place, I saw the fight and can vouch for its honesty. In the second place, I interviewed Tom Flanagan, noted Canadian athlete and trainer who prepared Jack Johnson for the Willard engagement.

Discussing Johnson's "confession," he said to me some years after the fight, "This is the first time since the Havana fight that I have made a definite statement about it. The battle was on the level. Willard won because he was the better man. Johnson was not at his best, but this is not intended as an excuse for him. The truth is that Johnson, whose pride in holding the title was great, could not bear to think of another man winning it. Also he did not want his people to know that he was inferior to Willard and thereby lose their respect for his ability.

"Remember that Willard was trained to the minute and was bigger and more powerful in every way than Johnson. In the fourteenth round Jack threw caution to the winds and tried his utmost to land a knockout. That was when he bruised Jess so badly about the cheekbone. When Jack found Jess took everything he had and was fighting back harder, he just lost heart. Johnson was not knocked cold, but he was out so far as offering further resistance was concerned and went down in the twenty-sixth round from sheer exhaustion.

"That is the true version of the contest. Jack was a wonderful defensive fighter and a very clever fellow even outside of boxing. It is too bad he made the statement about throwing the fight."

The deposed king eked out an aimless existence in foreign lands until depleted funds and homesickness drove him to surrender to the United States authorities. During the latter part of his exile he won a few unimportant fights from comparatively unknown boxers, but age and free living had robbed him of much of his former strength and agility, and he was but a pathetic shadow of the once formidable battler who defeated the best men of his time.

Having served his penitentiary sentence, the ex-champion attempted a comeback. But he was no longer a drawing card. The public had lost interest in him, and promoters passed him by. Jack Johnson's ring days were ended.

Yet if at the conclusion of his active service within the ropes Johnson had nothing left out of the fortune he had made, he still possessed good health and the ability to earn a livelihood. Settling down in New York, he capitalized on his popularity among the large Negro population by opening a gymnasium and training quarters. He was also an orchestra leader, a lecturer, a physical-culture director, a trainer of fighters, and a vaudeville entertainer.

In 1946, while Jack was on his way home after an engagement in the South with a circus, his car jumped the road and he was killed. The fatal accident took place at Raleigh, North Carolina, June 10.

After years devoted to the study of heavyweight fighters, I have no hesitation in naming Jack Johnson as the greatest of them all. He possessed every asset. He was big and strong and endowed with perfect co-ordination. He was a fine boxer, a good hitter, and a powerful counterpuncher. He could block admirably and was a master in the art of feinting. In all-around ability, he was tops.

CHAPTER 15

THE GIANT COWBOY

FOR A short period after defeating Jack Johnson, Jess Willard basked contentedly in the sunlight of fame as befitted the man who had restored the heavyweight crown to the white race. Yet his popularity did not long endure. His great bulk, which overawed most of his opponents, was a drawback rather than an asset in winning favor with the rank and file of fight followers.

It is axiomatic in ring circles that a crowd's sympathy is nearly always with the smaller man. When a giant scores a victory over a foe of slighter physical equipment, there is a general disposition among the onlookers to give the winner scant credit. And when the giant prefers, as did Willard, to loaf along quietly, merely extending himself sufficiently to outpoint an adversary instead of crushing him with a hurricane attack, the spectators usually unite in wishing that by some miracle the little fellow could take the measure of the lethargic Goliath.

Fight fans were quick to sense that the tiger instinct was altogether lacking in Jess's make-up, and they resented a champion who was merely a good-natured boxer. A great popular champion is the man who loves to fight. John L. Sullivan and, later, Jack Dempsey were the representatives par excellence of this class of battler. Featherweight champion Terry McGovern was another—a high-geared scrapping machine that, once set going, was bound to destroy something or wreck itself in the attempt.

Born near an Indian reservation in Oklahoma, on December 29, 1883, Jess spent his boyhood days among the redskins, riding, hunting, and indulging in other outdoor activities. Later he became a plains teamster.

There was enough legitimate Wild West background to warrant publicizing him as a former cowboy when he became prominent as a glove wielder. But there was really nothing of the romantic adventurer or the movie hero of the chaps-and-lariat type about Jess Willard. His tastes were quiet and domestic. No man living ever possessed less of the knight-errant spirit. Soon after he won the heavyweight title a story was printed to the effect that Jess, immediately upon hearing of Jeffries' defeat, threw up his teamster job and declared that his sole ambition was to whip Johnson. Which was all pure buncombe.

Willard simply wanted work that would provide him a better living than driving horses. Had he been a man of less physical strength, the thought of taking to the ring would never have entered his mind. But he had read of the big purses paid to star boxers, and as time went on and the frantic hunt for a "white hope" continued, it was slowly borne in on the big chap's mind that prize fighting was a trade in which his extraordinary strength and size might be turned to his financial advantage. He was twenty-eight, rather late in life for a pugilistic beginner, when he first donned the gloves in a gymnasium at Tulsa in 1911.

Inexperience resulted in his losing his first fight on a foul to Louis Fink. But Jess clearly had held the upper hand when the contest terminated, and a few months later he knocked out Fink in three rounds at Oklahoma City. Then he won a succession of bouts from other local fighters. But the purses were small in Oklahoma, and Jess went further afield.

In Springfield, Missouri, big Jess went to see Billy McCarney, a promoter, manager, and jack-of-all-trades in boxing, and one of America's most widely known fistic characters at the time. McCarney wasn't impressed with the amiable teamster's bulk and to get rid of him he slipped him along to Jimmy Bronson, who, besides working for McCarney as an aide in matchmaking, was handling a few battlers on his own.

"I'll never forget my first look at big Jess, a six-foot, six-inch giant scaling 260 pounds then," Bronson has related. "His pants stopped just below his knees and his sleeves ended around his elbows. How he got into the outfit no one will ever know! The whole rig was topped off with a huge black sombrero. I learned that his manager, a fellow named Brock, was having difficulties with the law at the moment, and the big guy was almost starved.

"After listening to his tale of woe, I slipped him a five, told him to go out and get a meal and not to forget the change. When he returned I asked him what he had, and he replied, 'Ham and eggs,' but never mentioned the difference. I found out later that Willard had gone through $2.75 worth of ham and eggs. Since one order only cost two bits in those days, figure out just how much of the stuff he had put away.

"A 'white hope' named Joe Cox was the big noise down in Springfield at the time. Not too bad a fighter, but the fans wanted to see him licked. Willard looked big enough (if nothing else) to turn the trick, so back down to McCarney at Springfield we went. Just about the same time a vaudeville strong-man act known as the Great Romanos hit town.

"The day after their arrival, the biggest Romano showed up in McCarney's office, announced he was a fighter, and challenged Joe Cox. Since Willard was ready to meet Cox, too, McCarney suggested the two meet in the gym with the better man getting the Cox shot. Both agreed. It came off before a packed gymnasium at fifty cents a head. Bill had figured that all out, and Willard made the other guy quit.

"I wonder if Victor McLaglen remembers that one, for that's who the Great Romano was—Victor McLaglen, the movie actor!

"Now Jess Willard wasn't a bad fighter, as Dempsey will tell you. He had a great left, and he was punching Cox around for a while. But along about the middle of the fight Cox landed a hard right and Jess maneuvered me—the referee—in between himself and Cox, stepped out of the ring, and called it an evening."

From Springfield Jess hit the trail eastward and landed in Chicago at the time the Windy City was the center of boxing in the Middle West. Like his predecessor on the pugilistic throne, Willard found Chicago a cheerless place for an unknown scrapper who was minus funds and friends. Times were very hard for him when Charles "Kid" Cutler, attracted by the vast dimensions of the young giant, steered him to the snug harbor of the Cutler flat on the North Side.

Cutler was then a wrestler of national prominence. He had previously followed the ring, in which he was fairly successful, and had spent a year touring with John L. Sullivan as a sparring partner. He grew dissatisfied with his slow climb up the pugilistic ladder, and since wrestling was enjoying a boom throughout the country he turned his attention to the mat sport. He was very successful as a grappler and made a small fortune.

Under Kid Cutler's tutelage in "Professor" Billy O'Connell's training quarters, Willard learned a lot about the finer points of boxing. The veteran heavyweight, himself a six-footer, took extraordinary pains with his charge, with such good results that in a battle at Fort Wayne, Indiana, with John Young, Jess scored a six-round knockout. Two other knockout victories were added to Willard's record while he was under Cutler's direction, and soon the Kid began to entertain hopes of seeing his protégé reach the topmost fistic heights.

At this juncture the tempter entered Cutler's pugilistic den in the guise of Tom Jones, managerial impresario and sometime pilot of Ad Wolgast, ex-lightweight champion. Mr. Jones saw and coveted the huge person of Willard. He had a secret interview with Jess, in which he pointed out that under his management he could achieve fame and fortune. He urged the big fellow to accompany him to New York, where, he assured Jess, he could gain the prominence necessary to advance him toward a match for the championship.

It might be supposed by the innocent that a sense of obligation would have prevented Willard from forsaking his benefactor, Kid Cutler. But gratitude is not, as a rule, much in evidence among professional fighters, as anyone who has had dealings with them will testify. Willard proved no exception. That night, while the Cutler family slumbered peacefully, their huge guest, grip in hand, stole down the stairs as softly as he could and faded into the outer darkness.

Great was the wrath of Charlie Cutler when he awoke in the morning to find that the bird he had hopes of making the cock of the roost had flown, leaving him nothing save bitter remembrances and a broken contract. Cutler swore vengeance on the villain who had coaxed his personal giant into abandoning Chicago for New York.

Several years elapsed. Mr. Jones was making a Chicago stop-over and was standing at the bar of the Morrison Hotel when the avenger struck his trail. Jones's jaw offered a fair target, and Kid Cutler unleashed a right hook that hit its mark squarely. When Jones recovered his senses he confessed his crime against his conqueror. In addition, he paid him five thousand dollars as compensation for the victor's violated contract and injured feel-ings—and if there is any moral in connection with the unfor-tunate Mr. Jones's come-uppance, it takes the form of a warning that no one (least of all, a fight promoter) should ever stand at a bar with his guard down.

Jess invaded Gotham in 1912. Big, hulking heavies trying to make a "white hope" rating were a dime a dozen then, and Willard's astute mentor knew that he must introduce some advertising novelty in order to arouse public curiosity and stim-ulate interest in his charge. So he hit on the idea of having Willard introduced to every fight gathering as the Oklahoma cowboy who had deserted ranch life with the sole notion of qualifying as an opponent for Johnson.

Willard was given instructions to climb into the ring just before a main bout started. Wearing his high leather boots and immense broad-brimmed black hat, he looked at least seven feet tall, and the spectators were duly impressed as this mighty figure stood beside the announcer, who was completely dwarfed by his huge presence.

The newspapers gave Jess plenty of publicity, and it was not long before he obtained a match with Arthur Pelkey. Arthur, destined to figure the following year in a tragic combat at Cal-gary, Canada, with Luther McCarty, which resulted in McCarty's death, was defeated by Willard in ten rounds. At that time no decisions were rendered under New York State boxing law, but the newspaper verdicts were all in Willard's favor.

The ill-fated Luther McCarty was Jess's next opponent. Luther was by all odds the best-looking prospect among the white heavyweights, and it was generally expected that Willard would be beaten. McCarty rushed from the start, while Jess boxed in his usual nonchalant manner.

Suddenly McCarty smashed a right over Willard's left eye that stung Jess and galvanized him into a momentary outburst of anger. The giant leaped forward, thrust his long left into McCarty's face, sent him back on his heels, and followed with a right uppercut which sent his antagonist staggering across the ring. McCarty recovered quickly, but he had learned respect for his opponent and remained on the defensive. If Willard had followed up his assault he might have stopped McCarty. But Jess relapsed into his former peaceful mood and was content to jab lazily until the final bell.

After both of these contests Willard was severely criticized by the sporting writers for his lack of energy. They could not deny that he had won, but with the tremendous physical advantages he possessed, the general feeling was that he should have stopped his opponents.

The adverse criticism stirred the easy-going giant sufficiently to make him a trifle more active in his next battle, which took place in Buffalo, with Sailor White. Jess, instead of playing a waiting game, headed briskly for the ex-tar when the gong clanged. In the slugging that followed, White was helpless. The charging giant hammered and beat him to the floor with ponderous blows, and White was counted out before half a round had elapsed.

A supposedly harder test was given Willard when he was matched with Soldier Kearns. While not quite so tall as the Westerner, Kearns was well over six feet and scaled 210 pounds. He could hit and had a long list of knockouts to his credit.

Against the Soldier, Jess reverted to his old, exasperating methods. Grinning amiably as the crowd angrily urged him to "go in and fight," he held Kearns off with his long reach and was content to jab in a desultory manner.

They were well into the eighth round when Kearns, ducking under a left lead, stabbed an awful right just above Willard's belt, and it actually appeared as if the glove had sunk to its wristband in the giant's stomach. Willard was badly hurt, and he reacted to the stimulus of pain. Uttering a gasping bellow of rage, he charged like a wounded buffalo and swung an upper cut from his hip that caught Kearns fairly on the chin. The Soldier was lifted from his feet and dropped as if struck with a sledge hammer. He lay motionless and was carried to his corner.

This victory convinced the doubters. Jess had established himself as a good drawing card, and after a couple of knockouts scored over Frank Bauer and Jack Leon he was matched to box Gunboat Smith before a San Francisco club on May 20, 1913. On form, Willard looked like a sure winner. In addition, he had an advantage of fifty pounds in weight and several inches in height and reach. Sailor White, whom Jess had eliminated in less than a round, had held Smith even in a ten-round bout.

Yet Gunboat, whose main reliance in action was a powerful overhand right swing with which he had run up a long string of knockouts, carried the fight to Willard for twenty rounds and was awarded the decision. There were no excuses for Willard. He was well trained and in perfect health, but his pacific temperament reasserted itself at the wrong time, and the frantic pleadings of his seconds failed to induce him to take the offensive.

Willard lost additional prestige the following month when Charley Miller, three times a victim of Smith's knockout punch, held him to a four-round draw. Yet the California promoters possessed enough faith in his ability to give him another match, and on August 22 he met Bull Young at Vernon. On this occasion Willard, spurred by the reflection that his career was at stake, fought with unusual venom and such deadly effect that Young was knocked unconscious in the eleventh round.

The loser remained in a state of coma. It was impossible to revive him, and he died after an emergency operation. Willard was arrested on a manslaughter charge and promptly exonerated. But he brooded greatly over this tragic accident, and there is no doubt that for a while he was more cautious than ever when in action. On November 17 he allowed Boer Rodel to stay the limit in a ten-round no-decision bout at Milwaukee, although it was plainly evident that he could have won in a hurry had he chosen to do so.

Arriving in New York toward the end of 1913, he was matched

with an opponent nearly as gigantic as himself, Carl Morris of Fulton, Kentucky. What followed was as slow and uninteresting an exhibition as New Yorkers had ever seen. Morris, who had a fair record, studded with knockouts, was unable to land with effect on Willard. And had Jess been a spectator instead of a principal, he could scarcely have appeared less concerned with the outcome. It was a no-decision bout in which Willard had a slight advantage, but both fighters were roundly scored by the newspapers for their miserable showing.

Jess's manager needled him into a state of synthetic ferocity, and nine days after the Morris fiasco, he scored knockouts in rapid succession over "One Round" Davis and his former opponent, Boer Rodel. Then once again Jess resorted to extreme caution and failed even to win a decision over Tom McMahon, a very ordinary fighter, in twelve rounds, on St. Patrick's Day, 1914. The same trouble that beset him in the Morris contest, the haunting vision of the deceased Bull Young, caused him to spare McMahon.

This time Tom Jones really took Jess apart. Willard's pride was aroused, and when he fought Dan Daily at Buffalo on April 13, 1914, he dropped him quickly. On April 28 he closed accounts with his old foeman, Boer Rodel, by stopping the South African in six rounds.

Then followed a long spell of idleness—a full year. Willard refused all offers of matches and went to California, where he basked in the sunshine, put on flesh, and enjoyed life thoroughly. But if Jess was idle, his manager was not. He interrupted the holiday with orders to start training for a title match with Jack Johnson.

Much as Willard hated the stress and turmoil of glove warfare, this was too big a chance to be missed, and he somewhat sourly consented to start the grind in preparation for the greatest battle of his career. It was a physical ordeal of exceeding grimness. Jess's long layoff and easy mode of living had combined to pile fat on his immense frame, and he tipped the scales at 320 pounds at the time articles were signed for the battle. He waddled when he walked.

Simon Legree of plantation fame had nothing on Manager

Jones when it came to coercing an unwilling worker. True, Legree had a blacksnake whip to aid his arguments. Jones had only his tongue, but it was a stinging and convincing weapon. Willard was big enough to have eaten Mr. Jones for lunch, but under his master's vocal lash he toed the mark.

Training began at El Paso, Texas, the battle originally having been scheduled for Mexico. But Johnson, en route from South America, refused to land in Mexico—a rumor had become current that bandits were planning to seize the Negro and hold him for a big ransom under threat of delivering him to American authorities. Nothing could convince Jack that his liberty wasn't endangered again, and he went to Havana. Thus the Cuban capital became the site of battle.

Big Jess trained faithfully. When he was pronounced fit, his weight had come down from 320 to 263 pounds. Also, his temper had grown uncertain, a sure sign that he was on edge. Fighters normally develop an irritable streak on the verge of an important battle for which they have undergone a heavy training siege, and Willard was no exception to the rule. Altogether, Jess was in the grandest condition of his life in April, 1915, and at no future period did he reach such a state of athletic perfection.

The battle, listed for forty-five rounds, terminated, as before related, with Johnson lying prostrate in the twenty-sixth. The newly crowned champion had fought carefully and, with few breaches, according to instructions. Once in the fifth, and again in the seventh and fourteenth, Johnson landed blows that stung the giant into sudden fiery action. On those occasions Jess waxed momentarily vicious and rushed his opponent, sending in body punches that made the Negro wince and seek safety in the clinches. Except for these brief outbursts of temper, Willard fought carefully and wore down Johnson by steady, methodical punching.

Immediately after winning the title, Willard declared that he was willing to rest indefinitely upon his laurels. His heart had never been in the fighting game, and had his finances permitted, he would undoubtedly have quit the ring then and there for good. But he returned to the United States not very much better off in pocket than before his departure. Besides Tom Jones, several other gentlemen of the managerial tribe were stock-holders in what might be described as "Jess Willard, Inc." The boxer had signed away about 75 per cent of himself to these astute speculators, this being one of the earliest instances of "syndicating," a practice that afterward reached such absurd proportions as to call for interference by the New York State Athletic Commission.

Consequently Willard, although the title brought him some lucrative offers from showmen throughout America, had little cash left after he had bought himself free of most of his "owners." But he never succeeded in ridding himself entirely of these para-sites, even up to the day when he lost the championship to Jack Dempsey, a little over four years after he won it.

Even so, Jess put off his re-entry into the ring for almost a year. The Havana battle took place on April 5, 1915, and Willard did not face another opponent until March 25, 1916. Then he boxed ten rounds with Frank Moran in the old Madison Square Garden in New York.

During the months that passed after he became champion, Willard had put on a good deal of flesh. He did not train very hard for the contest with Moran and was rather unwieldy when he entered the ring. But the champion trusted to his long reach to outpoint his adversary and his superior bulk to offset Moran's assaults.

Moran's best asset was a tremendous right swing, referred to by the sporting scribes as the "Mary Ann." He had knocked out several antagonists with this punch—a blow that, with Moran's fighting weight of 210 pounds behind it, was extremely effective. But against Willard, Moran, always aggressive, always trying hard, was so thoroughly outclassed that the bout did not prove particularly interesting. Trying to stir Jess into rapid action when he was in a good temper was about as great a waste of time as flogging a dead horse. And since Moran never hurt him, Willard simply kept on grinning and outjabbing his rushing foeman until the final bell.

It was a no-decision bout, but the newspapers were unanimous in awarding victory to the champion. Jess came in for considerable adverse criticism through his failure to stop Moran, but he didn't mind this. Ring glory meant little to him at any time. He was satisfied to be known as the man who brought back the championship to the white race. That was fame enough. For the rest, it was merely a matter of using his title to collect what money he could in the easiest way possible.

Several years were to pass before Willard would defend his title. During the intervening period he filled circus and theatrical engagements and made a few appearances in exhibition boxing bouts.

Financially, Jess's long rest from active service was not very fruitful. After the excitement attending his defeat of Johnson had subsided, fight fans lost interest in him, nor did he ever become a great attraction in the show business. Athletically, it was even worse. Always prone to obesity, Jess's huge frame gradually assumed the mammoth proportions it reached in the days before he started training for the Havana battle. It seemed unlikely that the champion would ever fight again, and then a remarkable gentleman named Tex Rickard, a fight promoter from the West, decided to try his hand on the Atlantic seaboard.

Of all the heavyweights then in the public eye, a tough pug called Jack Dempsey seemed the most likely man to pit against the Goliath who wore the crown. Smaller in every way than Willard, he had fought his way upgrade steadily, compiling an extraordinary list of knockouts over all comers. To Rickard, Jack looked like an ideal challenger, and, having obtained Willard's signature to fight any man in the world for a guarantee of one hundred thousand dollars, the promoter had no difficulty in concluding an agreement with Dempsey and his manager, Jack Kearns.

The battle took place in an open-air arena on July 4, 1919, at Toledo, Ohio, and by the end of the third round Jess Willard had been pounded into a helpless pulp. For the first time since the glorious days of John L. Sullivan, the United States had a heavyweight who was an idol as well as a champion.

Dempsey proved that he was more than a fighter. He was the greatest tornado the boxing game had ever seen. One minute and fifty-eight seconds after the gong had sent them on their way, Willard received a pile-driving right to the point of the jaw, and down he went. Seven times in that round Willard hit the canvas.

Not in the memory of the oldest fan had a champion taken such punishment as did Willard from Dempsey. Yet Jess, responding as he did after every knockdown by arising to absorb still more punishment, proved that he was gameness personified. He was not the quitter some critics would have us believe because he failed to come out for the fourth round. No man with a yellow streak in him would have endured the agony he experienced through those nine minutes of battering. In defeat, he gave an amazing exhibition of courage.

Before the first round ended, he was reeling around in the ring, dazed, not knowing where he was, completely at the mercy of his younger opponent. Dempsey almost had Jess in that first round. When it ended, the champion was sitting on the canvas, his wide-open mouth streaming blood, his eyes glassy, blood shot, staring wearily and aimlessly into space. His seconds had to drag him to his corner.

Pandemonium reigned. The crowd had gone mad. The bell had not been heard—even by Ollie Pecord, the referee. He raised Dempsey's hand after counting Willard out, and Jack, also believing he had won the championship by a first-round knockout, jumped from the ring and was on his way to the dressing room before Timekeeper Warren Barbour, later United States senator from New Jersey, could explain to Pecord that Willard had been down for only seven seconds when the bell sounded ending the round. The referee then ordered Dempsey to return and resume the battle.

Blood was still flowing from Willard's mouth. Two front teeth had found their way to the canvas. His right eye had begun to close, and the right side of his head was enormously swollen. He looked as if he had been repeatedly struck by a blackjack.

Yet when the bell sounded for the second round, Willard rose feebly from his chair, ready to continue the hopeless battle. A pitiful object, he staggered toward Dempsey. His appearance was revolting, and many in the throng urged the referee to stop the fray.

CHAPTER 16

THE MANASSA MAULER

JACK DEMPSEY in the fistic records, William Harrison Dempsey according to his baptismal certificate, was born at Manassa, Colorado, June 24, 1895. By the time he was twenty he had begun to attract attention as a sort of bush-league knockout specialist. His only reversal during the next few years was a knockout in 1917 at the hands of Jim Flynn, a veteran who in 1907 had made an unsuccessful bid for the championship title held by Jack Johnson. But the year following, Dempsey evened matters by putting Jim away in seventy seconds.

At the start of his fighting career Dempsey was just a tough young hobo with a neck like a bull, a granite jaw, and fists like iron. He wandered about the country, riding the brake beams when unable to pay for softer means of transportation, taking matches wherever he could get them, and generally putting his opponents to sleep without wasting any time boxing with them. Life to Dempsey was a rough proposition—you either walloped or got a thrashing yourself. Blackly scowling, he would sit in his corner, glaring across at his antagonist, waiting for the bell. Once it sounded, Jack leaped to the fray like a hungry beast and habitually devoured his man with the unpitying fury of a jungle terror.

It was fortunate for Dempsey that he finally joined with a manager who had no hampering scruples, knew the fight game from A to Z, and was equipped with a degree of cunning that outmatched even the subtle craft of the fight promoters. The man was Jack Kearns. From the day he and Dempsey went into partnership, the fighter's stock began to boom in the pugilistic market.

Kearns and Dempsey barnstormed through the country with

considerable success. Whenever opponents ran short, the astute Mr. Kearns could always rise to the occasion and dig up someone who, for a consideration, would "take it on the jaw and turn a somersault." One of these handy men was Al Norton, an old playmate of Dempsey's and true friend of his manager. Under various names, Norton "fought" Dempsey in the four-round bouts then permitted by law on the Pacific Coast and in ten-round engagements elsewhere.

It is an open question whether Kearns was really responsible for Dempsey's rise to glory, or whether, unaided by Kearns's diplomatic methods and his managerial strategy, Jack could ever have climbed to the giddy heights. Undoubtedly Kearns had in Dempsey one of the greatest knockout artists of the age to exploit; conversely, in the hands of a less crafty pilot Dempsey could easily have fared a great deal worse. After Dempsey and Kearns had disagreed and split the combination, the fighter liked to point to the money he took in from matches he personally made with Jack Sharkey and Gene Tunney—three fights that grossed a total of five million dollars. But by that time, Dempsey was doing business in conjunction with the late Tex Rickard, one of the greatest showmen who ever coaxed the dollars out of an easily excited public.

For a long time Dempsey was under a cloud on account of his war record, or rather his lack of one. He felt no overwhelming urge to join the ranks of the A.E.F. Instead, his name was on a shipyard pay roll.

It is no wonder that a prominent boxer like Dempsey should have found himself the target for unlimited abuse as a slacker. Yet Jack's failure to enlist was typical of the fistic fraternity, whose members were conspicuous by their absence in World War I. They considered a bayonet a poor substitute for the padded glove and were loath to risk life and limb in a quarrel without gate receipts. (Jack made up for his faulty decision by doing a real job in World War II. An officer in the Coast Guard, he trained thousands of men, made them physically fit, and finally braved the shells and bullets of the Japs by leading a landing party to the shores of Tarawa.)

Les Darcy, middleweight champion of Australia, visited the

United States in search of matches while the war was on. He was subjected to such a storm of abuse by the newspapers all over the country for not having enlisted in the Allied ranks that he suffered a nervous breakdown, caught a fever, and died in Memphis, Tennessee, on May 24, 1917. Dempsey's nerve was not so easily broken. Yet it was nearly a year after his successful fight for the title before Jack could appear in the ring without hearing loud hisses mingling with the cheers. During that period he knocked out Billy Miske in three rounds and Bill Brennan in twelve.

By the time the Manassa Mauler stepped into the ring to defend his title against Georges Carpentier of France on July 2, 1921, in Jersey City, the spectators were ready to accord him a hearty greeting in which there lingered no trace of the old animosity. Though Carpentier received a greater volume of applause, many in that huge gathering felt that an American sports crowd could hardly do otherwise than hail Jack as the defender of national pride against a foreigner.

The match itself was an unconscionable imposition on the public. Carpentier at no time in his career scaled over the light-heavyweight limit. As a middleweight he had been stopped by Frank Mantell and Billy Papke. His heavyweight engagements had been entirely with opponents of less than championship caliber.

Carpentier trained in secret to conceal his shortcomings from the outside world. Tex Rickard, who promoted the affair, visited Dempsey in his dressing room just before hostilities were to commence and pleaded with the champion to go easy and allow Carpentier to make a good showing for a little while. Rickard was naturally anxious to please his patrons and feared the effect upon future gate receipts of a too sudden flop by the popular but sadly overrated Frenchman.

The fight had been preceded by a magnificent ballyhoo. Carpentier had served with distinction all through the Great War as a soldier of France, and the publicity corps had no difficulty in selling him to the public. Even the aid of George Bernard Shaw was enlisted to brighten up the public view of Carpentier's chances; he gave an interview in which he pro-

claimed Georges a ring marvel who would conquer the re-
doubtable Dempsey. But Shaw, author of a novel entitled
Cashel Byron's Profession, which had a ring champion of the old
days for its hero, proved a poor prophet, for Carpentier, except
for one momentary flash in the second round when he set
Dempsey back on his heels with a straight right drive to the
chin, never landed a blow that so much as jarred the champion.
Carpentier, incidentally, wrecked his right hand completely
when it hit the target, a flattering testimonial to the rocklike
quality of Dempsey's jaw. Dempsey played with his man until
the fourth, when he hammered him down and out.

Except for a one-round knockout of an obscure boxer named
Rioux in Montreal, Dempsey's ring record for 1922 was a blank.
Jack took life easy, savored the sweets of popularity, posed for
moving pictures, built up his bank account, and created around
himself that atmosphere of invincibility which only the great
Sullivan before him had lived in.

On July 4, 1923, Jack was awarded a decision in fifteen rounds
over Tom Gibbons at Shelby, Montana. His showing against
Gibbons was a decided disappointment to his admirers, for
Tom was much the smaller man, and the Dempsey adherents
fully expected that Jack would destroy him in his customary
hurricane fashion. But Gibbons was a perfect master of self-
defense, a tricky boxer, and a cunning general who knew how
to side-step and take advantage of every inch of the ring.

The question has often been asked how the money was raised
to pay Jack Dempsey the sum guaranteed him for his fight with
Gibbons. Before the summer of 1922, Shelby was nothing more
than a cow burg with a population of about five hundred, a
town that was regarded in the West as one of the poorest in this
country. A few starved dry-dirt farmers, a handful of cowboys,
and some sheepherders constituted the population. Traveling
salesmen for big concerns always made certain that this dreary
hamlet would not be one of their stopping places, and persons
who had survived the calamity of spending even so little as a
few hours in the place trembled violently years afterward at the
mere mention of the word Shelby.

Then in 1922 they struck oil near the whistle-stop nightmare.

Sam Sampson was the man most responsible for putting Shelby on the map. One cold night in January, 1923, a few months after the oil strike, several of the Shelby big shots were whooping it up in a little all-night saloon, the kind that had never heard of the Eighteenth Amendment or of the quaint law that was supposed to prevent the ingestion of alcoholic beverages. But the gentlemen in the saloon were not merely whooping it up. They had come together with the serious purpose of discussing what could be done to let the world know that the discovery of oil had made Shelby a great town. They knew what oil strikes had meant to communities in Oklahoma and Texas, and they were going to see to it that their own Shelby got the same kind of break.

Seated at the table beside Mayor Jim Johnson was the afore-mentioned Sampson, proprietor of an army-goods store. He had been making money lately. Suddenly an idea smote him.

"Why not let's stage a championship fight here?" exclaimed Mr. Sampson. "That will draw many fight fans here and put Shelby on the map. Let's get Jack Dempsey and Tom Gibbons. Both are popular, and we can fill an arena."

Everyone agreed that it was a wonderful idea, and Sam Sampson was elected manager of the enterprise. Wires were immediately sent to Dempsey and Gibbons, but there was no response.

On March 10, about two months later, Mike Collins, veteran newspaper man, promoter, manager, and publisher of *Boxing Blade*, was located at the Republican Club of Milwaukee, where he received a telegram from Sampson asking him to come to Shelby and look over the prospects for staging a world heavyweight championship fight out there on Independence Day. Mike agreed to make the trip.

When he got into Shelby, Collins gave it the once over. Then he remarked to Sampson, "So this is Shelby—are you guys all crazy?"

His hosts unhesitatingly rejected the possibility.

"I found several business houses, three rooming houses, the Silver Grill Hotel, the Great Northern depot, a mountain on the south, an oil field on the north, and the Great Northern Railroad running east and west," Collins told the reporters who attended the fight. "I felt I was stung but didn't have the heart to quit these guys who felt so confident they could put the fight over. I said to Sampson, 'You'll be the laughing stock of the fistic world. A hick town, a little cow pasture with a population of about five hundred, trying to outbid big Eastern cities of several million people and millions of dollars' backing for the big attraction you say you want. It is simply ridiculous.'

"There was no way of stopping them. They were determined. Their only answer was, 'Well, we will do it, and what do you know about that! If you feel otherwise, we're sorry we bothered asking you here.'

"How could you quit such people?" concluded Collins.

Mike called a meeting of Mayor Johnson and his friends to find out how the project would be financed. Mose Zimmerman, well-known horse salesman of St. Paul, who had bought up the best land in Shelby and was reselling it at a big profit, was supposed to furnish three hundred thousand dollars to stage the show that would boost Shelby, but he failed to show up at the meeting. A scouting party was sent out to bring him in, and they did. Mose appeared to be irritated when he joined the group.

"What in hell are you fellows thinking about?" he demanded. "Are you all crazy?"

Mose said that he had agreed to put up some money if others would do the same, but that he never had promised to finance the venture with such a fantastic sum as three hundred thousand dollars and that if he had uttered the words he was only kidding.

Collins then decided to quit all this foolishness, and he went back to his hotel to pack up and go home. But just before train time he had two visitors in his room, Carl Schwarz and John Dwyer. They pleaded with Mike to change his mind and come to the town hall, where Mayor Jim Johnson and others would speak at a mass meeting.

Mike agreed. A big cheer greeted him on his arrival. All hands had considerable faith in him and firmly believed that if anyone could put the fight across for them, the man was Mike Collins.

The Mayor asked Mike to speak. He spoke. He told the group

what was needed to stage such a gigantic affair. The most essential thing in such promotion was cash, and plenty of it.

"Get some money up and show your good faith, and I'll stick with you," said Mike.

Mayor Johnson and Sampson asked how much was necessary.

"We must have a hundred thousand to start with and another hundred thousand in thirty days," replied Collins.

It took exactly eleven minutes to raise the first twenty-six thousand dollars. Then vouchers for ringside seats were given for that amount, and the money was banked.

"Now will you wire the managers of Dempsey and Gibbons and have them come out here to settle matters with us by signing them for the fight?" asked Sampson.

"No, not that way," Collins replied. "I won't enter this thing until I see the hundred thousand dollars raised. When you have that amount, I'll promise you I'll get Dempsey and Gibbons to fight here."

It took eight days to obtain the rest of the guarantee. Lou Molumby, state commander of the American Legion, and Collins traveled around Montana by automobile and plane, making some sixty speeches at Rotary Club and Chamber of Commerce meetings and got 110,000 dollars subscribed instead of the 100,000 dollars, on the strength of Mike's promise to sign up the fighters—a promise that might be knocked into a cocked hat if either principal refused the offer.

Then Collins wired Jack Kearns and Eddie Kane, respectively managers of Dempsey and Gibbons, and each wired his eagerness to go through with such a match. This was the first that either had heard about the earth-shaking saloon conference, but they were ready for action.

Articles for the big show were signed on May 5, 1923. It was stipulated that Dempsey was to receive three hundred thousand dollars and that Gibbons was to get 50 per cent of the gate above that sum—and not one penny before. Gibbons had been offered the choice of taking fifty thousand dollars in cash or the percentage, and he decided on the gamble. It was a sad mistake, for he didn't collect one sou for the fight.

Collins returned to Shelby to get started on the arena. That was a serious problem since no money had been subscribed for the structure. Every citizen of Shelby owned lots, and everyone was eager to have his lot included in the arena. There was plenty of land but no fund with which to lease any part of it.

Things were becoming desperate when an idea struck Collins that the only man in Shelby who had plenty of credit was Mayor Johnson. He approached the Mayor with the proposition that he accept the post of treasurer so that the townsfolk would have faith in the project and loosen up their purse strings.

And so it was arranged. Within twenty days an arena went up seating forty thousand persons—not paid for, but built!

Then the ticket sale began, and some cash began to flow into the treasury. Meanwhile the owner of the lumber mill had become anxious, and he demanded payment for his lumber. He refused to wait any longer.

Mike Collins came up with another bright idea: Why not make Major Lane, whose company had furnished the lumber, a member of the directorate?

"Good!" cried Mayor Johnson. "Let's call him in."

Thus Major Lane became part promoter by being made president of the Dempsey-Gibbons fight. It was an honor to be cherished at the time, but it brought him severe headaches later.

This is the only fight on record that was promoted on absolutely nothing and put over on scheduled time—though it did appear, until twenty minutes before the event got under way, that there would be no fight.

Dempsey got his money. Gibbons and the investors in the project got nothing.

When all was over, Shelby had practically been wiped off the map. Three banks had failed, the big shots of the town were broke, the boom that had been expected as a result of the fight didn't follow, and the original promoters, including Mayor Jim Johnson, Lou McCutcheon, Sam Sampson, Lou Molumby, and James Speer had learned all they cared to about promoting a fight.

Two and a half months after the Shelby affair, which was profitable only for himself, Dempsey fought Luis Angel Firpo.

Against the Wild Bull of the Pampas, who had recently thwarted Jess Willard's comeback attempt, Jack, although he won in singularly melodramatic style, came within an ace of losing his crown.

Firpo, a big, rough, savage performer, could hit like a mule, but unfortunately for himself, his ring knowledge was scant. Had the South American commanded even a little ring science, he might have won the crown.

The champion floored Firpo seven times in the first round and twice in the second before Luis was counted out. A short right uppercut to the jaw ended the contest. But in those three minutes and fifty-seven seconds of warfare was crowded more action than ordinarily is seen in fifteen rounds of a championship bout. In those scant minutes of whirlwind milling, Dempsey was knocked once clear through the ropes and out of the ring—and had he not been helped up by the friendly hands of newspapermen, he would have returned to the site of battle too late to resume the bout. A second time Dempsey went down to his knees, just before he gave Firpo the finishing blow.

Firpo gave as marvelous an exhibition of gameness as ever has been seen in a ring. Battered and bloody, groggy from a terrific bombardment of lefts and rights, Firpo showed a fighting heart by coming back with an attack of crushing drives that all but had Dempsey out in the opening session. The contest was the most dramatic in the history of the heavyweight division. It surpassed the terrific fray in Toledo in which Dempsey tore the laurels from the head of Jess Willard and the knockout, years later, of Max Schmeling by Joe Louis. It even topped in excitement the knockdown of Gene Tunney by Dempsey in their second contest in Chicago.

Had Firpo possessed brain power in proportion to his enormous strength, he would have been crowned that day as heavyweight champion of the world. The Wild Bull, with all his powerful strength to give and take punishment, showed that he lacked the one essential quality to pugilistic greatness. He saw Dempsey with his back against the ropes, his jaw an open target, his hands hanging loosely at his sides, stunned from the impact that had sent him into the laps of the newspapermen at the ringside. But Firpo's brain was not quick. When he finally did come to the full realization that a beaten man stood before him and a championship was at his feet, his opportunity was gone. Luis gave Jack time to recover. In a moment the Manassa Mauler shifted into action, and then there was no stopping him.

After defeating Firpo, Jack Dempsey, like Jeffries, Johnson, and Willard in their day, seemed to have fought himself out of opponents. No white heavyweight then in view appeared capable of giving the Manassa Mauler a decent argument.

Harry Wills, a Negro, stood out as the best of his race and repeatedly challenged Dempsey, but neither the latter nor his manager were inclined to recognize Wills's claim to a battle. Dempsey, in reply to those who criticized him for not meeting the Negro, stated that he was perfectly willing to box Wills, provided some responsible promoter could be found to stage the bout. Tex Rickard, monarch of fistic showland, stated that, having due regard to the confused condition of affairs caused by the Jeffries-Johnson contest in pugilistic circles, he would never seek to match Negro and white in a heavyweight championship bout. Rickard added that he had also been told that New York's governor, Al Smith, was opposed to the mixed match.

Thus was Harry Wills safely sidetracked from the main line leading to the championship goal. Judging from his later record he would probably have proved an easy victim for Dempsey. He was eliminated as a threat to white supremacy in 1926, when he lost to Jack Sharkey on a foul, after making a poor showing.

This was the age of "Coolidge prosperity" and the "permanent bull market." It was the age of the flapper, the hip flask, and the coonskin coat. It was the jazz age. And not unnaturally, the era of wonderful nonsense became also the era of the million-dollar gate. More and more, boxing assumed the proportions of big business, and following the practice of big business, Rickard and his peers employed every trick of publicity to dazzle the customers. So adroit was Tex in the art of ballyhoo that in 1926 some 120,000 enthusiastic clients were persuaded to gather in Philadelphia to watch the champion put away an earnest young man by the name of Gene Tunney. Gene was almost universally regarded as a second-rater. But what did it matter—it was to be the Battle of the Century, wasn't it? Tex had said so. That was enough.

It was inevitable that a long period in inactivity should have had an adverse effect on Dempsey's fighting powers. The same thing had happened to all of Jack's predecessors, and he was no exception. In addition, Jack had made a lot of money, and he lacked some of his old zest for physical strife. He had also undergone a plastic operation to transform his battered nose from a button to a more classic formation. When the news came out, the wise old boys of pugdom shook their heads sadly. To them it was a sure sign of decadence, a hint that Dempsey would not submit his now genteel proboscis to the massaging of an opponent. At the very least, it meant that Jack Dempsey, the human tornado, had decided to forsake the role of slugger for that of careful boxer.

None of these views was correct, yet it cannot be denied that Dempsey at the age of thirty-one, when he was preparing to defend his title against Gene Tunney, had passed the peak of his fistic ability. His heart no longer cherished a real love for the rough game, as it had in the days when he was a carefree, reckless young hobo, ready to fight for the mere joy of combat. The youthful brake-beam traveler had been replaced by the mature man of business, a world-famous athlete who had accumulated riches and was hailed with frantic enthusiasm by the mobs.

Not that his physical condition had been altogether neglected. Dempsey's pride in his splendid body prompted him to take enough exercise to keep down the fat. He played handball and golf and occasionally worked out in a gymnasium with the gloves. To the inexperienced eye he still looked formidable enough to whip any man in the world.

But hard training had become a wearisome task instead of a pleasure. Something of the old do-or-die spirit had passed away. He could and did perform his road work faithfully, and he could still make his sparring partners suffer in their camp sessions. But the Dempsey who used to revel in the rough stunts of preparation for combat was now a man who had to drive himself and was glad when the day's toil was finished. The champion was also under the strain of defending a lawsuit that had been brought against him by his former manager, Jack Kearns, after they had parted company. Dempsey finally won in court, but there is no doubt that the burden he was bearing at the time increased his nervous tension.

Yet the reports from the champion's training camp were satisfactory, and outwardly Jack appeared to be his old self as the battle date of September 23, 1926, drew near.

The bout, for ten rounds, was scheduled for the Sesquicentennial Stadium in Philadelphia, and despite the unusual shortness of the route for a championship fight, it aroused universal interest and drew a gate that paid Dempsey 711,868 dollars and Tunney 204,000 dollars. Tunney, three years younger than Dempsey, a tall, well-proportioned athlete, had been holder of the American light-heavyweight title. After defeating Battling Levinsky for that crown, he won decisions over Harry Greb (twice), Dan O'Dowd, and Martin Burke and knocked out Erminio Spalla, Italian heavyweight champion, Georges Carpentier, Jack Herman, Bartley Madden, and Tom Gibbons. By stopping Gibbons in twelve rounds, Gene accomplished a feat that Dempsey had failed to achieve in fifteen.

Scientific to the extreme, a hard though not terrific hitter, Tunney had won most of his battles through skilled generalship and a cultivated knack of wearing his opponents down by degrees. The Tunney-Dempsey match paralleled the bout thirty-four years earlier between James J. Corbett and John L. Sullivan in that representatives of two schools of pugilism—a boxer and a slugger—were pitted against each other. And as in 1892, few persons were willing to accord the boxer more than an outside chance.

The great gathering of 120,557 persons in the Quaker City open-air arena were soon to learn that the challenger was no setup. At the sound of the gong he sprang forth to meet Dempsey's rush and landed a straight right on the jaw that shook the champion. That first punch, delivered with unerring accuracy and plenty of power behind it, not only jarred Dempsey physically but robbed him of his confidence. He remarked afterward, "No one ever did that to me before!"

As the fight went on and Tunney's counters offset Dempsey's fiercest efforts, at the same time battering Jack's features, it was obvious that unless the champion could connect with one of his famous left hooks to the jaw, he was a whipped man. The canvas, made heavy by a drenching rain, didn't help Dempsey any. It slowed him more than it did Tunney.

Once in the fourth round the Dempsey left hook glanced off Tunney's jaw and sent the challenger against the ropes. Even though his head rolled with the blow, Gene was almost dropped by that punch.

Dempsey rushed again, but Tunney stepped nimbly out of danger. It was now apparent that Dempsey's chief weakness lay in his legs. The speed had left his underpinnings. Though the old vicious hitting power still lurked in the gloves of the Manassa Mauler, his ability to follow up a successful assault was lacking.

After the fourth round Tunney had the fight well in hand and knew it. Methodically, as coolly as if he were boxing a rough novice instead of a world's champion, Gene jabbed and ripped Dempsey to pieces. Jack was exhausted, dazed, and staggering at the final bell. He barely escaped a clean knockout.

Dempsey's dethronement was almost as sensational as Sullivan's downfall at the hands of Corbett. The masses had been carefully tutored by the propagandists into believing the Manassa Mauler unconquerable. And most of the Dempsey adherents, despite the clean-cut nature of Tunney's victory, were still of the opinion that the ex-champion was the better man. The temper of those who had bet heavily on Jack was such that they were willing to sponsor any kind of scandal rather than admit Tunney's superiority to the erstwhile ring terror.

Thus the new champion, even in the first flush of success, encountered in many quarters the same dislike that had plagued Jim Corbett after he disposed of the Strong Boy of Boston. He who overthrows an idol does not gain the thanks of its worshipers, and the toppling of Dempsey from his pedestal was speedily followed by a demand that the object of worship be returned to its former proud position.

That was fine for the promoters. The echoes of squabbling over the rights and wrongs of that Philadelphia battle had scarcely died away before the possibilities of a return match were being discussed wherever the fight fans came together. Tunney had done his work neatly, as a master workman should, but it was plainly evident that the wrecked idol would be repaired and set up for him to try to demolish anew some time in the near future.

The story of the second meeting between Dempsey and Tunney will be told in the next chapter, but before going into the career of the new champion, a few more words on the character and contributions of the old champion—the second figure in the annals of American boxing who deserved the title of the Great—are in order.

To this day Jack Dempsey's appeal is universal. "The most popular man in boxing"—that's what Jack Dempsey has been acclaimed. The boys worship him; street gatherings stampede him when he arrives in a city on a special mission; feminine hearts flutter in his presence; a joyous acclaim greets him at every meeting he attends. The man who listened to the hisses and boos after World War I is today—nearly twenty-five years after he lost the title—still the greatest living figure of the squared circle. In popular esteem, he continues to be the champion among champions.

CHAPTER 17

THE FIGHTING MARINE

GENE TUNNEY, the new champion, was the complete antithesis of the man from whom he won the title. Tunney was essentially a ring scientist, Dempsey a ferocious slugger. Tunney was reserved in manner, self-contained, and self-sufficient; Dempsey was tempestuous, gregarious, and a complete extrovert.

Jack was obviously of the sporting genus. His swarthy, rugged features suggested the dangerous fighter. Far from handsome, he yet possessed in full what has been described as "a personality which fairly exuded mob appeal"—a quality his conqueror certainly never had.

Above all, it was Dempsey's prowess as a knockout hitter which established him firmly in the hearts of fandom. A clever boxer is merely tolerated by the same crowd that goes frantic with enthusiasm over a demon puncher. Though Tunney could hit with deadly efficiency on occasion, as his record of forty-seven knockouts proves, his wearing-down mode of attack was far less satisfactory from a box-office standpoint than the spectacular methods employed by the Manassa Mauler.

Had Tunney been a "good mixer" like Dempsey, he might have eased himself into the fickle affection of the masses. But Gene's tastes and desires did not incline toward the sporting element. What is known as "night life" in the big cities held no lure for him. A boxing enthusiast at the beginning of his career, he had not long been a professional before he became thoroughly acquainted with the sordid side of the prize ring and developed a lasting scorn for the gamblers and parasites who infested the game.

Call it fastidiousness or what you will, there was something in Tunney's nature that revolted against the jovial shoulder slap of the blatant politician, the familiarities of the millionaire bootlegger, and the coarse congratulations of underworld leaders and their henchmen. If popularity depended upon such favors and such men, Gene wanted none of it.

The new champion knew the seamy side of life. He learned the inside of things thoroughly during hard years spent struggling upward to the goal of his profession. He could not avoid contact with sinister persons whom he despised, but neither could he bring himself to their level of boisterous comradeship. He was, in a sense, with the gang. He was certainly never of it.

When success began to come his way, he grew more and more self-centered and withdrew more and more from the companionship of the ring "regulars." Once he became champion, he restricted his personal relationships to the people he really liked and trusted. What people in general said about him was a matter of perfect indifference.

Finding himself in a position to order his life as he saw fit, Gene Tunney did so. He was utterly oblivious to adverse criticism by aggrieved promoters, plundering managers, peeved journalists who found him an inferior source of copy in comparison with the energetic, sociable Mr. Dempsey, and the scathing "high-hat" accusations hurled at him by morons to whom he remained an exasperating mystery.

Little minds are always suspicious of the unfamiliar. The bulk of fight followers never understood—or wished to understand—Gene Tunney. Still other persons disliked him for professional reasons. Certain sports writers, annoyed by his failure to minister to their vanity or bow to their edicts in the traditional fashion of the average boxer on the lookout for advertising, took particular pains to ridicule and abuse Gene. Some of these scribblers berated the champion for his lack of appreciation of what the press had done for him.

Tunney owed little to the newspapers. He was not a publicity-made champion but one who had fought every inch of the way for his honors. When he became news value, the papers gave him plenty of space simply because he was too important to ignore. Of praise he received none beyond the minimum due his worth. While his match with Dempsey was in the making, nine out of ten critics confidently predicted his rapid extermination.

Tunney's preference for quiet society and good literature proved a fruitful source of ridicule for his detractors. At first his attitude was looked upon as a publicity pose, or so the Tunney-baiters termed it. When it became evident that such a rare bird as a fighter who admired and even enjoyed good books and who preferred educated companions to roughnecks really existed, a howl of indignation went up from those who had found Tunney anything but a soft touch for their predatory schemes. These birds of prey made it their business to circulate the report that the champion was a fellow of insufferable conceit. He pretended to be educated!

As everybody knows, the indispensable prerequisite of an American hero is the quality of being "average." In his own specialty—running for touchdowns, hitting home runs, being President of the United States, or punching an opponent on the jaw—he may be supreme. But in all other respects, he must be just like everybody else. Look what had happened to poor Frank Moran, the Pittsburgh heavyweight who fought and lost to Johnson and Willard:

There had been a press discussion as to the relative athletic merits of pugilists and football players, during which several writers expressed surprise that no powerful young chap from the gridiron had ever won high honors in the ring. This gave Moran's publicity agent a notion that he proceeded to exploit. Shortly afterward, articles appeared in the daily papers stating that Moran had played football on a Pennsylvania college team and attributing much of his ring success to the training he received while chasing the elusive pigskin. Frank was depicted as a student of uncommon ability, an ardent lover of the classics, who might have occupied a high place in the world of literature and society had not his ambition to become world's heavyweight champion led him to forsake all else for the strenuous life of the ring. Some day, it was predicted, when he had won the title, Moran would return to his cloisters and assume his proper place among the great minds of the age.

The reaction to these revelations was not exactly what Frank or his ingenious press pilot had expected. Had Moran been accused of burglary, bootlegging, arson, murder, and rape combined, he would have found plenty of sympathizers and admirers among those who cheered him when he swung his trusty right in the padded arena. In fact, the rank and file of ring followers would probably have viewed any offense against the law as a laudable testimonial to the perpetrator's good nerve. But to be, or even to have been, highbrow was unpardonable. Moran's popularity immediately sank to zero and his closest pals eyed him with loathing, even though he assured them that "the whole thing was a josh!"

"It might be," they said frigidly. "But how can you prove it? There it is in print. A guy can't be too careful of his rep. It looks damned bad."

Fortunately for Moran's damaged prestige, scarcely three weeks elapsed before a letter from the president of the college mentioned in connection with Frank's biography was published in every New York paper. This epistle set forth in caustic, dignified fashion the fact that Mr. Frank Moran had at no time been a student. Ample space, with appropriate comment, was given this communication by the sports columnists, and Frank Moran loudly gave thanks that a hideous stumbling block had been removed from his professional path. He had been saved from a fate worse than death. The stigma of education no longer stained his reputation. A forgiving Providence had restored him to good standing in the ranks of his fellow pugs.

Gene Tunney was not a university alumnus. Brought up in New York City, he attended St. Veronica's School and De La Salle Academy, both Roman Catholic institutions. When he was seventeen he acted as a gymnasium instructor in Greenwich Village. He also taught boxing, and his skill attracted the attention of Billy Jacob, then matchmaker of the old Sharkey Athletic Club, who pitted the tall, slender 152-pound lad against one Bobby Dawson.

Bobby was a rough battler of considerable experience, and it was a real test for Gene to go ten rounds with such an opponent. Nevertheless he won the first real bout of his career. Even at that early age Gene could use a straight, cutting jab to good advantage, and he stopped Dawson cold in the seventh round.

The official record books do not mention the bout with Dawson, which took place in 1915, nor, for that matter, are several other early victories chronicled. According to accepted records, Tunney's professional career is shown as commencing in 1919. This apparent oversight was due to Gene's own wishes. He was very proud of having been a United States Marine and preferred that the public should think of him as a direct product of that fighting service. But the fact remains that he was far from being a novice when he enlisted, and he won several boxing contests in Paris later on, among them a victory over Bob Martin, of whom much was expected by the fistic experts.

Although Gene had twenty-nine victories and not a single setback on his record when he defeated Battling Levinsky for the American light heavyweight championship in 1922, it was not until then that his star began to shine brightly on the pugilistic horizon. As previously mentioned, Tunney was a poor hand at winning publicity, and his reserved demeanor handicapped him considerably in forging to the front. His conquest of Levinsky, cleanly and decisively administered, brought him for the time being into the spotlight. But he returned to the shadows after his next encounter, in which he dropped his newly gained title to Harry Greb in a fifteen-round decision.

Tunney was badly beaten by Greb. Harry, a wily ring general and one of the fastest boxers who ever held the middleweight title, had a habit of stepping out of his own class and defeating much bigger men. He knew too much for Tunney, and his singularly perplexing two-handed whirlwind style of attack was hard to solve. It has frequently been said, and it is probably true, that Tunney took more punishment in that first battle with Greb than he ever sustained before or after.

Such a defeat might have taken the heart out of a less resolute person than the ex-Marine, but Tunney was not easily discouraged. In losing to Greb he gained considerable knowledge of his curious fighting methods and at once set his active intel-

ligence to work on the problem of discovering a way to coun-
teract them. That he had profited by his lesson became evident
a few months later, on February 23, 1923, when he again faced
Greb in New York and regained his title by winning decisively
in fifteen rounds.

Tunney had redeemed himself, and never again was he to
appear in a losing role. Greb, surprised and chagrined, demanded another trial and was accommodated. Tunney defeated
him a second time before Greb reluctantly admitted that he
had met his master. After their third encounter Greb paid
honest tribute to Gene, stating that he was by far the best man
he had ever fought and prophesying that Tunney would be
the next heavyweight champion.

In 1924 Tunney breezed triumphantly through the ranks of
his rivals in the light heavyweight division, one of his many
victims being Georges Carpentier. Next year, he entered the
heavyweight class and scored knockouts over Tommy Gibbons
and Bartley Madden. He also defeated Johnny Risko in twelve
rounds. Then, in 1926, he defeated Dempsey for the world title.

From a slender though sinewy athlete, he had developed
into a splendidly muscled specimen, with massive shoulders,
deep chest, and stalwart frame. His weight and punching power
increased without sacrificing the agility and speedy footwork
for which he was celebrated. Not the least surprising thing
about the Philadelphia meeting with Dempsey was the unsus-
pected strength of the victor, which enabled him to tie up and
control in the clinches a pugilist who had hitherto been deemed
invincible in a test of roughing it at close quarters.

A second encounter between Dempsey and Tunney was inevitable. Although after the first bout Dempsey, soured by
defeat, intimated that he was through with the ring, few believed him. There was a general demand that the ex-champion
be given another chance at the title. Tex Rickard, keenly alive
to the fact that no other fighter he could select as an opponent
for Gene would prove such a tremendous drawing card as the
loser in the Quaker City fracas, brought his powerful influence
to bear upon Dempsey. He pointed out to Jack that there was

another million-dollar gate in view, besides the chance of the championship again changing hands.

That chance looked excellent to many prominent sport devotees, among the number being the venerable William Muldoon, ex-champion wrestler, the same man who nearly forty years before had trained Sullivan for his victory over Kilrain. Muldoon, then a New York boxing commissioner, asserted that all Dempsey needed to retrieve his crown was a thorough course of judicious training. He was upheld in this opinion by a multitude of Dempsey adherents who could not abandon the notion that Jack's defeat had been due to a combination of overconfidence, carelessness in preparing for the encounter, and the annoyance caused by Kearns's suit.

For a while Dempsey refused to declare himself. He could not deny the temptation of the huge profits involved in another Tunney match. But not until he had spent several months roughing it in the mountains and satisfying himself that his stamina was still intact did he announce his return to the ring.

Despite the blind faith of Dempsey's mass of supporters in their favorite, he had been so badly beaten at Philadelphia that a demand arose for the ex-champion to show himself worthy of a second meeting with Tunney. To give the former titleholder his due, he made no attempt to dodge this issue and agreed to box any man who might be selected as his opponent.

The fighter chosen to give Dempsey a tryout was Joseph Paul Cukoschay, otherwise known as Jack Sharkey, who loomed as the outstanding figure among the big fellows plodding toward the championship goal. Sharkey had a good record, his most noteworthy performance being a victory over Harry Wills, the Negro gladiator who for years had vainly challenged Dempsey. It was his removal of what had come to be known as the Black Menace from the roster of title contenders that boosted Sharkey's stock and gained him the match with the ex-champion.

The bout took place at the Yankee Stadium, New York, on July 21, 1927, Dempsey winning by a knockout in the seventh round. In the contest's early stages, Sharkey elected to fight at long range; a fast boxer, he outpointed Dempsey, whose speed did not equal that of his antagonist. But Sharkey, abandoning his cautious attitude, unwisely went in to mix matters—a style of milling that exactly suited the iron-fisted Dempsey. He pounded Sharkey's body savagely, and in the seventh round he landed a stomach punch at close quarters that seemed to many of the spectators to be a trifle low. Sharkey imprudently turned his head to protest to the referee, and in the same instant Dempsey smashed a hook to the jaw that sent him down and out.

Great was the tumult following Referee Jack O'Sullivan's action in awarding Dempsey the verdict. Opinion about the questionable punch was about evenly divided among the spectators, and a similar division existed among the sports writers. There was no doubt at all that Dempsey had fought a rough fight and that some of his body punches landed close to the line between fair and foul. Most important, from the point of view of Dempsey's faithful followers (to say nothing of the promoters) was that he could still hit with stunning force.

Tex Rickard went ahead with his plans for holding the second Tunney-Dempsey fray, which was scheduled for Soldier's Field, Chicago, on September 22, 1927, and limited to ten rounds. Since Dempsey was on fighting edge from the long training spell he had undergone while preparing for Sharkey, it was not hard for him to keep himself in good condition for the Windy City battle. Also, he had what most of the experts considered a decided advantage over his rival in that he had experienced the strain of actual combat once since the Philadelphia affair, whereas Tunney had not fought since defeating Dempsey a year before.

Tunney, however, was undisturbed by any dismal reflections and went through his training period calmly.

A crowd of 104,943 paid the record sum of 2,658,660 dollars to see the return battle. As was expected, Dempsey forced matters from the outset. Tunney countered continually with straight lefts. Occasionally he stood up to his rushing foe, blocking carefully and ever on the watch for Dempsey's most potent weapon, the left hook to the jaw with which Jack had vanquished so many of his opponents in his stormy past.

It was plain, however, that Tunney "had the legs on Dempsey." The champion's speed of foot carried him safely out of range of Dempsey's most furious assaults, while his busy left jab, interspersed with occasional short rights to the head, piled up points in Gene's favor.

In the third and fourth rounds Dempsey began to show signs of the punishment to which he was being subjected. Some of the viciousness had gone out of his attacks, although he was ever pressing forward. The fifth and sixth were a continuation.

It was the seventh that furnished the thrill that brought the spectators to their feet yelling hysterically. During a sudden rally near the ropes, Dempsey rushed desperately and lashed a long left hook to the jaw. It reached its mark with deadly effect. Tunney's feet shot from under him, and he fell heavily, remaining in a sitting posture, with one hand grasping at the nearest rope.

Immediately Timekeeper Beeler started his count. *But Referee Dave Barry did not count!*

According to the rules of the Illinois State Athletic Commission, a fallen boxer is not considered down until his opponent goes to the corner farthest from the man he has downed. This rule had been thoroughly explained to both Tunney and Dempsey and was thoroughly understood by each. Dempsey did not obey it.

Instead, after scoring the knockdown, the ex-champion walked around the referee toward his own corner, just a few feet from where Tunney reposed. There he stood watching Gene. Referee Barry, carrying out his instructions to see that the upstanding boxer should go to the corner farthest from the fallen man, waved Dempsey away before beginning his count. But Dempsey wouldn't budge, and Barry held off the count until Dempsey went to the proper corner. Seconds passed before Barry's arm began to rise and fall in tolling off the count.

At "four" Tunney made a motion as if to rise—then, either of his own volition or in obedience to a signal from his seconds, he sank back and listened, his lips moving in unison with Barry's waving arm. At "nine" he sprang to his feet. Dempsey leaped at him savagely. But Tunney's noted agility stood in good stead. He back-pedaled, making use of every inch of the arena.

In vain did Dempsey plunge toward the lithe, swiftly moving

figure. Once the ex-champion stopped dead in his tracks and, with a sneer, motioned to Tunney to fight. But Gene, cool, methodical, his head quickly clearing from the stunning effects of the knockdown, smiled contemptuously and continued his retreating tactics. He was far too skilled and wary a general to be lured into fighting Dempsey's kind of battle.

The eighth round found Tunney fully recovered and bent on vengeance. Three times he stabbed Dempsey's face with his long left, then feinted him into an opening and crashed a short right hook to the jaw that toppled Jack to the floor. Up in an instant without taking a count, Dempsey rushed again.

By this time the effects of Tunney's viperish jabs were beginning to show on Dempsey's swarthy features. Raw, red gashes gaped above both his eyes, his lips were cut and bleeding freely, his mouth was puffed out of shape. Even to the most inexperienced observer it was clear that Dempsey was a beaten man. He still kept trying doggedly, but the force had left his blows. He was floundering and groggy.

Tunney, ever cautious but confident, now took a hand at forcing the issue. He staggered Dempsey with right-hand smashes over the heart and jabbed him incessantly, making Jack's head bob back as though on springs. Worried and desperate, Dempsey resorted to roughhouse tactics and was repeatedly warned by the referee for striking low.

In the tenth and final round Jack closed with Tunney and wrestled him down, but Gene sprang up swiftly and resumed his pitiless jabbing attack. The last bell found Dempsey weak, almost out on his feet, still blindly aggressive. But the ex-champion had clearly been whipped, and the referee so decided.

A protest by the Dempsey forces to the Illinois State Athletic Commission that Tunney should have been counted out and the verdict awarded to Dempsey on a knockout in the seventh round was denied by the members of that organization. The commission pointed out that Dempsey had not conformed to the rules after flooring Tunney, hence the seconds that elapsed before Referee Barry began his count could not be taken into consideration.

The bout has gone down in fistic history as the Battle of the

Long Count. That it was—but justly so. The referee was merely enforcing the rules, and his conduct of the battle at the critical moment in the seventh round was not only correct but commendable.

However Dempsey and his friends stormed over the decision, there can be no doubt in the light of after events that the ex-champion knew that he had met his master. Although he was offered a third match with his conqueror, a proposition to which Gene was perfectly agreeable, Dempsey refused on the plea that his eyes had suffered as a result of ring injuries and he feared that blindness might ensue if he fought again.

Nearly a year passed before Tunney again defended his title. This time Tom Heeney, known as the Australian Hard Rock, was selected to oppose him. Out of a ruck of rather mediocre heavies in an elimination tournament conducted by Tex Rickard at Madison Square Garden, Heeney and Sharkey had forged to the front. A meeting between the two resulted in a draw, but since Sharkey had already been knocked out by Dempsey, the Australian was awarded the match for the championship.

Tunney and Heeney met on July 26, 1928, at the Polo Grounds in New York City. The fight was halted by Referee Eddie Forbes eight seconds before the conclusion of the eleventh round when Heeney, game to the core, but literally cut to pieces by the champion's unerring punches, was blind and utterly helpless. From first to last Heeney never had a chance. The man who had stood off the best of the heavyweight contenders was little better than a novice in the hands of the most scientific pugilist since the days of James J. Corbett.

Financially the bout was a dismal failure. It was the first championship battle staged by Rickard that resulted in a loss; he dropped 152,000 dollars in the fight. The glamour and color of the vivid Dempsey were missing. Despite the most frantic efforts of press agents, the public remained coldly indifferent as to what would happen to Tom Heeney. There was nothing spectacular about the man from the Antipodes. He was a persevering, dogged, plodding fighter, and the fans guessed correctly in advance concerning his fate.

Speculation about Tunney's next opponent ceased suddenly

when the champion announced his retirement. There were no "ifs" about Gene's statement. It was short, definite, to the point. The champion was through forever with the ring, and his contemporaries could fight among themselves to decide who should occupy the vacant throne. He did not even follow the precedent set by some of his predecessors of naming his successor. Instead, Gene made it plain that it was of no interest to him what became of the title he was tossing away.

Gene Tunney was finished with the fight game. He had attained his objective of making a fortune, and no offer, however generous, could tempt him to re-enter the squared circle.

At first the promoters and rank and file of the fighting brigade scoffed at the notion of a champion in his prime quitting while there was still an easy million or two to be picked up. But when another announcement was forthcoming to the effect that Tunney was engaged to Miss Polly Lauder of Greenwich, Connecticut, an heiress and one of society's elect, the incredulous ones were forced to admit that Dempsey's conqueror seemed determined upon severing all relations with the sport in which he had become the most commanding figure.

As might have been expected, there was much grumbling among the promotorial tribe over what they termed Tunney's ingratitude in refusing to make any more money for them. Even some of the sporting journalists took this view and criticized Gene's action unfavorably. But they were the ones who had never missed an opportunity to blow off steam at a man who went his way without paying the slightest attention to their vituperations, and it is not on record that Tunney was in the least degree affected by their parting shafts. The retired champion merely smiled when a final frenzied appeal was made to him to fight just one more battle, with Jack Sharkey as his opponent. He sailed for England in August, 1928. A month later he was followed by his fiancée. They were married in Rome on October 3.

Tunney was given a commission as officer in the Marine Reserve Corps, an honor which he probably prized above the title of heavyweight champion. In World War II, he became a captain in the Navy and had charge of the physical-training program of the boys in blue.

With the passing of the years one may expect to find a growing appreciation of the retired champion's merits. He will some day be acknowledged, if he has not yet received his due, as one of the truly great holders of the heavyweight title.

CHAPTER 18

A CHAMPION FROM GERMANY

GENE TUNNEY'S retirement left the heavyweight situation as lacking in interest as a melodrama without a hero. There was no champion. Fighters there were plenty, but none possessed either Dempsey's spectacular appeal or the skill and generalship that distinguished Dempsey's conqueror.

Even had Tunney consented to fight once more, with Dempsey avoiding him, no other boxer would have been conceded a chance of defeating Gene. And the financial failure of Gene's farewell performance, with Tom Heeney as victim, proved conclusively that the public would not patronize one-sided exhibitions. It was the combination of Tex Rickard and Dempsey, promoter and star, respectively, that registered the latter as the ring's greatest money-maker. Altogether, Dempsey brought in a gross of more than ten million dollars for Rickard, a figure no other promoter has ever approached.

Rickard died suddenly at Miami, Florida, January 6, 1929, following an appendicitis operation. At the time of the showman's demise, Dempsey had been associated with him in several business deals, including the holding of a ten-round fight at Miami Beach between Jack Sharkey and William "Young" Stribling. After the promoter's death, Dempsey announced his intention of carrying out Rickard's plans for the Miami affair. In this, the ex-champion had the powerful backing of the Madison Square Garden Corporation, whose directors were temporarily aghast over the sudden loss of their chief executive, and the bout took place as originally scheduled.

There was no million-dollar gate, as Rickard had prophesied there would be, but the receipts totted up to 395,369 dollars. That the show was a financial success was principally due to the fact that everything was wide open at Miami Beach, with a race track operating, betting flourishing, and gambling resorts running full blast. Thither flocked the "best people" in search of amusement, as well as a choice aggregation of racketeers of all grades. It was a heterogeneous gathering, with genuine fight fans in the minority.

Perhaps the absence of the faithful was the reason why no hostile demonstrations took place during one of the most uneventful exhibitions ever seen between two boxers of supposedly high class. Had a large number of experienced fight followers been present, the protagonists would probably have been hissed out of the ring. As it was, they boxed languidly through ten tame rounds, with Sharkey, as the lesser offender, being awarded the decision.

The most promising heavyweight developed during the year following Tunney's relinquishment of the title was Max Schmeling, a young German who first attracted attention in American rings because of his close facial resemblance to Jack Dempsey. Schmeling's European record was not particularly formidable.

Max began boxing in 1924 and gradually became known as the possessor of a telling knockout punch—largely in consequence of having put away a number of minor pugilistic lights in short order. He was twice disqualified for fouling, lost one decision to Jack Taylor, and in 1928 he was stopped in a round by Gypsy Daniels, a mediocre British pug.

Nevertheless, shortly after his visit to America in the latter part of 1928, he shot into prominence by knocking out Joe Monte in eight rounds. The following year he administered a similar treatment to Johnny Risko of Cleveland in nine. It was the Cleveland fight that sent Max's fistic stock booming sky high, for Risko, though never a champion, had proved a stumbling block in the paths of many ambitious fighters and only once before, in 1925, at the hands of Chuck Wiggins, had he suffered the ignominy of taking the full count. Even Tunney, although he decisively defeated Risko, merely won on points from the tough Clevelander.

It was evident that the German youth with the dangerous right-hand punch had to be taken seriously as a contender.

When, a few months later, he won a clean-cut victory over Paulino Uzcudun of Spain, who was looked upon as a likely aspirant for Tunney's title, Max was unanimously listed by the boxing experts as a good choice to send against Sharkey in an endeavor to place a new leader at the head of the heavyweight division.

Schmeling, however, was sidetracked for the time being in favor of Phil Scott, England's heavyweight champion. Scott was matched to go against Sharkey at Miami on February 27, 1930, the understanding being that the winner would be paired with Schmeling in a fifteen-round bout at the Yankee Stadium the following June.

Scott, six feet, three inches tall, and weighing 215 pounds, was a clever but unreliable boxer. In 1927 he paid his first visit to America and was knocked out by Knute Hansen in one round. Later he lost a decision to Johnny Risko.

Scott got decisions over Pierre Charles and Roberto Roberti in ten rounds in 1928. In 1929 he beat Ludwig Haymann of Germany in fifteen rounds and won on a foul from Ted Sandwina in London in seven. Returning to America, he was awarded a decision in ten rounds over Vittorio Campolo, the Argentine giant. In a bout with Otto Von Porat in Madison Square Garden, Scott dropped to the canvas in the second round, claiming a foul. Few of the spectators believed the Briton was seriously hurt, but Scott was declared victor.

On the whole, Scott was not very highly regarded in this country, and Jack Sharkey entered the ring in Miami a strong favorite.

Sharkey was outboxed in the opening round. In the second he rushed Scott into his own corner and half punched, half pushed the Englishman to the floor. Scott took a six count and held Sharkey off with his long left when he arose. It was a fairly even round.

In the third, Sharkey dropped Scott with a left hook to the stomach. Scott went down, arose at the count of six, protesting to the referee that he had been fouled. No attention was paid to his complaints, and almost immediately Scott went down under a second stomach punch. Twice more the Briton was floored by body wallops, and on the fourth occasion he yelled "foul" so insistently that the referee, Lou Magnolia, halted the proceedings.

Scott was dragged to his corner and examined by a physician, who declared him capable of continuing. Phil once more raised his voice in protest but was told to go in and fight. The combat was resumed, and Sharkey dived madly at his adversary and sank him in a neutral corner with another body blow. Scott flatly refused to take another chance, and the referee announced that Sharkey was the victor.

While "Phainting Phil's" behavior earned him the contempt of the fans, there was little in Sharkey's victory to arouse enthusiasm. Not only did Sharkey fail to justify the long betting odds in his favor, but he actually came within an ace of losing on a foul. The net result of the battle was that many ring followers conceded Schmeling an excellent chance of beating Sharkey.

The prediction was fulfilled. Max was proclaimed victor by virtue of a foul stomach punch that left him reposing on the floor in the fourth round of their engagement on June 12, 1930. It was a powerfully driven, but wildly wandering punch to the body that stretched out Schmeling. Up to the moment when the foul punch was administered, Sharkey had looked like the winner, although the German was game as a bulldog, continually on the aggressive, always the true fighting man.

What surprised the crowd was Max's splendid endurance, his ability to stand punishment, and the speed with which he recuperated after each round. That Schmeling had been outpointed up to the moment of the foul was generally admitted, but there was always the chance that he would have taken everything Sharkey had to offer for perhaps half the battle and then come on to win.

Under the circumstances, there was nothing to do but proclaim Schmeling the world champion, and as such he was officially recognized by the New York State Athletic Commission, a verdict concurred in by the rest of the country. For the first time, a Teuton athlete reigned as heavyweight monarch. Oddly enough, it was the battle in which the world title passed from America that drew the best gate since Tunney had made his farewell appearance against Heeney; Schmeling and Sharkey played to 79,222 spectators, with receipts grossing 749,935 dollars.

The New York boxing-commission members were strongly in favor of having Max give Sharkey a return match at an early date, and it was afterwards stated that it was with this proviso that they agreed to invest the German with the title. However, when Max returned to this country in 1931 after a protracted stay in his native land, trouble developed between the commission and the man it had crowned.

The officials were anxious to rush Schmeling into a match with Sharkey. Joe Jacobs, manager of the champion, would not be rushed, and the result of the argument that developed was an announcement by the state body that Schmeling was no longer recognized as champion. Instead Jack Sharkey was named as "defending champion," whatever that might mean.

During Schmeling's absence, Young Stribling, the Georgia heavyweight, had moved under the spotlight by scoring swift knockouts over Von Porat and Phil Scott, stopping the former in one round at Chicago and the latter in two before a London club. Stribling's record boasted the longest string of knockouts ever run up by a modern heavyweight, even though most of them had been scored in the hinterland at the expense of mediocre boxers who were never heard of outside their own particular bailiwicks.

Stribling was generally unfortunate in matches in the "big time." Twice, in battles with Mike McTigue and Paul Berlenbach, he failed to capture the light heavyweight title, and later, when campaigning among the big fellows, his record was spotty, to say the least. Yet Stribling, by virtue of the Scott and Von Porat victories, established himself in public esteem as a far more attractive personality than the erratic Sharkey. It was therefore not surprising that Joe Jacobs, unable to come to reasonable terms with the New York boxing commission, accepted the offer of a match with Stribling to take place at Cleveland, Ohio, July 3, 1931, with the world title at stake. The battle took place on schedule, Schmeling winning on a technical knockout in the fifteenth round, when Referee George Blake, seeing that Stribling was helpless and whipped to a frazzle, stopped the

fight and declared Schmeling the victor fifteen seconds before
the end of the round.

In this encounter Schmeling proved himself to be a very
much improved boxer. In the past he had been an open target.
Against Stribling his blocking was perfect, and at the same time
he fought with an aggressive fury that never lessened throughout the entire contest. Willy did not seem to hit Max one solid
punch. Schmeling carried the fight to him all the way, and after
the sixth round it was only a question of how long Stribling
would be able to stand up under the merciless bombardment to
which he was being subjected.

Perhaps the most surprised people in the crowd were the
attending boxing critics. With few exceptions, the metropolitan
scribes had picked the Georgian as a sure winner.

Financially, the show was a failure—as it would probably not
have been in a New York setting. That it was held in Cleveland
was due to the immovable opposition of the New York boxing
commission, which exercised its right of barring Schmeling
from the rings of the Empire State.

Two years and nine days after winning the championship on
a foul, Max engaged Sharkey in a return match in Madison
Square Garden's open-air arena on Long Island, and this time
Sharkey came through with a victory at the end of fifteen rounds.
No sooner was the decision rendered than the German raised the
cry of "robbery" and demanded an investigation by the boxing
commission.

Max protested without avail. The majority of spectators and
sports writers, myself included, thought that Sharkey had lost
to Max and sided with the German in his contention that the
officials erred in awarding the crown to his Boston opponent.
The loser made most of the fight and inflicted most of the punishment. He was up against a cool, clever boxer who was none
too easy to hit, and he made the most of it under the circumstances. It is difficult to say which one looked more bewildered
and amazed when the verdict was rendered—Sharkey, the winner,
or Schmeling, the loser.

Schmeling's next fight of importance was with Mickey Walker,
on September 26, 1932, three months after he had lost his crown

to Sharkey, and Max knocked out the former middleweight king in the eighth round of a thrilling battle. Schmeling was the acme of perfection in that bout, and the 60,000 persons who saw him vanquish his game foe thought that it was his best performance since first landing on these shores.

The final round of that contest will live in the memory of those who witnessed it; in those three minutes of fighting there was more action than New York fans had seen in ten previous heavyweight contests. Floored in the first round, Mickey shaded his opponent in the second, and at the end of the seventh round he was in the lead, four rounds to three. Then the tide turned. Schmeling had solved Walker's style and went out to get his man. He battered Mickey's body and face until he had his antagonist groping blindly after being floored with a powerful right. With blood spurting from Walker's nose and mouth and one eye closed, he was helpless. Schmeling appealed to the referee to stop the slaughter. Doc Kearns, manager of Walker, quickly answered Max's request by calling a halt.

In June, 1933, Schmeling was stopped by Max Baer in the tenth round at the Yankee Stadium, and that setback was followed by a loss in twelve rounds to Steve Hamas in Philadelphia. With those defeats chalked up against him, Max went back to Germany and remained overseas for about a year and a half. He drew with Paulino Uzcudun in twelve rounds at Barcelona, stopped Walter Neusel in eight rounds, Steve Hamas in nine, and defeated Paulino in a return bout in Berlin in twelve rounds. Then he was ready to return to the United States for another campaign.

Joe Louis was at the time coming along in great style. He was the talk of the fistic world. After many victories, he was being primed by Mike Jacobs for a title shot, and it was figured that the best way to convince the public that Joe was ripe for such a bout would be a match with Max. The contest was arranged for June 19, 1936, and in that affair, held in the Yankee Stadium, the German rose to the heights again by knocking out the Negro in the twelfth round. His victory brought the foreigner right back into the heavyweight picture.

So thoroughly and masterly a job did Schmeling perform that

the 42,000 spectators sat in their seats dumfounded at what they were witnessing. Instead of the American being the executioner, as had been almost universally predicted, it was the German who swung the ax.

A more determined, courageous, battling Schmeling had never faced an opponent than the Schmeling of this fight. Experience mastered youth. Schmeling knew just what to do when he had Joe going, and he grasped every opportunity and made the most of it.

Schmeling now was hot on the trail of Jimmy Braddock who in 1935 had won the world title from Max Baer. The German figured that his knockout triumph over Louis had earned him the title shot, but Braddock's manager thought otherwise—and so did those who were handling the affairs of Louis.

Even though the contracts had been signed for a Schmeling-Braddock title contest, it seemed doubtful from the very beginning that it would ever take place. The fear that Schmeling might win and take the championship back to Germany, where it probably would rest, had much to do with the decision of Braddock not to go through with the bout. Furthermore, Braddock decided that if he had to lose the title he, like the great John L. Sullivan, preferred to lose it to an American.

Most important, there was the dispute between Madison Square Garden, holder of the contracts, and Mike Jacobs, who handled the affairs of Louis. Jacobs readily induced Braddock to take on Louis instead of Schmeling. Thus, the fight was scheduled for Comiskey Park, Chicago, instead of New York City.

On June 22, 1937, as was expected, Louis won the crown from Braddock, and Schmeling was left holding the bag. But Max was a persistent challenger. He had beaten Louis once and was certain he could do it again. Joe was willing to make such a match, and exactly a year after he had won from Braddock, he and Schmeling faced each other in a return engagement.

Schmeling took one of the worst beatings a challenger in a heavyweight bout ever experienced, not excepting the thrashing Jess Willard received from Dempsey. Max was knocked out in two minutes and four seconds of the first round. The details of the fight are given in a chapter covering the career of Joe Louis.

That defeat ended the career of Schmeling in this country. He went back to Germany, where he stopped Adolph Heuser in one round. In due course he was drafted into the Nazi army. He was wounded at the battle of Crete, where he suffered a leg injury. After the war, he encountered many difficulties with the armies of occupation. Following his release from military custody, he settled down in Berlin. His money gone, he turned to his old profession. He is now a boxing instructor.

CHAPTER 19

ANOTHER BOSTON STRONG BOY

MANY champions chose the ring in boyhood as the best means of making a living. Jack Sharkey, although he was a big, robust lad, was not one of these. Jack was pushed into the ring.

Sharkey was born Joseph Paul Cukoschay on October 6, 1902, in Binghamton, New York, of Lithuanian parentage. While attending school in the town, young Cukoschay was never known as a picker of fights among his mates. The fights in which he did take part were, however, one-sided affairs. Joseph was strong and uncommonly well developed for his years.

As a youngster during World War I, Sharkey tried without success to join the Navy. Under age, he was shooed away from every recruiting station from Binghamton to Boston.

It was not until 1920, nearly two years after the war had ended, that he was finally admitted to the Navy. His mates at Newport, Rhode Island, where he was stationed at first, saw in his well-developed shoulders and arms just the make-up for a man of the ring. Stripped to the waist, he looked every inch the fighter, and after his first impromptu battle, Sharkey had no choice in the matter.

His first fight took place one day while he was in charge of a work party at the naval station. A boy selling boxes of ice cream was robbed of his entire wares and then cuffed around by several of the men. When Sharkey heard what had happened, he denounced the act in characteristic sailor fashion. One of the men resented his tone, and after an exchange of genealogical compliments, the two stripped for action. At the end of their mill, both were a bloody mess. It was the opinion of the sailor spectators that neither man had given or taken more than the other.

Shortly after that fight, Jack and his mates shipped to sea. Sharkey's vessel, the U.S.S. *South Carolina,* was the scene of his first ring bout. A mustached petty officer was his opponent. They fought three battering rounds to a draw, and each was awarded a box of chocolates, which neither could eat. The ship was on a run to Norway, and before the trip was over Sharkey had been in his second fight. His opponent was a finely built Negro, a mess attendant. Sharkey won this bout easily, and by the end of the cruise he had made something of a reputation for himself.

Biff Crawley, who later promoted bouts at Mobile, Alabama, holds the only decision over Sharkey while he was in the service. Crawley had fought Jack Dempsey in an exhibition bout previously and been stiffened by the Manassa Mauler. Sharkey and Crawley fought six vicious rounds. The judges disagreed and ordered an extra round. In it Sharkey dislocated his shoulder, lost the decision, and was out of the ring for eighteen months as a result.

"Big Skee," as Sharkey was called, in addition to twenty or more bouts as an amateur, engaged in three professional fights during his enlistment. All of them took place in Boston. Johnny Buckley had heard of the Lithuanian's fistic activities and dispatched Jack Conway, sports editor of the *Boston American,* and William Canty, a local alderman, to look the boy over. Taking their word on the gob's ability, Buckley signed him to a contract.

On February 23, 1924, after serving three years and eight months in the Navy, Sharkey was honorably discharged. Then he seriously entered upon his career as a ringster.

Jack Sharkey is one leading fighter who never had a teacher; what he learned of boxing he gained by his own experiences in the ring. When he began to think seriously of a fighting career, the original Tom Sharkey and Jack Dempsey were his idols. But he did not attempt to emulate the style of either. It was from the original Sharkey, an Irishman, that he took his ring name.

When he came to New York in 1926 to fight Eddie Huffman, the Lithuanian was an unknown quantity among the heavyweights. Sharkey recalls that he was generally regarded as "another big bum." But he beat Huffman easily and in subsequent bouts produced enough evidence of his fistic ability to alter that opinion.

In his thirteen years as a professional, Jack amassed a fortune. The engagements in which he participated grossed upward of five million dollars, of which his share was one million five hundred thousand dollars. He fought every good heavyweight of his time, with the exception of Gene Tunney, who would never consent to a meeting with the Boston tar. Sharkey clashed with Jack Dempsey, Harry Wills, Max Schmeling, George Godfrey, Tommy Loughran, Charlie Weinert, Floyd Johnson, Young Stribling, Primo Carnera, Jim Maloney, Mike McTigue, King Levinsky, K. O. Christner, Tom Heeney, and Johnny Risko.

Sharkey was one of the colorful men of the period. Brash and self-confident, he regarded all opponents as his inferiors in fighting qualities and felt that he could whip any heavyweight in the world. Generally popular with the fans, he was erratic and temperamental. He was also a clever boxer and a fairly good hitter.

One of the high spots of his career was his furious battle with Jack Dempsey in 1927, a fight already described in the Manassa Mauler's career. Though he lost because of carelessness, he showed that fear had no place in his make-up. Up to the time he was knocked out, Jack had been well ahead on points. He came close to knocking out the Tiger Man, and Dempsey admitted after the fight that it was one of his toughest and that Sharkey had hit him harder than any other of his opponents.

Sharkey's first major victory was scored over Floyd Johnson, but it was not until after he had defeated Dempsey's Nemesis, Harry Wills, in thirteen rounds, that the Bostonian became famous. Jack Dempsey and Gene Tunney, it will be recalled, refused to have anything to do with the Black Panther. Just prior to beating Wills, Jack had won a ten-rounder from George Godfrey in Boston, and Godfrey, like Wills, was avoided by most of the top white heavyweights.

The triumphs over Godfrey and Wills put Jack in line for the big-money fights that followed. In the first of these, he stopped Mike McTigue in twelve rounds, and in his next, he had his third meeting with Jimmy Maloney, the Boston Fishmonger. On this occasion he disposed of his rival in five rounds at the Yankee Stadium.

Then came the mill with Dempsey. That was his biggest money bout since joining the pro ranks. Sharkey's share of the gate of 1,083,000 dollars was 211,000 dollars.

Thereafter, with the exception of a loss in fifteen rounds to Johnny Risko, he had little trouble in his climb to the top. Tom Heeney, Jack Delaney, Leo Gates, Arthur DeKuh, K. O. Christner, Stribling, Loughran, and Phil Scott went down in that order. These victories lead to the Schmeling bout for the championship, which Sharkey lost on a foul.

Before he could get a return engagement for the crown, Sharkey was first asked to fight Mickey Walker, the middleweight, who then had heavyweight championship aspirations, and the former gob had all he could do to battle on even terms with his smaller adversary. The bout ended in a draw in fifteen rounds.

A victory in fifteen rounds over Primo Carnera, who was being primed for a title shot, qualified Sharkey for his second bout with Schmeling in 1932, in which he gained the heavyweight crown. He didn't hold on to the title for long. A year and a week after winning it, he was halted by Carnera in six rounds.

When he lost his championship to Carnera, the first Italian to carry off this important title, Sharkey stunned a gathering of forty thousand persons at the Garden Bowl in Long Island City. A right-hand blow to the chin turned the trick. The punch dropped Sharkey in his tracks and provided the huge gathering with the thrill they paid to see but which few had expected because Sharkey's conqueror was regarded as an ordinary fighter, a clown who had no business in the same ring with Jack.

Under the impact of the blow, Sharkey was stretched motionless on his face. Not a quiver of the body could be noted as the count was completed and a new world heavyweight king was crowned. The crowd was utterly bewildered, for there had been no indication previous to the delivery of the finishing blow that Carnera would win by a knockout. Until that moment the Italian had shown little except grim determination, and Sharkey had won three of the preceding four sessions by a big margin.

There was a cry from the Sharkey handlers that Carnera had some object concealed in his gloves, but the charge was ignored. Many in the gathering insisted that an "invisible" punch had scored the knockout!

Sharkey tried a comeback but was unsuccessful. In September of that same year he lost two important bouts, one to King Levinsky in ten and the other to Tommy Loughran in fifteen. Then he hung up his gloves for a year. When he returned to combat, the few battles in which he engaged demonstrated that he was too far on the down grade to figure any longer as a heavyweight threat. His kayo at the hands of Louis on August 18, 1936, was the final convincing evidence.

Sharkey took a cruel beating. He took counts of nine and eight in the second round, a count of eight in the third, and an instant later he was floored again, this time for the full count. The ex-sailor was through with the ring.

CHAPTER 20

AN ITALIAN GOLIATH

THE heavyweight ranks have produced a strange
assortment of ringmen during the long history of boxing, but it
is doubtful if there ever has been a stranger specimen than Primo
Carnera.

Carnera definitely was not born to be a fighter. Though a
giant in size and powerful in physique, standing six feet, five
and three-quarter inches, and weighing 260 pounds, he did not
have the temperament, the killer instinct, so necessary in a real
champion. Primo was an easy-going, good-natured sort, and his
simple, unimaginative nature made him gullible prey for schem-
ing exploiters who were not averse to taking every possible
advantage of him.

Even so, Primo did become a fair sort of boxer for one of his
tremendous proportions. For a fellow of his mammoth dimensions, he learned to move around fairly well. He developed a
good left jab, and his towering hulk made him a formidable
foeman at close quarters. His chief liability was inability to take
a hefty punch. His not-too-rugged chin constantly got him into
trouble and eventually caused his downfall.

Carnera was born in Italy, October 25, 1907, in the village of
Sequals, some miles northeast of Venice. As a youngster he
worked as a carpenter's apprentice. Primo had little interest in
school, preferring to spend his spare time wandering about the
countryside. The yearning to travel inspired him to leave home
at fourteen and make his way to France, where he tried his hand
at many occupations but found none of them fascinating enough
to keep him stationary.

During one of his periods of unemployment, Carnera, then
sixteen, chanced to stop in front of a street circus, and this

apparently harmless gesture was to prove a turning point in his unusual career. His great size made him conspicuous, and the circus manager, on the lookout for new attractions, picked him out of the crowd and offered him a job as strong man. The financial returns weren't calculated to make Primo a modern Croesus, but the job at least offered him bed and board and an opportunity to travel. He accepted the offer; for two years Carnera remained with the circus and saw plenty of the French landscape.

It was early in 1928 that Paul Journée, veteran French heavyweight, happened along as Carnera was carrying a light piano on his back for a local furniture mover. The youngster's gigantic frame and tremendous strength inspired Journée to experiment with the idea of developing Primo into a boxer. Paul introduced him to Léon See, prominent Parisian promoter. Journée and See joined forces, Léon as manager and Paul as coach and trainer.

In September of that year Carnera made his first appearance as a boxer. Though clumsy and awkward, he proved too powerful for his opponent, Léon Sebillo, and won by a knockout in the second round.

Primo registered two more knockouts over hand-picked opponents in Paris, stopping Joe Thomas in the third and Luigi Ruggirello in the fourth; next he gave his countrymen a chance to look him over, tackling Islas Epifanio in Milan. Epifanio proved a more capable opponent than had been anticipated, and Carnera was unable to knock him out, though he won clearly enough in ten rounds.

Now Carnera's desire to travel really had a chance to be gratified. Léon See had done a remarkable job of ballyhooing the giant, and promoters all over the Continent, as well as in Britain, were eager to show him. In the next year, Primo fought in Berlin, Leipzig, San Sebastián, Marseille, Dieppe, Paris, and London. Among the better-known heavyweights carefully selected for him were Ernest Rosemann and Franz Diener of Germany, Moise Bouquillon and Marcel Nilles of France, and Jack Stanley of England.

With only fifteen bouts under his competitive belt, Carnera

was matched with Young Stribling in London on November 18, 1929. It was a severe test for the overgrown youngster from Italy. His shortcomings were evident in that match. Primo's crude, lumbering tactics could not compete with the speed, cleverness, and ring generalship of the lighter but more seasoned Stribling. Yet he fought doggedly, and his bull-like strength made things uncomfortable for Stribling at close quarters.

The American was concentrating on body punching, but during a furious exchange in the fourth round one of his left hooks crashed into Carnera's groin. The giant collapsed in agony, and the referee promptly disqualified Stribling.

The unsatisfactory ending of the bout led to a rematch in Paris three weeks later. This meeting also was destined to wind up in a disqualification, but this time Carnera was the offender. As in their first clash, Stribling was well out in front on points when the bell clanged the end of the seventh round. The American dropped his arms and turned toward his corner just as Carnera started a ponderous right. The blow caught the unsuspecting Stribling on the back of the head, and down he went. The referee immediately declared him the winner on a foul.

A third match between the two was suggested, but before it could be arranged, Stribling returned to the United States.

Meanwhile, Walter Friedman, veteran New York boxing manager, then visiting Europe, interested See in an American tour. Friedman convinced See that regardless of how good or bad a fighter Primo actually was, the giant would be a tremendous novelty and box-office attraction in the United States. Friedman was representing Bill Duffy, a New York night-club owner and racketeer who dabbled in fighters as a side line. The deal was closed, and manager and fighter arrived in New York on December 31, 1929.

Probably no heavyweight in history has ever been subjected to such a gaudy ballyhoo campaign as was Carnera. The job accomplished by Duffy, Friedman, and their colleagues would have done justice to Phineas T. Barnum at his peak.

Primo was given ample opportunity further to satisfy his craving for travel. In nine months he made no less than twenty-four appearances in American rings, his tour, conducted with all the giddy fanfare of a four-ring circus, carrying him all over the United States.

He opened his jaunt in Madison Square Garden. Subsequently he appeared in Chicago twice, Newark twice, Oklahoma City, New Orleans, St. Louis twice, Jacksonville, Kansas City, Memphis twice, Denver, Philadelphia twice, Los Angeles, Oakland, Portland, Detroit, Omaha, Cleveland, Atlantic City, and Boston.

A most interesting assortment of opponents had been rounded up for the unusual tour. Duffy and his associates weren't taking any unnecessary chances of having anything happen to their well-exploited giant, but they did experience a couple of close calls, particularly with the veteran George Godfrey in Philadelphia, and Leon "Bombo" Chevalier in Oakland. In several other cities their performances didn't meet with the unqualified approval of the fans and critics. For the most part, worn-out campaigners like Chuck Wiggins, Pat McCarthy, Big Boy Peterson, Cowboy Bill Owens, Farmer Lodge, Sully Montgomery, Neil Clisby, K. O. Christner, and George Cook were resurrected from the fistic graveyard for the occasion. In most of the "contests," the setup was of the kind that made it almost impossible for Carnera not to win.

Everything closely followed schedule until Carnera's twenty-fourth start, which pitted him against Jim Maloney in Boston. Until then, Primo had been undefeated in his American junket, registering twenty-two knockouts and winning the other, the Godfrey affair, on a foul.

Not too much difficulty had been expected with Maloney, whose chin was notoriously fragile. But the Boston Irishman uncovered a surprisingly good exhibition and outboxed the Italian giant to take a ten-round decision. He had too much pride to permit himself to be included in the list of Primo's "victims."

Shortly after this defeat, Carnera returned to Europe to whip Paulino Uzcudun in Barcelona and knock out Reggie Meen in London. He came back to New York early in 1931. In his first start, he was matched with Maloney again, this time in Miami, and he squared accounts with Jim by punching out a verdict in ten rounds.

Then followed another barnstorming jaunt for Primo, with setups the order of the day, and these bouts netted him a string of knockouts over Pat Redmond in Brooklyn, Umberto Torriani in Buffalo, Bud Gorman in Toronto, Knute Hansen in Rochester, Roberto Roberti in Newark, and Armando De Carlos in Wilmington, Delaware.

All this time Primo was showing steady improvement in his boxing, and his managerial board of directors felt that the Italian mastodon had reached the stage where he could make a serious bid for titular consideration.

Accordingly, he was matched with Jack Sharkey at Ebbets Field, Brooklyn, for fifteen rounds, on October 12, 1931. Though beaten by the faster, cleverer, more experienced Sharkey, Carnera convinced his handlers that he could now well stand on his own two ample feet. They were willing to have him take his chances with the better heavyweights in the future.

After whipping the dangerous King Levinsky in Chicago and knocking out the Argentine giant, Vittorio Campolo, in Madison Square Garden, Carnera went back to Europe early in 1932. He knocked out Moise Bouquillon and Maurice Grizelle in Paris, George Cook in London, and Hans Schoenrath in Milan, and punched out decisions over Ernest Guehring in Berlin, Pierre Charles in Paris, and Don McCorkingdale in London. But he ran into a surprise defeat by the veteran Canadian, Larry Gains, in London.

Returning to New York in July, Carnera embarked upon another busy barnstorming junket for the next year. Barring one unexpected loss to clever Stanley Poreda in Newark, the Italian swept everything before him. His triumphs included knockouts over Jack Gross and José Santa in New York, Jerry Pavelec in West New York, New Jersey, Jack Gagnon in Tiverton, Rhode Island, Ted Sandwina in Tampa, Jack Taylor in Louisville, Les Kennedy in Boston, John Schwake in St. Louis, Big Boy Peterson in Grand Rapids, K. O. Christner in Omaha, Jim Merriott in Tulsa, and Jack Spence in Dallas. Primo also won decisions over Hans Birkie in New York, Art Lasky in St. Paul, King Levinsky (for the second time) in Chicago, and Jack League in San Antonio.

It was on February 10, 1933, that Carnera engaged in his tragic match with Ernie Schaaf in Madison Square Garden. Schaaf, former Navy champion, ranked as one of the world's top heavyweights. (Eight months before, Jack Sharkey had won the heavyweight title from Max Schmeling, and the Garden officials were looking around for a suitable opponent for him. Carnera, despite his previous defeat by Sharkey at Ebbets Field, looked like an acceptable opponent in a title match.)

"Sure, I'll fight Primo—if he can beat Ernie," the champion declared. Sharkey at the time was part owner of Schaaf's contract.

So Carnera and Schaaf were matched.

Schaaf was strong and rugged, an exceptionally good boxer and a vicious puncher with either hand. But something was radically wrong with Ernie that night. He fought a dull, uninspired fight, walking doggedly into Carnera instead of boxing him. As round after round went by, the fans and writers, accustomed to strange doings behind Carnera's activities, began to view the proceedings with suspicion. It looked as if Schaaf were deliberately trying to lose, to insure Carnera the title match with Sharkey.

When Ernie suddenly collapsed from an apparently light punch in the thirteenth round and Referee Bill Cavanaugh counted him out, the cry of "fake" immediately resounded through the vast expanses of the Garden.

It was not until three days later, when Schaaf died in a hospital, that the true facts were revealed. Ernie had never fully recovered from head injuries suffered in a bout with Max Baer in Chicago a year before, though no one had realized just how seriously he had been affected.

Following the customary investigation, Carnera was exonerated. But it looked for a while as though he would be denied his chance at the title. Bill Muldoon, venerable chairman of the New York State Athletic Commission, announced not only that Primo would be barred from fighting Sharkey but that he was "too big" for the average heavyweight and in the future would be permitted to meet only "superdreadnoughts," opponents nearer his own tremendous physical proportions.

Muldoon subsequently repealed his edict, and Carnera was

given his opportunity to battle Sharkey for the championship. The bout was set for June 29, 1933. This match, won by Carnera by a knockout in the sixth, has already been described in the chapter on Jack Sharkey.

Carnera made two successful defenses of the title in the next nine months. On October 22, he outpointed the veteran Paulino Uzcudun in fifteen rounds in Rome. Then he returned to the United States to whip the aging Tommy Loughran in another fifteen-rounder in Miami the following March 1.

By this time Max Baer was looming menacingly on the heavyweight horizon. The colorful Californian had climaxed a sensational campaign by knocking out the former champion, Max Schmeling, in ten rounds at the Yankee Stadium. Big and powerful—he measured six feet, two and a half inches, and scaled 210 pounds—Max shaped up as a dangerous contender for the title and the most formidable opponent in view for Carnera.

Madison Square Garden officials encountered no difficulty in getting Baer and Carnera together. The match was set for June 14, 1934, at the Long Island Bowl.

The battle was one of the weirdest in heavyweight championship annals. Ten times the giant Carnera was floored before he was halted in the eleventh round. Thrice in the second stanza, both champion and challenger became entangled and wrestled to the canvas. But in between his frequent trips to the floor Primo fought back desperately, and there were times when it looked as though he might outlast Baer.

With a pull of 53¼ pounds in weight and further advantages in height and reach, Carnera was the general favorite. Primo was considered too big and too powerful for Baer, and as the first round got under way, it looked as if the Californian felt pretty much the same way. Seemingly worried and perhaps frightened, Max backed constantly as Carnera stalked him about the ring for the first minute or so.

Suddenly Baer's right fist lashed out. It caught the Italian flush on the chin, and he toppled, a grotesque heap, almost in his own corner. Hurt though he was, Primo refused to take advantage of a count. He rolled over and rose unsteadily, only to run into the blazing fury of the challenger's attack. Twice more the giant went down, but the overanxious Baer was unable to keep him there, and Primo reeled drunkenly to his corner at the bell.

Carnera was still groggy when he came out for the second. Staggered by another right, he grabbed Baer in desperation; the two fell to the canvas, rolling over each other like wrestlers. A moment later both were down again, Carnera clutching Baer as he was rocked by another thunderous right to the chin. The Californian continued his vicious assault. A right to the jaw rocked Carnera, and the Italian, falling forward, grabbed at his opponent, and for the third time the two rivals wound up in a tangle on the mat.

Carnera seemed to have shaken off most of the ill effects of those two riotous rounds as he came out for the third. He began to peck away with an annoying left to Max's chin. The Italian appeared to be getting stronger as the round progressed, but shortly before the bell he ran into another right to the chin and went sprawling again.

Carnera actually outboxed and outfought Baer in the fourth. Baer had the better of the fifth when he shook Primo several times. But the Italian came back to win the sixth, seventh, eighth, and ninth.

The giant was boxing well in the tenth, scoring repeatedly with left jabs and hooks and occasionally ripping in a right uppercut. Then over looped Baer's deadly right. Carnera floundered all over the ring. Referee Arthur Donovan stepped in for a moment to see whether or not Primo was in condition to continue.

Apparently convinced that he was, Donovan waved Baer on. The Californian needed no encouragement. Tearing into his reeling opponent, Max battered him with a furious barrage of rights and lefts. Carnera sank to the canvas. But once again he refused to stay down. At the count of four he pulled himself unsteadily to his feet just as the bell clanged.

Carnera was very wobbly when the eleventh started, and Baer sailed in to finish him. A right to the chin dropped the giant for a two count. Up again and groggy, he electrified the crowd by nailing the Californian with two rights. Then another right sent Carnera to the canvas for two. As he gamely pulled himself to his feet, he was so clearly beaten that Donovan decided the slaughter had gone far enough. The time of the round was two minutes, sixteen seconds.

Despite this defeat, Carnera continued to remain a factor in heavyweight activities for another year. Five months after losing his title, the Italian embarked upon a tour of South America. He whipped Vittorio Campolo in Buenos Aires and knocked out Seal Harris in São Paulo and Ervin Klausner in Rio de Janeiro.

Primo returned to the United States early in 1935 and was matched with another giant, Ray Impellitiere, in Madison Square Garden. The battle of the mastodons resulted in a nine-round knockout victory for Carnera.

The newly organized Twentieth Century Sporting Club, with Mike Jacobs as promoter, was operating in competition with Madison Square Garden. The promising Joe Louis was signed to box under the club's exclusive direction. His first appearance in a New York ring was set for June 25, 1935. Carnera was selected to box him at the Yankee Stadium.

Louis, living up to all the enthusiastic reports that had preceded him from Detroit, practically sounded the death knell for Carnera as a heavyweight headliner. Despite Primo's tremendous advantages in height, weight, and reach, Joe outclassed him completely, knocking him out in the sixth round.

The big Italian wasn't entirely convinced that it was time for him to call it a career. He continued to box, but after scoring a few minor successes at the expense of Walter Neusel and Isidore Gastanaga in New York, Ford Smith in Philadelphia, and Big Boy Brackey in Buffalo, he was knocked out by Leroy Haynes in three rounds in Philadelphia. Rematched with Haynes at Ebbets Field, Brooklyn, Carnera was topped again, this time in the ninth round.

Primo faded from the boxing picture after that. Returning to Europe late in 1936, he remained out of the ring for more than a year. When he did don the gloves again, it was to lose a decision to a Tony Duneglio in Paris, and this setback was followed by an even more crushing one, a two-round knockout by Josef Zupan in Budapest.

After remaining more or less in obscurity in Italy during World War II, Carnera returned to the United States in 1946 with a new trade. Primo is prospering now as a wrestler.

CHAPTER 21

THE MAGNIFICENT SCREWBALL

ONE of the most remarkable personalities in prizering history was Maximilian Adelbert Baer. Nature endowed him with a magnificent body and all the physical requisites of a great champion. But he lacked the mental poise to balance his ruggedness, strength, stamina, and terrific punching power.

A carefree, irresponsible sort, Baer gloried in being known as the Merry Madcap and the Magnificent Screwball. His career was one of continuous excitement—of sensational victories and disappointing defeats, of managerial tangles, annoying lawsuits, and frenzied excursions into the realm of romance. At one stage, early in his fistic youth, he sold or gave away a total of 110 per cent of himself to a varied assortment of managers. Out of all the confusion and court proceedings finally emerged Ancil "Pop" Hoffman, to pilot him to the heavyweight championship.

Baer was born in Omaha, Nebraska, February 11, 1909. He was only four when his family moved to Colorado, settling first in Denver, then in Durango. When Max was eight, the clan shifted again, this time to California. Stopping for a while in Oakland, Max's father finally established residence in Livermore, where he set up a butchering business.

At thirteen, Max was working in his father's shop. At sixteen he was an expert butcher and cattle killer, swinging an ax with plenty of power and vigor, and showing qualities of endurance that amazed his brawny dad. In later years, Max attributed the tremendous force of his punch to the powerful muscles he had developed wielding a meat ax.

Prospering as a butcher, the elder Baer purchased the Twin Oaks Ranch near Livermore and raised cattle for the market. Max went to high school for a year but quit to give all his time to helping his father on the ranch. At eighteen, Max was a husky youth, standing six feet in height and weighing 190 pounds.

It was at a dance in Livermore that Baer was first bitten by the pugilistic bug. He and four companions had purloined a demijohn of wine that belonged to a locomotive engineer, and when the owner discovered his loss, he was in no mood for explanations of boyish pranks. He rushed at the miscreants, swinging right and left. Max's pals scampered for safety, but Max himself was too slow getting under way. A haymaker caught him on the chin.

Max went crashing back against a wall. As the infuriated engineer rushed again, Max let go a wild right. It landed flush on the attacker's jaw, and down he went, out.

The thrill of that one-punch victory gave Baer ideas. He bought a punching bag and a pair of gloves and set up a small gymnasium on the ranch. A few informal set-tos with the cow-hands convinced Max that his destiny was in the ring. He de· parted the ranch for Oakland and got himself a job in a factory. Off hours he devoted to furthering his fistic aspirations. Ray Pelkey, veteran Oakland light heavyweight, coached him.

J. Hamilton Lorimer, son of the owner of the plant where Max was working, became interested in the possibilities of the strapping youngster and signed him to a three-year contract. As a bonus for signing, Lorimer turned over to Max a three-thousand-dollar automobile.

Max was just twenty when he made his professional debut in Stockton against an opponent known as Chief Caribou. The first lusty right that Baer uncovered was sufficient for the Chief, and Max's ring career was under way.

The youngster was a busy performer his first year in the industry. Only one blot, a loss on a foul to Jack McCarthy, marred an otherwise perfect record for 1929, a record that embraced knockouts of Tilly Taverna, Sailor Leeds, Al Ledford, Frank Rudjenski, George Carroll, Alec Rowe, Chet Shandel, and Tony Fuente, and decisions over Benny Hill (twice) and Natie Brown.

Max moved up against stiffer opposition in 1930. After

losing to Tiny Abbott, he came back to knock Abbott out and run off six more victories, a decision over Ernie Owens, a knockout of Owens in a return match and kayos over Jack Stewart, Tom Toner, Jack Linkhorn, and Buck Weaver.

So far, Baer's activities had been confined almost exclusively to the Oakland–San Francisco district. But now his fame had begun to spread, and Los Angeles beckoned. He was offered a bout with the experienced Les Kennedy, at the time one of California's top heavyweights.

Kennedy proved a bit too cagey and ringwise for the youngster and succeeded in outpointing him in ten rounds. Back to Oakland went Max to take on the veteran K. O. Christner. The Ohioan was no match for the hard-hitting lad from Livermore and was flattened in the second.

Baer by now had become one of the outstanding box-office attractions on the Pacific Coast. In his ninth bout he had drawn a purse of four thousand dollars and for his fourteenth battle he had been paid seven thousand dollars. A match between Baer and Frankie Campbell was now arranged by promoter Ancil Hoffman, with Max guaranteed ten thousand dollars for his end.

This fight was held in San Francisco, and in the fifth round of a furious melee, Baer knocked Campbell out—and Frankie failed to regain consciousness.

Max was broken up by the tragic ending of the battle, and for a while he talked of retiring from the ring. But Promoter Hoffman, greatly interested in the colorful youngster, prevailed on him to continue.

To get his charge away from the depressing environment of his unfortunate meeting with Campbell, Hoffman decided to head across the continent and show Max in New York. Not yet twenty-two and with only two years of professional boxing behind him, Baer made his Madison Square Garden debut on December 19, 1930, with strong, experienced Ernie Schaaf as his opponent. Schaaf proved too clever for the Californian and won the decision in ten hard-fought rounds.

Though defeated, Baer made an excellent impression on New York fans and critics by his aggressiveness and lusty thumping and was brought back to the Garden four weeks later to face the veteran Tom Heeney. Max pounded the ring-worn New Zealander into submission in the third round.

On February 6, 1931, Max appeared in the Garden again, this time against the elusive Tommy Loughran, who was probably the smartest boxer in the heavyweight ranks at the time. Tommy was entirely too fast for the wild-swinging Californian and treated him to a real boxing lesson. Baer and Hoffman then headed back to the Pacific Coast.

Max belted Ernie Owens out in the second round in Portland, Oregon. Then he and Hoffman trekked eastward again. In Cleveland Baer lost a ten-round decision to durable Johnny Risko.

At this point, Jack Dempsey announced that he would promote an Independence Day fight in Reno, Nevada; to give the show added appeal, he decided to stage it over the twenty-round route. Hoffman accepted terms for Baer to meet "the best opponent available." The rugged Basque, Paulino Uzcudun, was selected, and after twenty grueling rounds he was declared the winner. That was the last decision Baer was to lose for four years.

Max took a well-earned rest after his bruising brawl with Paulino. Returning to action on September 23, 1931, he knocked out Jack Van Noy in Oakland. Then, also in Oakland, he flattened the Portuguese giant, José Santa.

Johnny Risko was now imported from Cleveland, and Baer squared accounts with the Rubber Man by whipping him soundly in San Francisco. Another blot was erased when Les Kennedy, who had beaten Max in Los Angeles sixteen months before, was flattened in the third at Oakland. Following a victory over Arthur DeKuh in Oakland, Baer and Hoffman headed for New York again.

Awkward but dangerous King Levinsky was pitted against the Californian in the Garden on January 29, 1932. It was a wild slugging affair, but Baer hit harder and more often and won by a clear margin in ten rounds.

Tom Heeney, not content with the result of his previous meeting with Baer, clamored for a return match and was accommodated on February 22. This time the New Zealand veteran fared slightly better than he had in the first scrap. He escaped a knockout, but he was a thoroughly beaten man at the close of the tenth round.

Back to California went Baer and Hoffman. Walter Cobb was knocked out in Oakland and Paul Swiderski in Los Angeles.

Reno sportsmen had engaged Jack Dempsey to stage another big fight on Independence Day. Jack tried to fix up a return bout between Baer and Paulino, but the Basque had returned to Spain. When Hoffman agreed to have Max meet any heavyweight picked by Dempsey, King Levinsky was named.

The battle was a repetition of the New York meeting, though over twice the distance. At the close of twenty bruising rounds, Baer was a decisive winner.

Chicago, a city that had never seen Max in action, was now clamoring for a peek at him. Ernie Schaaf was suggested as an opponent, for August 31, and Hoffman accepted terms.

Baer was no longer the strong and willing but crude and wild-swinging slugger Schaaf had outfought in New York nearly two years before. Max was now a real master of ring technique. Going into the eighth round, Ernie was leading by a narrow margin, but it had been a desperate, bitter battle. Sensing that his opponent was weakening, Baer launched a furious two-handed assault.

Through the ninth the Californian continued his savage attack, and the former Navy champion began to wilt. In the tenth, Baer staggered his opponent with three thunderous rights and chased him around the ring with a vicious bombardment of face and body. Two seconds before the bell clanged the end of the fight, Schaaf collapsed from the fearful punishment. Only the gong saved him from being counted out. Several minutes passed before Ernie was revived sufficiently to leave the ring. It was the terrific battering he absorbed in this battle that was believed to be the real cause of Schaaf's tragic death, which took place not quite six months later in his bout with Primo Carnera in New York.

Baer returned to Chicago four weeks after his victory over Schaaf to clash with the veteran Tuffy Griffith. Tuffy proved no match for the devastating Californian and was hammered out of competition in seven rounds.

Baer had now definitely established himself as a real contender for the heavyweight championship. Hoffman began to eye a match with Jack Sharkey for the title, but to strengthen his bid for the bout, he offered to pit the Californian against Max Schmeling, Primo Carnera, or any of the other headliners. Meanwhile, it wasn't only his sensational exploits in the ring that kept Baer's name in the newspaper columns. The Merry Madcap had become involved in all sorts of tangles with various gentlemen who claimed to have managerial agreements with him, and much of Hoffman's and Baer's time between fights was spent in courtrooms and lawyers' offices. Then, too, spicy tales of Max's colorful and frequent amours played their part in helping to keep his name before the public. Baer added to the general gaiety by traveling around in an expensive limousine, with his own chauffeur and staff of "social secretaries," and he became a regular habitué of Broadway and Hollywood night clubs.

Following his knockout of Griffith in Chicago, Baer didn't swing back into fistic action until he squared off with Max Schmeling in New York's Yankee Stadium on June 8, 1933. Jack Dempsey, who promoted Baer's two twenty-round battles in Reno with Paulino and Levinsky, had been prevailed upon to compete against Madison Square Garden's fistic monopoly in New York. Taking out a promoter's license, Jack leased the Yankee Stadium and began to look around for the best attraction available. Max Schmeling, still protesting the decision that had cost him the heavyweight title in his match with Jack Sharkey the previous year, was working for another crack at the champion. But the Garden had already announced that Primo Carnera would be Sharkey's next opponent. Disgruntled, Schmeling promptly accepted Dempsey's terms to meet Baer. The German felt that a victory over the new sensation would go a long way toward forcing a popular demand for him to be matched with the Sharkey-Carnera winner.

And so Baer met Schmeling. By the end of the eighth round, the advance speculations of Schmeling's adherents had apparently been confirmed. Surviving Baer's early assaults, the German had come on steadily to take charge of the battle, and victory appeared to lie before him.

Assuming a vigorous offensive at the start, Max swarmed all over Schmeling, swinging his punches from everywhere. In his excitement, the Californian paid little attention to the rules. He backhanded, cupped Schmeling's head with one hand and hit with the other, punched low, and violated several other rules of clean boxing. Seven times Referee Arthur Donovan warned him.

Schmeling, undaunted by his opponent's roughhouse tactics, plodded along in his cool, methodical way, working into close quarters and beating a vicious tattoo on Baer's body. His incessant pounding began to make itself felt by the fourth round, and in the fifth, when Baer slowed down and went on the defensive, Schmeling took charge of operations. By the ninth round he appeared to have the match well in hand.

Then, suddenly, the Californian turned on the pressure again. He tore savagely into the German, ripping away with both hands. Schmeling rolled with many of the punches and blocked others, but enough of them whistled through to jolt him. At the bell, Schmeling didn't look any too strong or too confident.

Continuing his furious assault, Baer bounced out of his corner in the tenth and belabored Schmeling with rights and lefts. As Max paused for a moment, Schmeling came back to score with two stiff jabs. But Baer brushed them off and charged in with a thunderous right that staggered Schmeling. The former champion floundered on the ropes.

Referee Donovan pried the rivals apart, and Baer quickly stepped in with a sizzling left to the stomach. As the German, badly hurt, backed to the ropes near Baer's corner, the Californian let fly a looping right that dropped squarely on Schmeling's chin.

Down went the former champion. At the count of nine, he staggered weakly to his feet. Groggy, he covered his head with both gloves as Baer rained a shower of leather on him, driving him back to the ropes again. Schmeling teetered and fumbled for the ropes. Donovan, realizing his helplessness, stepped in and halted the massacre. The time of the round was one minute, fifty-one seconds.

That smashing triumph definitely established Baer as the outstanding contender for the heavyweight title, and when, three weeks later, Carnera relieved Sharkey of the laurels, there was an insistent clamor for the Italian giant to meet the dynamic Californian.

But another year passed before Max stepped into the ring of Madison Square Garden's Long Island bowl to face Carnera. In that year, Max, a big drawing card in the amusement world, cashed in on his tremendous popularity with boxing exhibitions, with stage and radio appearances, and as a motion-picture actor. He starred in *The Prizefighter and the Lady,* with Carnera appearing as Max's opponent in a ring battle.

Baer fought Carnera for the title on June 14, 1934, and, as told in the chapter on Primo Carnera, the Italian lost the championship.

As heavyweight champion of the world, Baer embarked upon another busy schedule of boxing exhibitions and night-club and radio performances. On his tour, he caught up with an old rival, King Levinsky, in Chicago. As a rule, the genial, easy-going Baer didn't take advantage of his opponents in exhibition tilts and was satisfied to clown his way through. But Levinsky elected to make a real fight of it. The King started tossing his heftiest punches in the opening frame, and that was too much for Max. In the second, the champion went to work. Driving Levinsky across the ring with a savage, two-fisted attack, he flattened the King with a terrific left hook to the jaw. It was the first time the rugged Levinsky had been knocked out.

Signed by Madison Square Garden to defend his title in June, 1935, Baer for some time lacked an opponent. Schmeling was clamoring for a return match with him, and Art Lasky and Steve Hamas were two other possibilities. Hamas, former Penn State football star, was favored on the strength of victories over Schmeling and Lasky, but he then made the serious mistake of fighting Schmeling a second time in Germany, and in this bout he was badly beaten. The Garden, with whom Schmeling was not too popular, decided to give Lasky the championship match. But first, Art was asked to whip the veteran James J. Braddock, who had been staging a remarkable comeback after his career had seemed finished.

On the form charts, Lasky figured to whip Braddock handily enough, but Jim completely upset the advance calculations by decisively outboxing and outfighting the Minneapolis boy. By his victory, Braddock qualified for the title match with Baer. The date was set for June 13, 1935.

Seldom if ever in the long history of heavyweight boxing has a challenger been given less chance to win than was Braddock. Baer himself refused to take the match seriously. Confidently predicting he would knock Braddock out inside of six rounds, Max trained in a slap-dash, careless manner—with the result that he was in far from his best physical condition when he squared off with the despised challenger. He paid, and paid dearly, and the boxing world was given a stunning shock. Braddock, waging a smart, determined fight, outboxed and outgeneraled the Californian all the way to win the unanimous decision and the heavyweight title.

A good puncher himself, Braddock did not make the mistake of trading lethal wallops with so dangerous a clouter as Baer. Instead, Jim boxed masterfully on the defense, steadily piling up points by consistent use of a left jab, and cleverly blocking or ducking under Max's ponderous swings. Even when Baer did manage to connect, his punches seemed to lack their one-time potency. Several times Max jolted Braddock, but Jim was never in distress. At no stage during the fifteen rounds did Baer even remotely resemble the devastating demon of the Schmeling and Carnera battles. He fought listlessly most of the way, and his poor physical condition was evident when he did try to uncover an offensive. His rallies were few and short-lived. Max was tired by the eighth round. At times, in desperation, he resorted to roughhouse tactics and was repeatedly warned by the referee, Johnny McAvoy.

Baer asserted after the bout that he had injured both hands in the fifth round, but beyond this he had no excuse to offer for his startling defeat. He did, however, express the desire to meet Braddock again.

Meanwhile Joe Louis was in training for his New York debut, a match with former champion Primo Carnera at the Yankee Stadium. The newly organized Twentieth Century Sporting Club, with Mike Jacobs as promoter, had Louis signed to operate exclusively under its aegis. Baer was sounded out on the possibility of meeting the young sensation in the event that the Negro whipped Carnera.

Twelve nights after Baer's defeat by Braddock, Louis toppled the giant Carnera in six rounds. A Louis-Baer match was arranged for September 24, 1935, at the Yankee Stadium.

Though he trained hard and faithfully for the bout, Baer again proved a bitter disappointment to his followers. He made few offensive gestures against the sharpshooting young Negro, and Louis battered him into submission in four one-sided rounds.

Discouraged by that setback, Baer announced his retirement from the ring. But he could not resist the temptation to try his luck once more, and in June, 1936, he embarked upon a busy barnstorming jaunt that saw him engage in eighteen bouts in three months. With the exception of a six-round decision lost to Art Oliver, his junket was a complete success.

Encouraged, Hoffman early in 1937 accepted terms for Max to cross the Atlantic and meet Tommy Farr, the British heavyweight champion, in London. The bout was held April 15, and the erratic Baer was beaten in twelve rounds. Max remained in London to take on Ben Foord, the South African, six weeks later. This time the Californian flashed some of his best stuff to knock Ben out in the ninth.

Returning to the United States, Max whipped Nash Garrison in a four-round exhibition in Oakland. Meanwhile, Joe Louis had taken the heavyweight title from Jim Braddock in Chicago and had already defended it against Tommy Farr in New York. Louis's inability to knock Farr out in fifteen rounds gave Baer an idea that Joe wasn't the annihilating puncher he was supposed to be.

With a Louis bout as his goal, Baer settled down to serious

training and was matched with Farr for March 11, 1938. The bout was arranged for Madison Square Garden, which had given up promoting on its own and had joined forces with Mike Jacobs and the Twentieth Century Sporting Club. Uncovering one of his best performances, Max handed Tommy a decisive whipping, winning easily in fifteen rounds and squaring accounts for the beating at his hands in London.

The Californian trounced Farr even more convincingly than had Louis, and the stage was now set for Max to meet Joe again. But Baer suddenly underwent a change of mind, headed west, and remained out of the boxing picture for several months. He returned to the ring again to knock out Hank Hankinson in one round in Honolulu. Another long layoff followed that performance, and it was not until June 1, 1939, that Max next appeared in fistic action. His opponent was a rival Californian, Lou Nova, and the bout was staged in New York's Polo Grounds. Badly beaten, Baer was stopped in the eleventh round.

It looked as if Max had reached the end of the boxing trail. But he still wasn't convinced. Late that fall he returned again to knock out Ed Murphy in Omaha and Babe Ritchie in Lubbock, Texas, and whip Nash Garrison in a four-rounder in Oklahoma City.

Another long layoff followed, and it wasn't until July 2, 1940, that Baer again donned the gloves to face Tony Galento in Roosevelt Stadium, Jersey City. Max, in one of his best fighting moods, battered rolypoly Tony into gory submission in eight vicious rounds. On September 26, Baer uncovered another impressive performance when, in the same ring, he flattened dangerous young Pat Comiskey in the first frame.

Baer now clamored for the opportunity to even scores with his fellow Californian, Lou Nova. He was accommodated in Madison Square Garden on April 4, 1941. Max proved unequal to the task. He fought desperately and several times in the early rounds had Nova in distress, but Lou weathered the rough going and came on to knock Baer out in the eighth round.

That defeat definitely eliminated Max from top-flight consideration, and once more he announced his retirement, this time for keeps.

Serving well as a physical-training instructor for the Army Air Forces during World War II, Baer, upon his discharge, turned to the stage. With another former boxing champion, light heavyweight Maxie Rosenbloom, he became a popular attraction in theaters and night clubs.

CHAPTER 22

THE CINDERELLA MAN

JIM BRADDOCK will never be rated as one of the ring's all-time greats. But his career unquestionably is one of the most remarkable in the history of boxing.

A year before he became heavyweight champion, Braddock, apparently finished as a fighter, was laboring on the docks of Hoboken's water front trying desperately to eke out a living for himself, his wife, and his three youngsters. His spectacular rise from near obscurity and poverty to the fame and fortune that go with the highest estate in the boxing realm represents one of the most amazing chapters in all sports history.

It was Francis Albertanti, nationally famous sports writer, who labeled Braddock the "Cinderella Man." It was a perfect appellation. Not even in his loftiest flights of imagination had Horatio Alger ever conceived a more fantastic, a more incredible from-rags-to-riches tale than the one actually lived by Braddock and brought into the spotlight by Albertanti.

Jim was born December 6, 1905, in the boisterous Hell's Kitchen district of New York's rugged West Side, where battling with the other kids was an accepted part of every youngster's daily routine. So Jim learned early how to handle his fists.

"I guess the Braddocks always fought," he told a reporter. "My dad was a handy fellow with his fists back in the old country. He used to hang around the boxing booths and the county fairs and stiffen those pound-a-round pros. He still boasts that he once knocked out a horse with a blow between the eyes. My uncle Jim was one of the best rough-and-tumble fighters in all Ireland. So I guess fighting came naturally to me."

Braddock was still quite young when his dad moved the family across the Hudson River and settled in New Jersey. He frequently was in battles with his schoolmates, and though a frail, skinny kid, he showed so much natural aptitude for the rugged business of trading punches that he was prevailed upon, when only sixteen, to try his luck in the amateur boxing ring. At the time, Jim was working as a printer's devil in a Jersey press shop.

Braddock did well as an amateur. But seeing no future in fighting for medals and watches, he decided to turn professional. He was training in Joe Jeanette's gymnasium in Hoboken when he was asked one day to put on the gloves for a round or two with a prominent welterweight from Brooklyn, Harry Galfund. Joe Gould, New York boxing manager, who was handling Galfund at the time, had been approached by a couple of Jersey businessmen who were eager to purchase Harry's contract. They asked Gould to bring Galfund over to Hoboken so they could see him in action at close range.

Braddock was a tall, lanky kid, and while he outweighed Galfund by perhaps twenty pounds, he was frail and inexperienced compared with the seasoned Brooklynite. Neither Gould nor his fighter expected the workout to prove anything more serious than just that—a workout. But the youngster proceeded to give Galfund a real battle. He made things so difficult for Harry that the prospective buyers of the contract lost interest in the deal.

"He can't be so good if a young, green, unknown kid can make things that tough for him," they stated as they walked out.

Joe Gould didn't mind. He was convinced that Braddock was an exceptional prospect, a lad who would bear a lot of serious watching. He was so impressed, in fact, that he arranged to take over the management of the young Irishman.

Braddock was a success from the start. In his first year of professional competition, 1926, he was undefeated in fifteen starts. He won eleven of those bouts by knockouts. He whipped some fair opposition, too, his best known victims being Phil Weisberger and Carmine Caggiano, who were flattened, and Lew Barba, whom he defeated on points.

Stepping up against stronger competition in 1927, Braddock continued along his winning way by scoring five kayos, winning eight decisions, and engaging in three no-decision bouts. Jim's only setback was a newspaper-decision loss to the clever, experienced Paul Cavalier. His chief triumphs were knockouts of Johnny Alberts, George La Rocca, and Stanley Simmons and official verdicts over Jimmy Francis, Jack Stone, and Vic McLaughlin.

It was late in 1928 that Braddock reached the headline class. Jim had been coming along steadily that year and had beaten, among other performances, Paul Swiderski, though he dropped a decision to Joe Sekyra in Madison Square Garden. Pete Latzo, former welterweight champion of the world, then staging a comeback as a light heavyweight, was matched with Braddock in Newark. Jim startled the form players by not only whipping Latzo in ten rounds but fracturing Pete's jaw in the process.

Just about that time the boxing world was becoming excited over the sensational punching feats of Tuffy Griffith in Chicago. Madison Square Garden signed Griffith for November 30 and began looking around for an opponent. After several other prominent light heavies had politely declined the match, Gould was offered the date for Braddock. Joe accepted for his charge, and young Jim rang up one of the year's most stunning surprises by knocking out Tuffy in the second round.

Braddock started 1929 by dropping a decision to Leo Lomski in the Garden. But he came right back with a sensational nine-round kayo of Jimmy Slattery, flashy Buffalonian, in the Garden. In consequence of this victory, Jim was matched with Tommy Loughran for the light heavyweight championship of the world.

The bout was held at the Yankee Stadium on July 18, and Braddock learned that a fighter needed more than willingness and a hefty wallop to cope with Loughran, one of the smartest, cleverest boxers of his time. Jim was little more than a raw pupil in the hands of a master.

That defeat seemed to knock a lot of confidence out of Jim, and for the next three years his record was very spotty. He lost to Yale Okun in Los Angeles, Maxie Rosenbloom in New York, Leo Lomski in Chicago, Billy Jones in Philadelphia, Babe Hunt in Boston, Ernie Schaaf in New York, Baxter Calmes in

Chicago, Al Gainer in New Haven, Charley Retzlaff in Boston,
John Henry Lewis in San Francisco, and Tom Patrick in Hollywood. His chief victories during this time were knockouts of
Jake Warren in New York, Phil Mercurio in Boston, and Jack
Roper in Miami and decisions over Joe Monte in Boston and
Dynamite Jackson in San Diego. It was not an impressive record,
and when a nasty gash over Jim's left eye forced the referee to
stop his match with Lou Scozza in the sixth round in San Francisco, it looked as if Braddock were definitely through as a headliner.

But Jim kept plugging along, winning here, losing there. In
1933, he engaged in nine bouts, knocking out Al Stillman in
St. Louis and whipping Martin Levandowski in Chicago, Les
Kennedy in Jersey City, and Chester Matan in West New York,
New Jersey. But he was beaten by Hans Birkie in New York
and Al Ettore in Philadelphia, and by both Levandowski and
Stillman in return matches in St. Louis.

Braddock cracked both hands in his bout with Abe Feldman
in Mount Vernon, New York, on September 25, and the referee
halted the affair in the sixth round, calling it "no contest."
Jim, utterly discouraged, announced his retirement from the
ring.

It was in the midst of the depression, and Braddock had saved
little from his ring earnings. The support of his wife and three
children quickly used up Jim's backlog, and he was flat broke
soon after he had hung up the gloves. He began looking around
for a job, any sort of a job, but the going was desperate. Occasionally he found work on the Hoboken docks, but not often
enough to keep the family regularly in groceries, and Braddock
found it necessary to have his name entered on the relief rolls.

Meanwhile, Primo Carnera had become heavyweight champion of the world and Max Baer had established himself as the
Italian giant's outstanding challenger. Madison Square Garden
had signed the rivals to meet at the Long Island bowl on
June 14, 1934.

A young Southern heavyweight, Corn Griffin, had aroused
the interest of boxing critics by his flashy performances as one
of Carnera's sparring partners, and Jimmy Johnston, Garden

matchmaker, offered to find Griffin a match in the semifinal
that preceded the championship bout. Looking around for a
likely opponent, Johnston came across the name of Braddock.
He got in touch with Joe Gould.

"Hey, if that fighter of yours can use a few dollars, I can put
him on with Griffin," he said to Joe.

"No, Jim's retired," Gould replied. Then, as an afterthought:
"But a dollar bill would look like manna from heaven to him.
Wait until I get in touch with him, and I'll let you know."

Braddock fairly leaped at the offer. "Sure, grab it, Joe," he
said.

Jim didn't appear to have a chance against the speedy, clever
Griffin. Supposedly through, he had been out of the ring nearly
nine months. But he buckled down to serious training and
whipped himself into the best physical condition he could
under the circumstances.

"At least, if I'm licked, I'll go down fighting," he told
Gould grimly.

The going was rough for Braddock in the first round. Griffin
swarmed all over him and dropped the veteran to the canvas.
Jim was shaky when he returned to his corner at the end of
the frame. But he came out punching in the second round, and
almost before the startled assemblage realized what had happened, Jim's lusty right had flattened Griffin. It was a sensational
performance—and the wily Gould knew how to make the most
of Braddock's comeback.

A few months later the Garden contracted with John Henry
Lewis for three performances; the Negro from Phoenix, Ari-
zona, fighting in spectacular form at the time, was being touted
by Pacific Coast authorities as the world's best light heavyweight. Matchmaker Johnston, eager to have Lewis get off to
a flying start in his first New York appearance, decided that
Braddock would be an ideal opponent for John Henry. Jim was
obviously too slow and too old for the flashy Arizonian. As a
youngster, he had beaten Braddock handily in San Francisco
two years before, and there seemed to be no risk involved for
the now mature Negro fighter.

The bout was held November 16, 1934, and the twenty-nine-year-old Braddock came through with another surprising performance. After ten blistering rounds, the officials awarded Jim the decision. The veteran, fighting with all the fire and dash of a youngster, clinched the verdict by knocking Lewis down in the seventh frame.

Fresh from his upset victory, Braddock was now selected to fight Art Lasky for the right to meet champion Max Baer The match was arranged for March 22, 1935, and once more Jimmy scrambled the classic dope. Giving away height, reach, and nearly fifteen pounds to his favored rival, he fought one of the finest, smartest battles of his career. The veteran took the play away from Lasky at the start, and with a clever, heady exhibition of boxing and accurate punching, he remained in front all the way. At the close of the fifteenth round, Braddock was a decisive winner.

By his clean-cut win over Lasky, Braddock established himself as a challenger for the heavyweight championship of the world. But Schmeling also was demanding a match with Baer. When Gould offered to settle the issue by matching Jim with the German, Schmeling refused. The Garden executives issued an ultimatum: Either Max would meet Braddock in a final elimination or Jim would be given the crack at the championship.

Schmeling continued adamant. Whereupon, matchmaker Johnston announced that Baer's defense of his laurels would be made against Braddock in the Long Island bowl on June 13. The details of Braddock's stunning victory have been set down in the chapter on Max Baer.

In one year, Jim Braddock had written the most fantastic volume in the heavyweight library—the improbable story of a climb from the docks to the heavyweight championship of the world, from poverty to the richest estate in the sports realm. He was indeed the Cinderella Man.

Gould and Braddock now reaped the golden harvest. For two years Jim toured the country, boxing and refereeing in exhibitions and making frequent stage and radio appearances.

During that time, the problem of Braddock's first defense of his title arose. Schmeling was still clamoring for a crack at the

1919: Jack Dempsey in his famous crouch against Willard as they battled for the championship in Toledo.

Willard helpless against the ropes. Dempsey won a three-round knockout when Willard, unable to continue, quit during the rest period between the third and fourth rounds.

1921: The first "million-dollar gate." Georges Carpentier and Dempsey before the start of their championship battle in Jersey City.

Carpentier taking a count. Dempsey knocked him out in the fourth round.

1923: Luis Angel Firpo knocking Dempsey through the ropes in the first round of their championship fight in New York. Helped back into the ring, Dempsey won by a second-round knockout.

Referee Barry urging Dempsey to a neutral corner before starting to count.

1927: The blow that floored Champion Gene Tunney in the seventh round of the "battle of the long count" in Chicago.

After the knockdown, Dempsey stood over Tunney for several seconds, then went to the corner nearest Tunney. The referee properly delayed his count until Dempsey retired to a neutral corner.

k Sharkey, who won the title in 2.

The ring's leading comic characters of the 1930's. Max Baer (who won the title from Carnera in 1934) is being butted by Two-ton Tony Galento.

Primo Carnera, the Italian giant who won the championship from Sharkey in 1933.

1936: Joe Louis' only defeat as a professional. Max Schmeling knocked him out in the twelfth round.

1937: Jim Braddock (who won the title from Baer in 1935) losing the championship to Louis.

1938: Louis squares accounts with Schmeling, winning by a first-round knockout, in two minutes, four seconds. Only Tommy Burns won a championship fight in less time. Thirty years earlier, in Dublin, Ireland, he knocked out Jem Roche in one minute, twenty-eight seconds of the first round.

1940: Louis wards off a savage attack by Arturo Godoy prior to knocking him out in the eighth round. In an earlier fight that went the scheduled fifteen rounds, Louis had taken a close decision from the Chilean.

1948: By knocking out Jersey Joe Walcott, Joe Louis defends his crown for the twenty-fifth time. This was the champion's last fight. He retired undefeated in 1949.

crown. And to his voice had been added the insistent tones of Joe Louis, an efficient young man from Detroit.

Braddock was under contract to Madison Square Garden; Louis was the exclusive property of the rival Twentieth Century Sporting Club. The Garden signed Schmeling to meet Braddock. But Jim, remembering Max's refusal to face him in an elimination match to determine Baer's logical challenger, had no intention of giving the German a chance now. He accepted a match with Louis instead, under Mike Jacobs' promotion, in Chicago's Comiskey Park for June 22, 1937.

Two years had passed since his title-winning fray with Baer, and at the advanced age of nearly thirty-two, Braddock was decidedly ring rusty.

Jim started well enough. In the first round he electrified the crowd by clipping Louis with a short right to the chin and dropping him to the canvas. Louis, more surprised than hurt, was up at the count of two.

After that opening-round flash, Braddock was never in the running. Louis was too young, too strong, and too vicious a puncher for the veteran. But Braddock went down fighting.

The eighth round had gone one minute and ten seconds when Louis nailed the weary champion with a terrific right to the chin. Down went Jim. He fell in the center of the ring, blood from his nose and mouth staining the canvas. He didn't stir as the official timekeeper stood up at the side of the ring and banged out the count in unison with little Tommy Thomas, the referee.

Braddock was completely out. But though he lost the title, he and his manager continued to retain an interest in the crown. They had a secret agreement with Louis whereby, if the Negro won, they would get 10 per cent of his earnings for ten years—and they have to date collected all but a small fraction of the amount due them.

It was generally supposed that Braddock would hang up his gloves after losing the title. His earnings as champion had been wisely invested, and Jim was apparently well protected against the future. But, like an old fire horse who cannot resist the call to a fire, Braddock returned to the ring seven months later to face Tommy Farr, the Welsh heavyweight, in Madison Square Garden. The bout was held January 21, 1938.

Farr, who had given Louis a stubborn fifteen-round battle at the Yankee Stadium only two months after Joe's title-winning effort against Braddock, was expected to prove too young and too strong for the veteran. But Braddock once again confounded the experts. Trailing Farr on points at the end of the eighth round, Jim uncovered a furious rally in the last two frames that swept him through to a brilliant victory.

That was Braddock's last official appearance in ring combat. Jim once more announced his retirement, and this time he made it stick, although he retained an active interest in the sport by teaming up with Joe Gould in the management of a stable of boxers and occasionally appearing in exhibitions or as a referee. He also became part owner in several lucrative business ventures.

During World War II, Jim served well as a captain in the Army Transportation Service.

CHAPTER 23

THE BROWN BOMBER

NO CHILD could have had a more humble beginning than Joe Louis Barrow. Born May 13, 1914, in a ramshackle cabin in the cotton fields of Alabama, Joe was the seventh child of Monroe and Lily Barrow, who had to struggle desperately to make a bare living for their brood.

Joe was only a small boy when his father, worn down by the ceaseless, discouraging battle to support his family, suffered a mental breakdown and was sent to a state institution. For several years, Lily Barrow fought doggedly to keep her children alive. Then, hearing that her husband had died, she remarried. Her second husband was Pat Brooks, a widower with a large flock of his own.

Brooks could see nothing but a dismal future for the combined clans in Alabama, so he moved them up to Detroit. Joe was then ten. He was only twelve when he got a job after school hours, working on an ice wagon. At fourteen, he entered a trade school to learn cabinetmaking.

It was quite by accident that Joe became involved in boxing. One of his pals, Thurston McKinney, who was doing well as an amateur, asked Joe to put on the gloves with him one day in the gymnasium. Though awkward, Joe displayed a natural aptitude for the sport. McKinney took him in hand, and after a few lessons Joe was encouraged to try his luck in competition. He was sixteen at the time he entered his first amateur tournament.

Joe was not an instantaneous success. In his first bout he drew an experienced boxer, Johnny Miler, as his opponent and Miler gave the youngster a thorough going over, knocking him down seven times in the first two rounds, and gaining the decision. But Louis, though disappointed, was far from discouraged.

Joe went on to become one of the outstanding performers in amateur ranks. In fifty-four bouts he lost only four decisions, and of his fifty triumphs, forty-one were by knockouts. In 1933, he reached the finals of the light heavyweight class in the National A. A. U. championships in Boston, only to lose a close, disputed decision to Max Marek. The following year he swept everything before him, and when the Nationals were staged in St. Louis, he punched his way to the top of the 175-pound division.

Louis now decided the time was ripe for him to step into professional competition. He talked the matter over with John Roxborough, whose interest in the youngster had done much to encourage his success.

"If I turn pro, John, will you manage me?" Joe asked.

"But, Joe, I'm not a professional manager. There's a lot about the business I don't know," Roxborough replied.

"Well, I don't know much either, so let's the both of us learn together."

The first thing Roxborough did was probably the smartest move he could have made. He hired Jack Blackburn to coach and train Louis. Blackburn, a great boxer in his day, had become just as successful as a trainer; among his pupils had been several world champions, notably Sammy Mandell, lightweight, and Bud Taylor, bantamweight. (Roxborough had meanwhile teamed up with Julian Black of Chicago in a business venture, and this association also was to carry over into the management of Louis.)

Blackburn worked for two months with Louis in the gymnasium to polish up his boxing. On July 4, 1934, Joe made his professional debut in Bacon's Arena, Chicago. His opponent was Jack Kracken. Louis belted Kracken out in one heat. The purse was fifty dollars.

Then followed knockout after knockout, against stiffer and tougher opposition with each succeeding bout. Only four of his first twenty-seven foes were able to last the distance—Jack Kranz, Adolph Wiater, Patsy Perroni, and Natie Brown.

Joe's first real prominence came with his knockout of Stanley Poreda in Chicago. Poreda, no mean puncher himself, was belted right into the timekeeper's lap with one punch. Joe followed up that fast job by stiffening Charley Massera, a good heavyweight. When he knocked out Lee Ramage in eight rounds, Louis really had the fans wondering, for Ramage had been a heavy favorite to halt the winning streak of the young Negro marvel.

By this time Joe Louis had become known as the Brown Bomber. He continued to bomb his opponents until his name was up near the top of the list of contenders for the heavyweight crown. His only setback in his upward climb was the knockout at the hands of Max Schmeling, and a year and three days after that, the boy who had come north from the Alabama cotton fields won the world heavyweight championship. Louis was only twenty-three years old when he gained the crown.

Joe has defended his title more times than any man in the history of boxing. His total of twenty-five championship battles more than doubles the record of any previous heavyweight king. The record includes other impressive accomplishments: seven title defenses attracting gates and crowds among the top thirty-two in all boxing history, seven defenses in one year, knockouts of twenty-two of the twenty-five challengers, an average of only six and a half rounds for the twenty-five battles.

But little things have made the Louis reign quite as significant as the big, important factors. These are the things that will be remembered when most of the statistics have been forgotten.

There was the night when Louis and Tommy Farr fought fifteen rounds two months after Joe had won the crown. What is most clearly recalled of that battle is the loud *crack* that sounded over the ringside when Louis lashed out with his first left hand of the fight and shattered his opponent's nose.

And there was the night that Joe appeared in California against Jack Roper in a title fight. When it was all over, Jack got on the air with Joe and remarked, "I zigged when I shoulda zagged."

Fans will not forget the last two battles of the Bomber before he hung up his gloves to enter the Army. He took no pay for them, having contributed both purses to the Army and Navy relief funds.

Already some Louis anecdotes are far better known than the fights that gave them currency. When John Henry Lewis was about to face the champion in 1939, one of the reporters cornered Joe on the afternoon of the weighing-in and asked whether he'd go easy on John Henry since they were pals.

"He's my pal, all right," Joe confessed, "so I'll put him away early. I'll make it quick for him, 'cause that'll be easier." The fight lasted two minutes and nine seconds of round one.

Tony Galento, the beer barrel who walks, gave the fans something to talk about when he made Joe hit the deck in the third round. As Louis landed on the canvas-covered floor, a ringsider jumped up and moaned, "Say it ain't so, Joe!" That's what they'll recall of the Galento fight, even more than Joe's knockout of Tony in the fourth.

There was the fight with Bob Pastor in Detroit, who had lasted ten rounds two years before by moving constantly backward. This time, trying to slug with Joe from the opening bell, he hit the floor four times in the first round. Jimmy Johnston, his manager, had suffered a heart attack a few days before, and his doctor had given him some pills to take. "Now, I'm warning you, Jimmy," he cautioned, "you mustn't work in the corner that night, and you must take things easy. And above all, you must always keep these pills handy so you can get them in a hurry."

When Pastor went down for the fourth time, Jimmy's doctor leaned forward, white and trembling, and tapped Johnston on the shoulder. "Those pills, Jimmy," he gasped. "Give me one of them in a hurry."

Just before that same fight someone asked Joe what he thought of Johnston.

"Jimmy's a nice little fellow," Louis answered.

"He's been saying nasty things about you all over the country," his questioner continued.

"Jimmy's all right," Louis said softly. "He's just saying those things to make us a little money."

In the dressing room after the first Pastor fight, somebody asked Louis if he had been hurt by the back-pedaling Pastor. Disgusted with the bad fight he had made, Joe answered, "No one hurt but the people who paid the money."

Then there was the unusual situation during Joe's second fight, in the summer of 1940, with Arturo Godoy, who had gone the route of fifteen rounds in their initial meeting. When Referee Donovan stopped the fight in the eighth, Godoy raced over to Joe's corner and tried to start slugging again. With imperial calm, Joe turned his back, started through the ropes, and motioned to his trainer, Jack Blackburn, to take care of Godoy.

Joe went down to Washington to fight Buddy Baer, Max's younger brother. Buddy opened the bout with his Sunday punch —and there was the champion knocked through the ropes and lying on his back on the ring apron in the very first round! As Joe went through between the top and middle strands, however, his foot caught in Buddy's leg, and the fighters remained in a tangle. But for that circumstance, Louis would probably have rolled right off the apron—with the result, had he failed to climb back by "ten," that a new champion would have been crowned.

Nor will they soon forget the night that Billy Conn nearly ended the Bomber's reign. After the twelfth round, in which Conn all but floored Joe with a left hook, John Blackburn worked over the champion and said quietly, "Chappie, you know you're losing the title—you gotta knock him out now."

"Guess I'll have to knock him out then, Chappie," Joe replied.

He did so in the next round after Conn made the mistake of opening his guard too wide. Billy's error was explained to him in simplest terms by his manager, Johnny Ray:

"Billy, if you had a Jewish head instead of an Irish head, you'd be the heavyweight champion right now."

In 1942, the day before he went into the Army, Joe took on Buddy Baer again in another benefit bout for the Navy relief fund. Jack Blackburn was in failing health, and although he should not have been in the champion's corner on the night of the fight, he showed up at the ringside anyway. Just before Joe climbed through the ropes, he said to his mentor, "I'll see you don't have to do any climbing these stairs between rounds, Chappie."

He kept his word by belting Buddy out in one round.

When Joe was leaving on his first overseas tour to entertain GI's in Europe, Billy Conn, who was then awaiting a similar assignment, called him on the telephone: "Now take good care of yourself over there, Joe. You and I have an important date as soon as the war's over, and I don't want anything happening to you."

"Don't worry, Billy," Joe came back. "I'll be very careful—for you, Billy." Joe took good care of himself, too, as Conn discovered when they met again in the ring after the war had ended.

It is pleasant to recall little items like the foregoing when one considers the career of Joe Louis, the boy from Alabama who became heavyweight king, the Negro who has not only proved himself the master boxer of his age but who has also demonstrated by his fine behavior in and out of the ring that the color of a man's skin is an irrelevant factor in determining his worth. Not the least of Joe's achievements was a reign of nearly twelve years without a single demand that he be dethroned by a *white* man. The explanation lies partly in the fact that the American people have become more mature since the days of Jack Johnson, partly in the fact that Louis was a great champion and a fine citizen.

He didn't have everything his way on his rise to the top. There were few setups among the fighters whom Joe was asked to meet before his clash with Braddock for the title. He took them as they came, and one after another they fell—until he came up against Max Schmeling in 1936.

That fight, ending in Joe's knockout in the twelfth round, was the crisis in the career of the Detroit battler. On the day of his meeting with the German, Joe Louis was the most interesting heavyweight in the world, a superman of twenty-two who had everything—boxing ability, punching power, the greatest gate appeal since Jack Dempsey—and it was clear to all the world that he was the coming champion. On the day after, Joe was just another heavyweight, a beaten fighter.

Yet the loss to Schmeling did perhaps more to make Louis a great fighter than any other thing in his career. It provided a test of spirit and plain guts, not in the ring—Joe never lacked courage when facing an opponent—but during the days and weeks that followed, when Joe was alone with his thoughts. The future was in his own hands. He alone could determine it. And he never doubted what it would be.

A comeback tour was at once arranged. Joe's first objective was to regain the prestige that his defeat had so greatly injured. There was only one way to do that—to roll up victory after victory over the knockout route.

Louis first took Jack Sharkey into camp. It was reasoned that a kayo victory over the Bostonian, added to those the Brown Bomber had scored over two other former champions, Carnera, and Baer, would bring Joe back into the challenger's post for a championship fight with Braddock.

The Brown Bomber was eager to get Schmeling into a return bout. He wanted that fight even more than he wanted to meet Braddock. It was very much a personal matter with him. Those who were handling Joe's affairs, however, decided differently. They knew that Braddock was ready to be taken, and they wanted Louis to put every worth-while contender out of the way. The important goal was the championship. Matches were therefore scheduled with the purpose of eliminating all other possible contenders—except Schmeling, who, as related in the preceding chapter, was being side-tracked by Braddock in favor of the Brown Bomber. Louis halted, in addition to Sharkey, Al Ettore, Jorge Brescia, Eddie Simms, and Natie Brown and won a ten-rounder from Bob Pastor to qualify for this mill.

The Braddock contest, already described, took place in Chicago on June 22, 1937, with Joe the winner by a knockout in eight rounds. A few months later, the new titleholder began his career of greatest fighting champion in history. The first of his twenty-five defenses of the heavyweight crown was staged with Tommy Farr of England.

Louis went into the ring to end the fight as quickly as possible. Instead, he caught a tartar, and it was lucky for him that Farr lacked a knockout punch. By staying the limit, Tommy routed the critics who had predicted his speedy fall. Tossing caution to the winds, he stood up for fifteen rounds of savage fighting, and at times he battled with a viciousness that made the thirty-six thousand spectators wonder whether he was really a representative of the country that in recent years had specialized in horizontal heavyweight kings.

Farr was a real fighter. He lost the decision to Louis but won the lasting respect of his conqueror, the critics, and the cash customers.

Joe felt that he was now ready to take on Schmeling again, but his board of managers vetoed that idea in favor of a couple more tune-up battles. They lined up two easy ones for Joe, a fight with Nathan Mann and another with Harry Thomas.

Then came the memorable return engagement with the German. Two years and ten fights had passed since Joe's knockout at his hands when the archenemies met on June 22, 1938.

At the bell, Louis tore into Schmeling with rights and lefts and bore the German to the ropes. Those drives were no long swings. The punches went barely eight inches, and they took all the fight out of Max. They paralyzed him.

Max glared at the Brown Bomber. He tried to think of all the things he had done to Louis two years before, of all the schemes he had worked out for a second triumph over the Negro, of all the ideas he had got from studying motion pictures of Joe's fights.

But Joe drove all notions and plans right out of the German's noggin. He backed Max into a corner. He shot a left hook to the head and then a right cross to Schmeling's eye. Another left hook to the head was followed by a murderous right to the jaw that staggered Max. He draped himself over the ropes. The referee, Arthur Donovan, shoved Joe back and started to count over the German.

They came to the center of the ring. Louis cut loose with a fusillade that sent Max to the canvas.

Donovan stopped the fight to prevent Max's being killed, he explained later. The time was two minutes, four seconds.

That first-round knockout stands as the high point of the Louis ring career.

With his crushing victory over Schmeling, Louis completed one of the most thorough house-cleaning jobs in all ring history. In his impressive list of conquests were the names of five former champions—Primo Carnera, Max Baer, Jack Sharkey, Jim Braddock, and Schmeling—and there was not a man on earth who could honestly be labeled a dangerous threat to the champion.

But fighting was Joe's business, and it became the problem of promoter Mike Jacobs to see to it that such an outstanding businessman be kept active. Accordingly, Mike surveyed the heavyweight field for possible opponents and finally decided upon another Negro, John Henry Lewis, the light heavyweight champion of the world.

Though a natural 175-pounder, Lewis had enjoyed consistent success against the bigger fellows, and he probably was sincere in the belief that his speed and cleverness would give him a good chance against the heavier and stronger Louis. Fast, clever, and a good two-handed puncher, Lewis, under Gus Greenlee's tutelage, had fought his way to the world 175-pound championship by whipping Bob Olin for the title in St. Louis.

Neither Louis nor Lewis was particularly keen for the match. Outside the ring they were close personal friends, and their trainers, Jack Blackburn and Larry Amadee, had often worked together. But business was business, and when Jacobs decided upon John Henry as Joe's next opponent, it was quite all right with the champion. The match was set for January 25, 1939, in Madison Square Garden.

Great boxer though he was, Lewis proved no match for the powerful heavyweight king. In the first round, John Henry was battered to the canvas three times; Arthur Donovan, the referee, stepped in to halt the slaughter after two minutes, twenty-nine seconds of fighting. A check against the motion-picture record later revealed that Louis had connected with a total of thirty-nine punches, most of them right-hand smashes, while John Henry, overwhelmed by the fury of the champion's onslaught, had scored with only three feeble jabs.

Promoter Jacobs decided to have Louis make his next appearance in Los Angeles, where he had last fought in 1934 in a knockout performance against Lee Ramage. The opponent selected was Jack Roper, veteran left-hook artist. The bout was held in Wrigley Field on April 17, 1939. Despite the fact that very few conceded Roper even an outside chance with the powerful champion, a crowd of 25,000, many of them film celebrities, turned out for the affair.

As had been generally expected, the bout didn't last long. The official count was two minutes, twenty seconds. But the assembled gathering was treated to one unexpected thrill when, almost with the first punch of the affair, Roper clipped Louis with a left hook that staggered the champion. Before the veteran could follow up, however, Joe recovered and overwhelmed him.

About this time one of the most cleverly handled build-up campaigns in boxing history was reaching its peak. Smart little Joe Jacobs was never one to remain long out of the spotlight or the money. After his German meal ticket, Max Schmeling, fell before Louis' dynamic fists, Joe promptly turned his attention to another heavyweight he was handling, Tony Galento of Orange, New Jersey, one of the most extraordinary characters who has ever appeared as a heavyweight title contender. Standing only five feet, nine inches, he weighed in the neighborhood of 225 pounds and was built along the graceful lines of a beer barrel. Which is no wonder, since Tony guzzled beer whenever and wherever he felt like it. He ate anything and everything and violated all the other accepted rules of training.

But Two-Ton Tony, regardless of his exceedingly unathletic appearance and his flagrant disregard of training programs, could fight. He was tough, and he could sock, particularly with a ponderous left hook. It was Galento's proud boast that he had never been knocked off his feet. Though he had been stopped a couple of times, those setbacks were of the "technical" variety, nasty gashes over his eyes causing the bouts to be halted.

With Schmeling definitely eliminated from the title chase, Joe Jacobs began to concentrate on building Galento into a possible opponent for Louis. Jacobs, who knew all the angles of ballyhoo, aided his campaign by lining up a series of victories for Galento that began to arouse the public's curiosity. The climax of the promotion campaign was Tony's two-round kayo of Nathan Mann in Madison Square Garden. That triumph convinced even the most skeptical that Galento would provide formidable opposition for Louis.

The match was set for June 28, 1939, at the Yankee Stadium, and the 35,000 fans who witnessed the set-to were amply repaid by a real Donnybrook Fair.

At the bell, Tony came out crouching and rushed in with a left hook to the body. Though Louis was staggered almost by the first punch Galento uncovered, he promptly tied up the challenger at close quarters. As they came out of the clinch, Joe jabbed two light lefts to Tony's scowling face, and then Galento suddenly crashed over a thunderous left hook to the champion's jaw.

Joe's legs buckled, his eyes became glassy, and he reeled back into a neutral corner. Louis was hurt, but he instinctively covered up, and the wild-swinging Galento was unable to reach him with another solid punch.

Louis, looking serious, boxed his way cautiously out of danger. Galento continued to chase the champion, pelting away with both hands, but found that Joe was a difficult target to hit. Just before the bell, Louis, getting the range, jolted Galento with a left and a right. Galento was credited with having the better of the opening stanza.

Louis went to work at the start of the second to make Galento pay with interest for his unseemly behavior in the first frame. Stepping out fast, Joe drew a trickle of blood from the corner of Tony's left eye with a jolting left. A hard right to the jaw almost lifted Galento off his feet. Louis followed with a left to the body and a right to the mouth that sent Tony wobbling into his own corner.

Louis, following his foe relentlessly, smashed away with both hands. But Galento fought back furiously. As Tony rushed in, Louis clipped him on the chin with a short uppercut that tilted his head back. Joe instantly smashed a right to Tony's wide-open jaw and hooked his left to the same spot. Galento was lifted off his feet and deposited on his broad beam.

Although Galento was badly hurt, he refused to take a count. He pulled himself to his feet and tried to fight back as Louis crowded him against the ropes. The bell came to his rescue. As

Tony stumbled to his corner, he was bleeding profusely from the right eye, nose, and mouth.

Continuing his vicious attack in the third, Louis was giving Galento a thorough going over when suddenly, as they were parting from a clinch, Galento whipped over a left hook. It caught the unprepared champion on the point of the chin, and as Louis dropped to his haunches the stadium became a veritable madhouse.

Bewildered by this unexpected turn of events, but not seriously hurt, Louis bounced up almost immediately. Infuriated, he tore into the challenger. But he found a willing mixer in Two-Ton Tony. Weary and battered though he was, Galento fought back desperately and forced Louis to the ropes. Tony, however, had fired his last ammunition. The champion had little difficulty in fending off his rolypoly opponent's attack.

Louis went out in the fourth to end the job. Grimly he hammered his stocky rival into submission. Galento reeled back drunkenly before Joe's determined assault. In his own corner, he fell back against the ropes and propped himself there while the champion hammered away at him. His legs sagged and he sank to the canvas, the upper half of his barrel-like body draped over the second strand of ropes.

Realizing Galento's helplessness, Referee Arthur Donovan stepped in at this point, pushed Louis back, and called off the massacre. The time of the round was two minutes, twenty-nine seconds.

No sooner had the tumult and the shouting died than Jimmy Johnston began a lusty beating of the tom-toms in behalf of his Bob Pastor. Jimmy's position was not unreasonable: Pastor had stayed the ten-round limit with Louis in Madison Square Garden only five months before Joe won the title.

"Louis is all right with the slow-moving fellows," was the gist of Johnston's contention, "but he doesn't look so good with the fast, clever boxers like Bob."

Johnston didn't have a particularly difficult problem to overcome. For one thing, Detroit had been clamoring for Louis to defend his title there. Although he had grown up in the Motor City and his family was still living there, Joe hadn't boxed in the Michigan metropolis since winning the championship. Another thing in Johnston's favor was the fact that Joe wanted to erase the memory of the first Pastor bout. Joe took a lot of pride in himself and his fistic accomplishments, and his disappointing performance against the former New York University football star set not at all well with him.

The bout was arranged for September 20, 1939, at Briggs Stadium, home of Detroit's baseball team, and scheduled for the twenty rounds permitted in Michigan. This was the first heavyweight title bout listed for anything beyond fifteen rounds since Jack Johnson lost the crown to Jess Willard in Havana in 1915. Not many persons expected the fray to go the full twenty rounds, but a few fans felt that Joe might need the long route to wear down his speedy opponent if Pastor pursued the same sprinting tactics he had used in their first engagement.

The first heavyweight championship match ever held in Detroit attracted a turnout of 33,638 and gross receipts of 347,870 dollars. And the fans were well repaid. Pastor, knocked down five times in the first two rounds, staged a gallant uphill battle, and at one point in the eighth frame it looked as if he might win. But Louis was not to be denied. His thunderous fists finally downed the gritty New Yorker in the eleventh.

It was not until February 9, 1940, that Louis swung back into fistic action. Jacobs had matched him with Arturo Godoy, rugged Chilean, in Madison Square Garden.

Godoy was a rough mauler, who had beaten Tony Galento twice, first in ten rounds at the New York Hippodrome, then in six rounds on the Louis-Braddock card in Chicago. The South American's main asset was a strong, durable physique and ability to sop up punishment, but he also had developed an awkward, crouching style that had proved troublesome to opponents. It was not expected, however, that Louis would find him too much of a problem.

Whether Joe felt the same way about it and underestimated the Chilean, or whether he just happened to run into an off night, has never been clear. But whatever the cause or causes, Louis turned in one of the most disappointing performances of his career.

Louis won the decision, but his margin was so close that a howl for a return match immediately went up from Godoy's camp. Promoter Jacobs accordingly announced that he would bring the rivals together in a summer ball-park show.

As a tune-up for his second meeting with the South American, Louis came back to the Garden on March 29 to face Johnny Paycheck, a native Chicagoan who had become something of a sensation in and around Des Moines. Touted as an exceptionally fast and clever big fellow and a dangerous puncher with either hand, Paycheck had piled up an impressive knockout record in Iowa rings.

Except for King Levinsky, no more frightened opponent ever squared off with Louis. Paycheck's legs were quivering as he came out of his corner for instructions. Johnny made no effort to fight. At the sound of the opening gong, he poked a feeble left in Louis's general direction and as Joe closed in on him, Paycheck started scampering backward. Louis stalked him slowly, but half the round elapsed before the champion succeeded in getting within firing range. Louis finally maneuvered Johnny into a corner and whipped a vicious right to the Chicagoan's chin.

Paycheck's legs collapsed and he sank to his knees, where he took the count of nine. Struggling to his feet, he started running backward again, but Louis quickly cornered him and dropped him again, this time with a left hook. Once more Paycheck took the count of nine before arising. Louis crowded him into a corner, and a whistling right to the jaw sent him sprawling for the third time. It looked as if it might be the finish, but Paycheck managed to pull himself up just as the round ended.

Louis lost no time winding up the affair in the second stanza. As Paycheck made a futile gesture of throwing a right hand, which Joe easily deflected, the champion shot over one of his own rights. It caught Paycheck flush on the chin and flattened him for the full count in forty-four seconds.

Louis now concentrated on his return match with Godoy which had been set for June 20, 1940, at the Yankee Stadium.

The criticism following his disappointing exhibition against the Chilean in the Garden had not set well with the champion.

Joe was a master craftsman who took great pride in his work, and it ruffled that pride to realize that he had looked like anything but a great champion in his first meeting with Godoy. Joe was determined this time to make the South American pay in full for the indignities he had inflicted upon him in their previous fray.

The champion fought one of his smartest battles that night. Godoy had apparently planned to operate along the same awkward, crouching lines he had followed so successfully in the Garden. But Joe was ready for him. Louis methodically stalked the Chilean, carefully measuring his punches and making every one count. Systematically, he wore Godoy down until, in the seventh round, the champion went out for the kill. The South American by that time was bleeding profusely from an ugly cut over his left eye. Louis jolted him with a series of rights and lefts to the jaw and finally dropped him to his hands and knees. The bell clanged at the count of six.

Louis wasted no time finishing his rugged adversary in the eighth. A barrage of rights and lefts sent Godoy down for the count of eight. Arturo gamely tried to fight back as he arose, but a lusty right to the chin dropped him again, this time for two. Referee Billy Cavanaugh then stepped in and called a halt. The time of the round was one minute, twenty-four seconds.

After that victory, Louis instructed Mike Jacobs to line up a fight a month for him, and in December, 1940, he began one of the most spectacular campaigns in championship history.

This campaign got officially under way in Boston on December 16 when Louis knocked out Al McCoy in the sixth round.

On January 31, 1941, the champion dropped into Madison Square Garden to flatten Clarence "Red" Burman in the fifth.

Philadelphia was selected for his February showing. Gus Dorazio was halted in the second stanza.

For his March engagement, Joe paid another visit to Detroit, where he found big Abe Simon a considerably tougher foeman than he had anticipated. Simon made things highly interesting for the champion, who required thirteen rounds in which to polish off the giant.

St. Louis had never seen Joe in action as a professional, and he felt he would like to appear in the city where in 1934 he had won the National A. A. U. light heavyweight title. So the Missouri metropolis was given the April assignment, with rugged, stocky Tony Musto as the party of the other part. Musto, with his awkward style, proved a tough nut for the champion to crack, but Louis finally stopped him in the ninth.

Washington was honored with the May date on the Louis calendar. By this time the champion's unusual program had prompted the late Jack Miley, of the *New York Post,* to coin a phrase that immediately caught the fancy of the populace. "The Bum-of-the-Month Club," Jack called it, and that became more or less officially the label for Joe's current activity.

Buddy Baer, ponderous younger brother of Max, was nominated for Louis' opponent in Washington. Baer was not in the least awed by the champion's reputation and made a fight of it from the start. In the first round he nailed Louis with a left hook that sent Joe reeling back to the ropes and out onto the apron of the ring. The timekeeper had tolled off four before Louis succeeded in getting back.

Though Baer was on the receiving end of terrific punishment in the next few rounds, he fought back stubbornly and several times jolted the champion. In the third, he forced Louis to the ropes with a barrage of rights—the effectiveness of this sortie was manifested by a mouse under Joe's left eye.

In the fifth, Buddy actually outfought the champion, one of his left hooks opening a cut under his opponent's right eye. Toward the close of the round, however, Joe cut loose with a flurry of rights and lefts that caused Buddy's legs to sag.

It was midway through the sixth round that Louis, during a furious swapping bee, suddenly exploded a thunderous right on Baer's chin. Down went Buddy. Badly hurt, he staggered up at the count of seven. Louis measured Baer for a one-two to the head, and again the big fellow collapsed.

As Buddy hit the canvas, the timekeeper stood up at the side of the ring and started to count. Baer, to all intents and purposes, was out. But as the seconds were tolled off, he began to show signs of life. As the count reached nine, Buddy made it, just as the bell clanged the end of the round. In all the noise and excitement, however, neither of the principals heard the gong, and as Baer wobbled to his feet, Louis nailed him with a vicious right that dropped Buddy to the canvas again.

Ancil Hoffman, Baer's manager, immediately rushed into the ring and demanded that Louis be disqualified. Meanwhile, Buddy's seconds hauled the unconscious fighter to his corner and worked frantically over him. He was still very groggy when the bell sounded to start the seventh round, and Hoffman refused to permit his charge to come out of the corner. He insisted that Referee Donovan declare Buddy the winner on a foul. Donovan refused and ordered Hoffman out of the ring. When Hoffman failed to leave, Donovan promptly announced Louis the winner.

Joe's victory over Baer marked the champion's sixth bout in six months. It had been a busy and wearying campaign of continuous training and fighting, but Louis wasn't prepared as yet to call it quits. He wanted to keep going. But the problem now confronting promoter Jacobs was to find a suitable opponent for the Bomber.

Billy Conn, brilliant light-heavyweight champion, had been clamoring for a crack at Louis. A flashy boxer, he had been enjoying consistent success against the bigger fellows, and a twelve-round kayo of Bob Pastor in Madison Square Garden had convinced him of his ability to cope with Louis.

But Jacobs was doubtful. Clever and speedy though he was, Conn did not appear to be heavy enough, strong enough, or rugged enough for the powerful heavyweight king.

Louis, however, wanted a June fight. Since Conn shaped up as the only possible opponent among the men willing to meet the champion, the match was arranged for the Polo Grounds. Nearly fifty-five thousand spectators were on hand for the battle.

Louis started as if he intended to finish his lighter opponent early, and in the first two rounds Conn was subjected to terrific body punishment. But Billy stood up gamely under the bombardment, and in the third his speed and sharp left hooks began to make themselves felt. The Pittsburgher held his own in that frame and actually had the better of Louis in the fourth. Conn was jolted several times in the next three frames, but he fought back doggedly.

As the eighth round got under way, it was obvious that Louis, not Conn, was tiring. Perhaps the wear and tear of his "Bum-of-the-Month Club" activities were the cause. In any case, Joe was wilting perceptibly, and Conn gradually but surely whittled down the champion's lead.

Louis was near exhaustion in the twelfth round, as Conn smothered him with a veritable deluge of flying leather. Toward the close, Billy ripped over a left hook to the chin, and Joe, legs buckling, eyes glassy, reeled back to the ropes. The champion was in bad condition at the bell.

Conn, cocky and confident, opened the thirteenth round by scoring with a one-two to Louis' face, then waded in with a vicious left hook to the body. He wanted to kayo the champ. Louis poked out a left that drew blood from Billy's nose and whipped over a right that grazed the Pittsburgher's chin. Conn came back to outslug the titleholder in a savage exchange. As Billy piled in, Louis nailed him with a right to the head. The Pittsburgher staggered.

Louis was never one to ignore opportunity. This was his moment. And he knew how to use it.

A right uppercut snapped Billy's head back. A volley of rights and lefts dropped the Pittsburgher to the canvas.

Conn struggled desperately to rise. But he could not make it before Referee Eddie Joseph had finished his count. The time of the round was two minutes, fifty-eight seconds.

Except for a brief visit to Minneapolis and a one-round kayo of Jim Robinson in an exhibition match in July, Louis forgot about boxing until he was notified by Jacobs that Lou Nova had been named as his opponent at the Polo Grounds on September 20.

On the strength of two knockout victories over Max Baer, first at the Yankee Stadium, then in Madison Square Garden, Nova had established himself as worthy of a championship match. A former amateur star, he was a good boxer, a fair puncher, and endowed with exceptional confidence. He was also a student of the occult. His glib comments on Yoga in general, and, in particular, on a mysterious weapon of his very own that he called the "cosmic punch," were turned into excellent ballyhoo. This combination of assets helped to attract 56,549 spectators and to swell the gate to 583,821 dollars. Louis' end, amounting to 193,274 dollars, lifted his total ring earnings above the 2,000,000-dollar mark.

The bout itself was tame and uneventful until the sixth round, when Nova made one of his infrequent gestures of aggression. After a slow start, the Californian scored with a short right that shook up Louis. More angry than hurt, Joe fired a vicious left hook, but missed. Nova, encouraged, tried again with a right that grazed the champion's chin. Once more Louis missed with a left.

Then it happened! The Louis right, with all its potent authority, suddenly lashed out and landed squarely on Nova's chin. It was a terrific wallop, and the challenger went down with a thud. Lou groped feebly for the ropes with one hand and at nine managed to stagger to his feet. But his knees were wobbly, and he was obviously befogged.

Nova instinctively covered up and tried to back away from harm. Around the ring the champion battered his reeling opponent, belaboring him with rights and lefts that opened deep gashes over both eyes. As the challenger sagged on the ropes in a neutral corner, Referee Arthur Donovan stepped in and stopped the massacre one second before the bell.

The victory over Nova represented Louis' nineteenth defense of the heavyweight title in four years and three months, a record for championship engagements never approached by any other heavyweight.

Then came the Japanese attack on Pearl Harbor. Joe immediately offered his services to the Army but was told to await further advices.

Not long after the war started, promoter Jacobs was approached by the United States Navy with a request to stage a bout for its relief fund. Jacobs got in touch with Louis. He said he would be glad to contribute his services.

Jacobs decided that Buddy Baer, on the strength of his fine showing against the champion in Washington, would make an ideal opponent. Baer was acceptable to Louis, who agreed to turn over his entire purse, less training expenses, to the fund. The match was arranged for Madison Square Garden January 9, 1942.

Baer had given Louis stiff opposition in their first battle but he proved an easy victim in the return match. Joe required only two minutes, fifty-four seconds of the first round to polish off the California giant. It was officially announced that 18,870 customers had paid a total of 189,700 dollars to see the bout.

Having contributed more than seventy thousand dollars to the Navy fund, Louis was next approached to help a similar cause for the Army. Meanwhile Joe, notified by the draft board in Chicago, where he was now living, that he had been classified 1-A, didn't wait for the call to service but entered the Army immediately in New York City.

It was late in February, a month after Joe's induction, that Promoter Jacobs and Army officials announced that Louis had been matched with Abe Simon in the Garden for March 27, with the champion's purse going to the relief fund.

Simon, mammoth New Yorker, had given Louis a stiff argument in Detroit a year before, but Joe had little difficulty with Abe this time. The champion won by a knockout in the seventh. The crowd, announced as 18,220, paid 132,430 dollars to see the fight. Joe's purse, contributed to the Army fund, amounted to about 75,000 dollars.

The Simon fight was Joe's first encounter as a professional that lacked the personal supervision of his beloved Jack Blackburn. Jack, who had been ailing for some time, was critically ill in a Chicago hospital. But the old warrior listened to the fight on the radio and was cheered immeasurably when he heard Joe's voice, at the finish, saying, "I hope you're satisfied, Chappie." A month later Jack was dead.

Louis was determined to become a good soldier. The Army first decided to make a cavalryman of him, and he was sent to Fort Riley, Kansas. But soon the big brass decided that Joe, as heavyweight champion, would be of more use in the field of morale and entertainment, and he was assigned to give boxing exhibitions and referee bouts between other soldiers at various camps.

On January 10, 1944, Joe began an extensive tour overseas. He went first to England. From there he went to Africa and then to Europe, often visiting the front lines.

On October 11, 1944, having traveled more than thirty thousand miles, the Brown Bomber returned from abroad. During the ten months that he was away, nearly five million servicemen saw him. For his services on behalf of the men in uniform, he received a citation from the government. During the war, as before and after, he remained a true champion.

Louis never kept close track of the number of exhibitions he gave during his Army hitch. Once, when asked to make an estimate, the Brown Bomber answered, "Must have been about a thousand, I guess."

Out of the service, Louis found himself involved in one of the hottest "naturals" the boxing profession ever had known. During his years in the Army, a return match with Billy Conn had been built up into tremendous proportions.

The bout was billed for June 19, 1946, at the Yankee Stadium. Jacobs set a ringside price of one hundred dollars. He predicted that the match would shatter all previous ones for receipts and hit close to the three-million mark.

Louis, when he started training, had reached the age of thirty-two, which placed him rather on the elderly side as modern boxers go. He had been away from active competition for nearly four years. What had the long layoff and the encroaching years done to him? Would he be the same old devastating fighter the public had known in the prewar era?

Joe set himself a rigid training program. At his camp in Pompton Lakes, New Jersey, with Mannie Seamon in charge, a formidable set of sparring partners had been rounded up.

Joe didn't look too well in his workouts. He admitted it frankly. He was rusty. That was what disturbed him, along with the thought that he might not be able to go the full fifteen rounds. "That's a long way to go when you're not used to it," he said.

But Joe's earnest preparation overcame the obstacles. He entered the ring in excellent condition and with confidence that he could overcome his antagonist.

It was the opposition that failed. Billy was a bitter disappointment. He made few offensive gestures. Louis, boxing warily, wasting little motion, stalking Conn relentlessly, finally got within range in the sixth round. He ripped a right to Billy's body, and the challenger sagged to one knee.

That was the beginning of the end. Louis speeded up in the seventh and caught Conn in the eighth. Coming out of a clinch, Joe hooked a left to the head and scored with a hard right. Louis then cracked home another right that drew blood from Conn's mouth. Once he had Conn going, Louis wasted no time in finishing him. A furious assault battered the Pittsburgher to the canvas, where he was counted out in two minutes, twenty-nine seconds.

The attendance fell considerably short of expectations. Even so, the turnout of 45,265 contributed 1,925,564 dollars, the second-largest receipts in all boxing history. The gate ranked second only to that of the Tunney-Dempsey match in Chicago, which drew 2,658,660 dollars.

Mike Jacobs now looked over the field of available heavyweights and decided that Tami Mauriello was the best opponent in sight. Mauriello was outstanding among the big fellows then in operation. A fair boxer and a dangerous puncher, he had polished off practically all the ranking heavies, and while he was conceded little better than an outside chance with Louis, it was felt that his gameness and hitting ability made him worthy of a try. The bout was set for September 18, 1946, at the Yankee Stadium.

The battle had gone only five or six seconds when Tami fired a right-hander that nailed Joe flush on the chin. Joe, off balance, went flying back against the ropes, and the 38,494 who paid a total of 335,063 dollars were stunned by the champion's undignified behavior. Joe was hurt, but Mauriello was too slow in following up his momentary advantage. By the time Tami snapped out of it, Joe had safely passed the danger spot.

Louis promptly went to work on Mauriello. A left hook to the jaw shook Tami to his heels. Another left, followed by a crushing right, toppled Mauriello near a neutral corner.

After taking a count of five, Mauriello was up, only to run into another blizzard of flying leather. He sank to his knees for another count, but at nine he pulled himself to his feet. Again the champion ripped into him with both fists, and again Tami went to the canvas.

Mauriello tried gamely to pull himself up. But though the spirit was willing, the flesh was weak. He fell against the ropes, and Referee Arthur Donovan tolled off the fatal ten.

With that fight out of the way, Louis decided to go on an exhibition tour. After paying deferred income taxes and taking care of prewar indebtedness to Mike Jacobs, he needed ready cash and figured that the exhibitions would be easy pickings. And they were.

He picked up thirty thousand dollars for six rounds in Honolulu, where he started the tour less than a month after his knockout of Mauriello. A fortnight later, he appeared in Mexico City against Perk Daniels in a four-rounder for which he had been guaranteed twenty-five thousand dollars.

Then came a tour of Central and South America, which began on February 7, 1947, in Mexico City with Arturo Godoy. Louis appeared in San Salvador, Panama, Chile, Colombia, and Cuba. The Carribbean jaunt netted him around 120,000 dollars.

With the windup of the exhibitions, Joe again sought action in a championship bout. Joe Baksi, then the ranking contender, was Louis' choice, but Baksi, offered a match, turned it down.

Louis was on the verge of retiring for the year, when concerted efforts on the part of the Garden and the Twentieth Century Sporting Club made the Bomber change his mind. He accepted Jersey Joe Walcott, veteran Negro heavyweight, as his opponent.

The bout took place in the Garden on December 5, 1947, and to the astonishment of an overflow gathering Jersey Joe went the limit and came within the proverbial hair's breadth of winning the championship.

The referee gave Walcott the bout, but the two judges saved the title for Louis by voting in his favor. The spectators and the millions who listened in generally favored Walcott. Jersey Joe was also favored by the majority of sports writers, who considered Louis a mighty lucky fellow to leave the arena with the crown still resting on his head.

The booing and hissing following the announcement of the winner, the thousands of telegrams and telephone calls that flooded the Boxing Commission, the Garden, the governor's mansion at Albany, and the box office, testified to the belief that the richest prize in pugilism belonged to bald-headed Jersey Joe. Only the Dempsey-Tunney "long count" in Chicago had provoked a greater controversy. Louis himself believed he had lost when the final bell clanged, and for the first time in his career he left the ring with the fans against him.

Joe had undeniably fought the worst battle of his life. He was awkward. He looked foolish as he tried to catch up with the sprinting Jerseyite. His timing was terrible and his co-ordination was lacking. He was listless. He often looked bewildered as he tried to get close enough for action. It was a depressing exhibition from a champion.

Yet it must be acknowledged that it was Joe Walcott's sprinting that made the champion look so foolish and awkward. Though Louis missed continuously, he was making the fight. The bout in many respects was a reminder of the first Louis-Pastor contest, in which Bob had kept away from Joe by circling the ring in every round.

Much of the time the milling was dull. But the bright moments were very bright indeed, and the gallery was amply rewarded by them. Three of the fifteen rounds were thrillers—the first, fourth and ninth.

In the opening session Walcott floored Joe with a clean right to the jaw after Louis had shaken the challenger with a right. Louis came up in a jiffy but looked bewildered as he faced his opponent. The Bomber, befuddled, tossed rights and lefts at his opponent's jaw, but they missed, while Walcott continued a steady rain of rights and lefts to the face and forehead. It was a round that caused the spectators to gasp in astonishment and made them feel that the show would be a corker, no matter how short it might be.

In the fourth round the crowd got its greatest thrill when,

after a short mix-up, Walcott again downed the titleholder with a solid right. The fans were in an uproar at the spectacle of the champion on his hands and knees. When Louis got up, after taking a count of seven, he held the challenger until Referee Ruby Goldstein ordered the men to break. It was one of the few times in Joe's career that he, rather than the other man, went into a clinch. Walcott didn't press his advantage after the break. He feared the outcome and was content to outbox his man instead of forcing him to fight it out while he was still groggy. Jersey Joe thus lost his most promising chance to knock out the riddled Bomber.

There was little excitement between the fourth and the ninth, in which Louis showed at his best. Thereafter, Jersey Joe sprinted around the ring, tossing a jab here and there and keeping out of danger, while Louis kept following him in a futile endeavor to nail him.

In the days immediately following Joe's depressing exhibition, it was rumored that the champion had fought his last battle. It was also rumored that Louis would shortly give Walcott a return match. The second rumor was correct. A championship bout was arranged for June 25, 1948, in Yankee Stadium.

For ten of the scheduled fifteen rounds, the 42,267 customers who had paid 841,739 dollars into the treasury of the Twentieth Century Sporting Club put up with as tedious an exhibition of fumbling and bumbling as most of them could remember. The fight lacked even the bright spots of the previous Walcott-Louis encounter, and the chorus of booing and hissing grew louder with each succeeding round. Referee Frank Fullam pleaded with the principals to give the fans some action.

It was not so much the coaxing of the referee that suddenly brought the spectators to life. Instead, it was Joe's realization that he might lose the fight on decision if he didn't wake up. And he was probably right in thinking so, for a check of the judges' cards after the bout showed that both of them had the challenger leading on points at the end of the tenth.

Joe remembered his close call in his first match with Jersey Joe, and in the eleventh he suddenly swept into action. When Walcott made one of his few offensive gestures of the fight, he

gave Louis the necessary opening. The champion first nailed
Walcott with three fast, numbing straight lefts to the head and
then drove a crushing right to the jaw.

All the fight left the Jerseyite. His legs became rubbery. He
caught a right to the body that brought his guard down, and
then came a hurricane of punches. He tried to hang on, but
nothing could save him from the fury of Louis' attack. Utterly
defenseless, he was spared further punishment only by collapsing
in his tracks. He was counted out in two minutes, fifty-six seconds of the eleventh round.

Joe Louis was still champion of the world. As he left the ring,
he could hear the pleasant thunder of cheers as he had so often
heard it in the past. He had erased the memory of his bad
performance six months before. He was still the Brown Bomber.

Joe Louis had now reigned eleven years as monarch of the
heavyweights. He had defended his crown in twenty-five battles,
twenty-one of which were knockout triumphs. He had scored
fifty-one knockouts in his whole professional career. It was a
magnificent record, and Joe was content. He wanted to retire.

"This is the end," he announced after the Walcott fight. "I
want no more training. I want no more competition."

But though the Brown Bomber was sincere in his intention
to hang up his gloves forever, only a few weeks later he came
out with a revised statement. In effect, he announced that he
would defend his title once more—provided a suitable opponent
could be found.

The key word was "suitable." It meant an opponent of
sufficient caliber to assure a large gate. Joe has always been an
astute businessman. Willing as he was to contribute his entire
earnings of two early wartime fights to relief funds, he has
never been a man to risk the championship without an adequate
guarantee. It was clear to all who knew anything about the
fight game that Louis would never expose his elderly chin to
just any pair of fists. Only the soothing jingle of the cash register
well in advance of a title bout could be expected to lure the
champion into another defense of his crown.

In the fall of 1948 Joe started off on another junket through
the Caribbean. Eighteen months before, he had made a similar

tour and netted more than a hundred thousand dollars from a series of exhibitions. The second tour was an even greater success than the first one had been, and, curious as it may seem on the surface, the success of this tour was one of the principal factors in the Brown Bomber's decision, announced publicly on February 28, 1949, to retire again, this time with all the emphasis of finality. Briefly, this tour had made more money for Joe than he could hope to earn in a fight with the title at stake. The man who had been champion since 1937 found himself in the odd position, through lack of a satisfactory opponent, of having to risk his crown for peanuts—and he wisely decided to call it quits.

At the moment, no fighter remotely to be compared with Joe Louis is in sight. It seems likely that at least three to five years must pass before some still unknown youngster appears who will be worthy of the crown. But somewhere in the United States today another Louis, Tunney, or Dempsey is growing up. Somewhere another Corbett or Jack Johnson is learning to handle his fists. The tradition of the great heavyweights is vital and enduring. Of that I am certain.

HEAVYWEIGHT CHAMPIONSHIP FIGHTS SINCE 1882

FEB. 7, 1882—Paddy Ryan was knocked out by John L. Sullivan at Mississippi City, 9 rounds. Referees, Alex Brewster, Jack Hardy.

JULY 8, 1889—John L. Sullivan beat Jake Kilrain, 75 rounds, Richburg, Miss. (Last bare-knuckle championship fight.) Sullivan scaled 198; Kilrain, 195. Referee, John Fitzpatrick.

SEPT. 7, 1892—James J. Corbett defeated John L. Sullivan at New Orleans, La., 21 rounds. (Used big gloves for first time.) Sullivan weighed 212; Corbett, 178. Referee, John Duffy.

JAN. 25, 1894—James J. Corbett knocked out Charlie Mitchell, Jacksonville, Fla., three rounds. Corbett, 184; Mitchell, 158. Referee, Honest John Kelly.

MAR. 17, 1897—Bob Fitzsimmons knocked out James J. Corbett, Carson City, Nevada, 14 rounds. Corbett, 183; Fitzsimmons, 167. Referee, George Siler.

JUNE 9, 1899—James J. Jeffries knocked out Bob Fitzsimmons, Coney Island, N. Y., 11 rounds. Jeffries, 206; Fitzsimmons, 167. Referee, George Siler.

NOV. 3, 1899—James J. Jeffries defeated Tom Sharkey on points, Coney Island, N. Y., 25 rounds. Jeffries, 215; Sharkey, 183. Referee, George Siler.

MAY 11, 1900—James J. Jeffries knocked out James J. Corbett, Coney Island, N. Y., 23 rounds. Jeffries, 218; Corbett, 188. Referee, Charley White.

NOV. 15, 1901—James J. Jeffries stopped Gus Ruhlin, San Francisco, Cal., 5 rounds. Sponge tossed in ring after bell ended the fifth round. Referee, Harry Corbett.

JULY 25, 1902—James J. Jeffries knocked out Bob Fitzsimmons, San Francisco, Cal., 8 rounds. Jeffries, 219; Fitzsimmons, 172. Referee, Ed Graney.

Aug. 14, 1903—James J. Jeffries knocked out James J. Corbett, San Francisco, Cal., 10 rounds. Jeffries, 220; Corbett, 190. Referee, Ed Graney.

Aug. 25, 1904—James J. Jeffries knocked out Jack Munroe, San Francisco, Cal., 2 rounds. Jeffries, 219; Munroe, 186. Referee, Ed Graney.

Lack of opposition forced Jeffries into retirement in March, 1905. He then named Marvin Hart and Jack Root as the leading contenders and agreed to referee their fight at Reno, Nev., July 3, 1905, with the stipulation that he would term the winner the world heavyweight champion. Hart stopped Root in 12 rounds. Hart, 190; Root, 171.

Feb. 23, 1906—Tommy Burns defeated Marvin Hart, Los Angeles, Cal., 20 rounds. Burns, 180; Hart, 188. Referee, Jim Jeffries.

Burns laid claim to the world title.

Another claimant to the throne was Philadelphia Jack O'Brien, who, on Nov. 28, 1906, at Los Angeles, had fought Burns a 20-round draw, with Jim Jeffries as referee. Burns weighed 172; O'Brien, 153½.

May 8, 1907—Tommy Burns eliminated Jack O'Brien by defeating him at Los Angeles, Cal., 20 rounds. Burns, 180; O'Brien, 167. Referee, Charles Eyton. Burns was generally acknowledged as world champion.

July 4, 1907—Tommy Burns knocked out Bill Squires, Colma, Cal., 1 round. Burns, 181; Squires, 180. Referee, James J. Jeffries.

Dec. 2, 1907—Tommy Burns knocked out Gunner Moir, London, England, 10 rounds. Burns, 177; Moir, 204. Referee, Eugene Corri.

Feb. 10, 1908—Tommy Burns knocked out Jack Palmer, London, England, 4 rounds. Referee, Eugene Corri.

Mar. 17, 1908—Tommy Burns knocked out Jem Roche, Dublin, Ireland, 1 round. Referee, R. P. Watson.

Apr. 18, 1908—Tommy Burns knocked out Jewey Smith, Paris, France, 5 rounds.

June 13, 1908—Tommy Burns knocked out Bill Squires, Paris, France, 8 rounds. Burns, 184; Squires, 183.

Aug. 24, 1908—Tommy Burns knocked out Bill Squires, Sydney,

New South Wales, 13 rounds. Burns, 181; Squires, 184. Referee, H. C. Nathan.

(These victories clinched world recognition for Burns.)

SEPT. 2, 1908—Tommy Burns knocked out Bill Lang, Melbourne, Australia, 2 rounds. Burns, 183; Lang. 187. Referee, Hugh McIntosh.

DEC. 26, 1908—Jack Johnson knocked out Tommy Burns, Sydney, New South Wales, 14 rounds. Johnson, 192; Burns, 168. Referee, Hugh McIntosh. Police stopped fight.

MAY 19, 1909—Jack Johnson and Philadelphia Jack O'Brien fought six rounds, Philadelphia. No decision. Johnson, 205; O'Brien, 161.

JUNE 30, 1909—Jack Johnson and Tony Ross fought 6 rounds, Pittsburgh, Pa. No decision. Johnson, 207; Ross, 214.

SEPT. 9, 1909—Jack Johnson fought 10 rounds, no decision, with Al Kaufmann, San Francisco, Cal. Johnson, 209; Kaufmann, 191. Referee, Ed Smith.

OCT. 16, 1909—Jack Johnson knocked out Stanley Ketchel, Colma, Cal., 12 rounds. Johnson 205½; Ketchel, 170¼. Referee, Jack Welch.

JULY 4, 1910—Jack Johnson knocked out Jim Jeffries, Reno, Nevada, 15 rounds. Referee, Tex Rickard. (Jeffries came out of retirement in an effort to regain title, but failed.) Johnson, 208; Jeffries, 227.

JULY 4, 1912—Jack Johnson won from Jim Flynn, 9 rounds, Las Vegas, N. M. Johnson, 195½; Flynn, 175. Referee, Ed Smith. (Police stopped bout.)

1913—Jack Johnson had trouble with the U. S. government during latter part of 1912, so the heavyweight champion went to Europe and remained in exile for several years. In the interval a tourney for white heavyweights was held in Los Angeles, Cal., and Luther McCarty, after defeating Al Kaufmann, Jim Flynn, and Al Palzer, was proclaimed champion white heavyweight of America.

On May 24, 1913, at Calgary, Canada, McCarty collapsed in the first round of a bout with Arthur Pelkey, and died from a brain hemorrhage. Ed Smith, referee.

Nov. 28, 1913—Jack Johnson knocked out Andre Spoul, 2 rounds, Paris, France. Referee, Georges Carpentier.

Dec. 9, 1913—Jack Johnson drew with Battling Jim Johnson, Paris, France, 10 rounds. (Referee called it a draw when Jack Johnson declared he had broken his arm.)

Jan. 1, 1914—Gunboat Smith won white heavyweight title by knocking out Arthur Pelkey in 15 rounds, San Francisco, Cal. Referee, Ed Smith.

June 27, 1914—Jack Johnson defeated Frank Moran, Paris, France, 20 rounds. Johnson, 221; Moran, 203. Referee, Georges Carpentier.

July 16, 1914—Georges Carpentier won white heavyweight title from Gunboat Smith on a foul, 6 rounds, London, England. Referee, Eugene Corri.

April 5, 1915—Jess Willard knocked out Jack Johnson, Havana, Cuba, 26 rounds. Willard, 230; Johnson, 205½. Referee, Jack Welch.

March 25, 1916—Jess Willard fought 10 rounds with Frank Moran, New York City. No decision. Willard, 225; Moran, 203. Referee, Charley White.

July 4, 1919—Jack Dempsey knocked out Jess Willard, Toledo, Ohio, 3 rounds. Dempsey, 187; Willard, 245. Referee, Ollie Pecord.

Sept. 6, 1920—Jack Dempsey knocked out Billy Miske, Benton Harbor, Michigan, 3 rounds. Dempsey, 185; Miske, 187.

Dec. 14, 1920—Jack Dempsey knocked out Bill Brennan, New York City, 12 rounds. Dempsey, 188¼; Brennan, 197. Referee, H. Haukaup.

July 2, 1921—Jack Dempsey knocked out Georges Carpentier, Jersey City, N. J., 4 rounds. Dempsey; 188; Carpentier, 172. Referee, Harry Ertle.

July 4, 1923—Jack Dempsey won on points from Tom Gibbons, Shelby, Montana, 15 rounds. Dempsey, 188; Gibbons, 175½. Referee, Jack Dougherty.

Sept. 14, 1923—Jack Dempsey knocked out Luis Firpo, New York City, 2 rounds. Dempsey, 192½; Firpo, 216½. Referee, Jack Gallagher.

SEPT. 23, 1926—Gene Tunney won world's heavyweight title from Jack Dempsey on points, Philadelphia, 10 rounds. Dempsey, 190; Tunney, 189½. Referee, Pop Reilly.

SEPT. 22, 1927—Gene Tunney again defeated Jack Dempsey on points, Chicago, Ill., 10 rounds. Dempsey, 192½; Tunney, 189½. Referee, Dave Barry.

JULY 23, 1928—Gene Tunney knocked out Tom Heeney, New York City, 11 rounds, and the following week he announced his retirement. Tunney, 192; Heeney, 203½. Referee, Ed Forbes. (Tunney retired after this victory.)

JULY 12, 1930—Max Schmeling and Jack Sharkey fought for the right to occupy heavyweight throne vacated by Tunney, New York City. In round 4 Schmeling was declared winner on a foul. Schmeling, 188; Sharkey, 197. Referee, Jim Crowley.

JULY 3, 1931—Max Schmeling stopped Young Stribling, Cleveland, Ohio, 15 rounds. Schmeling, 189; Stribling, 186½. Referee, George Blake.

JUNE 21, 1932—Jack Sharkey defeated Max Schmeling on points, Long Island City, 15 rounds. Sharkey, 205; Schmeling, 188. Referee, Gunboat Smith.

JUNE 29, 1933—Primo Carnera knocked out Jack Sharkey, Long Island City, 6 rounds. Carnera, 260½; Sharkey, 201. Referee, Arthur Donovan.

OCT. 22, 1933—Primo Carnera defeated Paulino Uzcudun on points, Rome, Italy, 15 rounds. Carnera, 259½; Uzcudun, 229¼. Referee, Maurice Nicord.

MARCH 1, 1934—Primo Carnera defeated Tommy Loughran on points, Miami, Florida, 15 rounds. Carnera, 270; Loughran, 186. Referee, Leo Shea.

JUNE 14, 1934—Max Baer knocked out Primo Carnera, Long Island City, 11 rounds. Baer, 209½; Carnera, 263¼. Referee, Arthur Donovan.

JUNE 13, 1935—Jim Braddock defeated Max Baer on points, Long Island City, 15 rounds. Baer, 209½; Braddock, 193¾. Referee, Jack McAvoy.

June 22, 1937—Joe Louis knocked out Jim Braddock, Chicago, Ill., 8 rounds. Louis, 197¼; Braddock, 197. Referee, Tommy Thomas.

Aug. 30, 1937—Joe Louis defeated Tommy Farr on points, New York City, 15 rounds, Louis, 197; Farr, 204¼. Referee, Arthur Donovan.

Feb. 23, 1938—Joe Louis knocked out Nathan Mann, New York City, 3 rounds. Louis, 200; Mann, 193½. Referee, Arthur Donovan.

April 1, 1938—Joe Louis knocked out Harry Thomas, Chicago, Ill., 5 rounds. Louis, 202½; Thomas, 196. Referee, Dave Miller.

June 22, 1938—Joe Louis knocked out Max Schmeling, New York City, 1 round. Louis, 198¾; Schmeling, 193. Referee, Arthur Donovan.

Jan. 25, 1939—Joe Louis knocked out John Henry Lewis, New York City, 1 round. Louis, 200¼; Lewis, 180¾. Referee, Arthur Donovan.

April 17, 1939—Joe Louis knocked out Jack Roper, Los Angeles, Cal., 1 round. Louis, 201¼; Roper, 204¾. Referee, George Blake.

June 28, 1939—Joe Louis knocked out Tony Galento, New York City, 4 rounds. Louis, 200¾; Galento, 233¾. Referee, Arthur Donovan.

Sept. 20, 1939—Joe Louis knocked out Bob Pastor at Detroit, Mich., 11 rounds. Louis, 200; Pastor, 183. Referee, Sam Hennessey.

Feb. 9, 1940—Joe Louis defeated Arturo Godoy on points, New York City, 15 rounds. Louis, 203; Godoy, 202. Referee, Arthur Donovan.

March 29, 1940—Joe Louis knocked out Johnny Paycheck, New York City, 2 rounds. Louis, 200½; Paycheck, 187½. Referee, Arthur Donovan.

June 20, 1940—Joe Louis knocked out Arturo Godoy, New York City, 8 rounds. Louis, 199; Godoy, 201½. Referee, Billy Cavanaugh.

Dec. 16, 1940—Joe Louis knocked out Al McCoy, Boston, Mass., 6 rounds. Louis, 202¼; McCoy, 180¾. Referee, Johnny Martin.

Jan. 31, 1941—Joe Louis knocked out Red Burman, New York

City, 5 rounds. Louis, 202½; Burman, 188. Referee, Arthur Donovan.

FEB. 17, 1941—Joe Louis knocked out Gus Dorazio, Philadelphia, Pa., 2 rounds, Louis, 203½; Dorazio, 193½. Referee, Irvin Kutcher.

MARCH 21, 1941—Joe Louis knocked out Abe Simon, Detroit, Mich., 13 rounds. Louis, 202; Simon, 254½. Referee, Sam Hennessey.

APRIL 8, 1941—Joe Louis knocked out Tony Musto, St. Louis, Mo., 9 rounds. Louis, 203¼; Musto, 199½. Referee, Arthur Donovan.

MAY 23, 1941—Joe Louis knocked out Buddy Baer, Washington, D. C., 7 rounds. Louis, 201¾; Baer, 237½. Referee, Arthur Donovan.

JUNE 18, 1941—Joe Louis knocked out Billy Conn, New York City, 13 rounds. Louis, 199½; Conn, 174. Referee, Eddie Joseph.

SEPT. 29, 1941—Joe Louis knocked out Lou Nova, New York City, 6 rounds. Louis, 202¼; Nova, 202½. Referee, Arthur Donovan.

JAN. 9, 1942—Joe Louis defeated Buddy Baer, in Naval Relief Fund bout, New York City, 1 round. Donated purse to Naval Relief Fund. Louis, 206½; Baer, 250. Referee, Frank Fullam. (Baer was disqualified when his manager refused to leave the ring after claiming his man had been fouled.)

MARCH 27, 1942—Joe Louis knocked out Abe Simon in Army Relief Fund bout, New York City, 6 rounds. Donated purse to Army Relief Fund. Louis, 207½; Simon, 255¼. Referee, Eddie Joseph.

JUNE 19, 1946—Joe Louis knocked out Billy Conn, New York City, 8 rounds. Louis, 207; Conn, 182. Referee, Eddie Joseph.

SEPT. 18, 1946—Joe Louis knocked out Tami Mauriello, New York City, 1 round. Louis, 211¼; Mauriello, 198. Referee, Arthur Donovan.

DEC. 5, 1947—Joe Louis defeated Jersey Joe Walcott on points, New York City, 15 rounds. Louis, 211; Walcott, 194½. Referee, Ruby Goldstein. Split decision, Referee voted for Walcott, judges voted for Louis.

JUNE 25, 1948—Joe Louis knocked out Jersey Joe Walcott, New York City, 11 rounds. Louis, 213½; Walcott, 194¾. Referee, Frank Fullam.

RULES OF BOXING

BROUGHTON'S RULES, 1743

1. That a square of a yard be chalked in the middle of the stage; and at every fresh set-to after a fall, or being parted from the rails, each second is to bring his man to the side of the square and place him opposite to the other, and till they are fairly set-to at the lines, it shall not be lawful for the one to strike the other.

2. That, in order to prevent any disputes, the time a man lies after a fall, if the second does not bring his man to the side of the square, within the space of half a minute, he shall be deemed a beaten man.

3. That in every main battle, no person whatever shall be upon the stage, except the principals and their seconds; the same rule to be observed in by-battles, except that in the latter, Mr. Broughton is allowed to be upon the stage to keep decorum and to assist gentlemen to get to their places; provided always he does not interfere with the battle; and whoever presumes to infringe these rules, to be turned immediately out of the house. Everybody is to quit the stage as soon as the champions are stripped, before they set to.

4. That no champion be deemed beaten unless he fails coming up to the line in the limited time; or that his own second declares him beaten. No second is to be allowed to ask his man's adversary any questions, or advise him to give out.

5. That, in by-battles, the winning man to have two thirds of the money given, which shall be publicly divided upon the stage, notwithstanding any private agreements to the contrary.

6. That, to prevent disputes, in every main battle, the principals shall, on the coming on the stage, choose from among the gentlemen present, two umpires, who shall absolutely decide all disputes, that may arise about the battle; and if the two umpires cannot agree, the said umpires to choose a third, who is to determine it.

7. That no person is to hit his adversary when he is down, or seize him by the ham, or breeches, or any part below the waist; a man on his knees is to be reckoned down.

LONDON PRIZE RING RULES, 1838
(REVISED 1853)

1. The ring shall be made on the turf, and shall be four-and-twenty feet square, formed of eight stakes and ropes, the latter extending lines, the uppermost line being four feet from the ground, and the lower two feet from the ground. In the center of the ring a mark to be formed to be termed a scratch.

2. Each man shall be attended to the ring by two seconds and a bottle-holder. The combatants, on shaking hands, shall retire until the seconds have tossed for choice of positions, which adjusted, the winner shall choose at his corner, according to the state of the wind or sun, and conduct his man thereto, the loser taking the opposite diagonal corner.

3. Each man shall be provided with a handkerchief of a color suitable to his own fancy, and the seconds shall entwine these handkerchiefs at the upper end of one of the center stakes. These handkerchiefs shall be called "colors" and the winner of the battle, at its conclusion, shall be entitled to their possession as the trophy of victory.

4. The two umpires shall be chosen by the seconds or backers to watch the progress of the battle, and take exception to any breach of the rules hereinafter stated. A referee shall be chosen by the umpires unless otherwise agreed upon, to whom all disputes shall be referred; and the decision of this referee, whatever it may be, shall be final and strictly binding on all parties, whether as to the matter in dispute or the issue of the battle. The referee shall be provided with a watch for the purpose of calling time; the calling of that referee only to be attended to, and no other person whatever shall interfere in calling time. The referee shall withhold all opinion till appealed to by the umpires and the umpires strictly abide by his decision without dispute.

5. On the men being stripped it shall be the duty of the seconds to examine their drawers, and if any objection arises as to the insertion of improper substances therein, they shall appeal to their umpires, who, with the concurrence of the referee, shall direct what alterations shall be made.

6. The spikes in the fighting boots shall be confined to three in number, which shall not exceed three-eighths of an inch from the sole of the boot, and shall not be less than one-eighth of an inch broad at the point; two to be placed in the broadest part of the sole and one in the heel; and in the event of a man wearing any other spikes, either in toes or elsewhere, he shall be compelled either to remove them, or provide other boots properly spiked, the penalty for refusal to be a loss of the stakes.

7. Both men being ready, each shall be conducted to that side of the scratch next his corner previously chosen; and, the seconds on the one side and the men on the other, having shaken hands, the former shall immediately leave the ring, and there remain until the round be finished, on no pretense whatever approaching their principals during the round without permission from the referee, the penalty to be the loss of the battle to the offending parties.

8. At the conclusion of the round when one or both of the men shall be down, the seconds shall step into the ring and carry or conduct their principal to his corner, there affording him the necessary assistance, and no person whatever be permitted to interfere in this duty.

9. On the expiration of thirty seconds the referee appointed shall cry "Time," upon which each man shall rise from the knee of his second and walk to his own side of the scratch unaided; the seconds immediately leaving the ring. The penalty for either of them remaining eight seconds after the call of time to be the loss of the battle to his principal; and either man failing to be at the scratch within eight seconds shall be deemed to have lost the battle.

10. On no consideration whatever shall any person except the seconds and the referee be permitted to enter the ring during the battle, nor till it shall have been concluded; and in the event of such unfair practice, or the ropes or stakes being removed or disturbed, it shall be in the power of the referee to award the victory to the man who, in his honest opinion, shall have the best of the contest.

11. The seconds shall not interfere, advise, or direct the adversary of their principal, and shall refrain from all offensive and irritating expressions, in all respects conducting themselves with order and decorum, and confine themselves to the diligent and careful discharge of their duties to their principals.

12. In picking up their men, should the seconds willfully injure

the antagonist of their principal, the latter shall be deemed to have forfeited the battle on the decision of the referee.

13. It shall be a fair "stand-up fight," and if either man shall willfully throw himself down without receiving a blow, whether blows shall have been previously exchanged or not, he shall be deemed to have lost the battle; but this rule shall not apply to a man who in a close slips down from the grasp of his opponent to avoid punishment, or from obvious accident or weakness.

14. Butting with the head shall be deemed a foul, and the party resorting to this practice shall be deemed to have lost the battle.

15. A blow struck when a man is thrown or down shall be deemed foul. A man with one knee and one hand on the ground, or with both knees on the ground, shall be deemed down, and a blow given in either of these positions shall be considered foul, providing always that, when in such position, the man so down shall not himself strike, or attempt to strike.

16. A blow struck below the waistband shall be deemed foul, and in a close, seizing an antagonist below the waist by the thigh or otherwise shall be deemed foul.

17. All attempts to inflict injury by gouging or tearing the flesh with the fingers or nails, and biting shall be deemed foul.

18. Kicking or deliberately falling on an antagonist with the knees or otherwise, when down, shall be deemed foul.

19. All bets shall be paid as the battle money after the fight is awarded.

20. The referee and umpires shall take their positions in front of the center stake outside the ropes.

21. Due notice shall be given by the stakeholder of the day and place where the battle money is to be given up, and be exonerated from all responsibility upon obeying the direction of the referee; all parties to be strictly bound by these rules, and in future all articles of agreement for a contest be entered into with a strict and willing adherence to the letter and spirit of these rules.

22. In the event of magisterial or other interference, or in the case of darkness coming on, the referee (or stakeholder in case no referee has been chosen) shall have the power to name the time and place for the next meeting, if possible, on the same day, or as soon after as may be. In naming the second or third place, the nearest spot shall be selected to the original place of fighting where there is a chance of its being fought out.

23. Should the fight not be decided on the day, all bets shall be

drawn, unless the fight shall be resumed the same week, between Sunday and Sunday, in which case the referee's duties shall continue and the bets shall stand and be decided by the event. The battle money shall remain in the hands of the stakeholder until fairly won or lost by a fight, unless a draw be mutually agreed upon, or, in case of a postponement, one of the principals shall be absent, when the man in the ring shall be awarded the stakes.

24. Any pugilist voluntarily quitting the ring previous to the deliberate judgment of the referee being obtained shall be deemed to have lost the fight.

25. On an objection being made by the seconds or umpires the men shall retire to their corners, and there remain until the decision of the appointed authorities shall be obtained; if pronounced "foul" the battle shall be at an end, but if "fair," time shall be called by the party appointed, and the men absent from the scratch eight seconds after shall be deemed to have lost the fight. The decision in all cases is to be given promptly and irrevocably, for which purpose the umpires and the referee should be invariably close together.

26. If a man leaves the ring, either to escape punishment or for any other purpose without the permission of the referee, unless he is involuntarily forced out, he shall forfeit the battle.

27. The use of hard substances, such as stones or sticks, or of resin in the hand during the battle, shall be deemed foul, and on the requisition of the seconds of either man, the accused shall open his hands for the examination of the referee.

28. Hugging on the ropes shall be deemed foul. A man held by the neck against the stakes or upon or against the ropes, shall be considered down, and all interference with him in that position shall be deemed foul. If a man in any way makes use of the ropes or stakes to aid him in squeezing his adversary, he shall be deemed the loser of the battle, and if a man in close reaches the ground with his knee, his adversary shall immediately loose him or lose the battle.

29. All glove or room fights to be as nearly possible in conformity with the foregoing rules.

Note on the Marquis of Queensberry

John Sholto Douglas, eighth Marquis of Queensberry, who succeeded to the title in 1858 and died in 1900, is one of the immortals of the sport of boxing. For it is the rules known by his name that in essence still govern both amateur and professional fighting.

Though variations have been adopted by boxing commissions in different communities, no basic changes have been made in the rules that prescribe ring conduct since fighting with gloves superseded bare-knuckle encounters.

It is only proper to note that the Marquis of Queensberry, though he was devoted to sports, and especially to boxing, was not really the author of the celebrated code that first appeared in 1867. The rules were written by John Graham Chambers, a member of the Amateur Athletic Club, who, in accordance with the convention of the times, sought a noble patron to lend his name. Queensberry graciously acquiesced and thereby gained a lasting fame that he does not wholly deserve.

The importance of the Marquis of Queensberry Rules lies in their shift of emphasis from the bruising type of fighting that thrived under London Prize Ring Rules to scientific boxing. Wrestling was eliminated, padded gloves took the place of bare knuckles or skin-tight "mufflers," rounds lasted three minutes instead of the time required for a knockdown, and the rest period between rounds was increased from thirty seconds to a full minute.

MARQUIS OF QUEENSBERRY RULES

1. To be a fair stand-up boxing match in a twenty-foot-long ring, or as near that size as practicable.

2. No wrestling or hugging allowed.

3. The rounds to be of three minutes' duration, and one minute time between rounds.

4. If either man fall, through weakness or otherwise, he must get up unassisted, ten seconds to be allowed him to do so, the other man meanwhile to return to his corner, and when the fallen man is on his legs the round is to be resumed and continued until the three minutes have expired. If one man fails to come to the scratch in the ten seconds allowed, it shall be in the power of the referee to give his award in favor of the other man.

5. A man hanging on the ropes in a helpless state, with his toes off the ground, shall be considered down.

6. No seconds or any other person to be allowed in the ring during the rounds.

7. Should the contest be stopped by any unavoidable interference, the referee to name time and place, as soon as possible, for finishing

the contest; so that the match must be won and lost unless the backers of both men agree to draw the stakes.

8. The gloves to be fair-sized boxing gloves of the best quality and new.

9. Should a glove burst or come off, it must be replaced to the referee's satisfaction.

10. A man on one knee is considered down, and if struck is entitled to the stakes.

11. No shoes or boots with sprigs allowed.

12. The contest in all respects to be governed by revised rules of the London Prize Ring.

GLOSSARY OF BOXING TERMS AND RING SLANG

ANNIE OAKLEY   A complimentary ticket. (So called because the tickets have had holes punched in them—as neatly as if they had been shot by the famous markswoman, Annie Oakley.)

BANTAMWEIGHT   A fighter who does not exceed 118 pounds.

BARNEY   A bout in which the principals attempt to give a good exhibition without hurting each other.

BELL   Since the adoption of the Marquis of Queensberry Rules, the beginning and end of each round has been indicated by striking a gong. Before the Queensberry era, when a round ended only after one of the contestants went down, no bell was used; the bout was resumed at the end of thirty seconds with the call of "time" by the referee.

BLOCK   To prevent an opponent's punch from reaching its target by interposing an open glove.

BLOW A DUKE   To lose a fight.

BOBBING   Moving the body up and down.

BODY BLOW   Any blow that lands between the neck and the waistline.

BOTTLEHOLDER   A second. (In the early days of boxing, one of the chief duties of a second was to hold a bottle containing water or a diluted stimulant.)

BOTTOM   Endurance.

BREADBASKET   The abdominal region.

BREAK   To separate after a clinch.

BRUISER   A fighter. (Eighteenth-century British slang.)

BUM   An extremely poor fighter, a ham, a stiff, a tramp.

BUNCH OF FIVES   A fist. (Eighteenth-century British slang.)

BUTTON   The point of the chin.

CARRY THE GUY   To let an inferior opponent last the limit instead of knocking him out.

CATCHWEIGHT   When two boxers of different weights, *e.g.*, lightweight vs. welterweight, are matched, they are said to fight at catchweights.

CHOPPER   A downward blow.

CHOPPING BLOCK   A glutton for punishment.

CLARET   Blood.

CLEAN SHOT   A fair blow to body or head that is not intercepted or deflected by hand, arm, elbow, or shoulder.

CLINCH   To hold or "hug" an opponent.

CLUB FIGHTER   A boxer who has been developed in a certain club and has built up a large following in his own neighborhood.

COASTING   Ceasing to be aggressive after gaining a comfortable lead. Loafing, taking things easy.

COCONUT   The head.

COME TO SCRATCH   See Scratch.

CONK   The head.

COUNTER   A punch delivered after an opponent's lead.

COUNTER PUNCHER   A fighter who habitually waits for an opponent to lead before delivering his own punch.

CRANK   A close student of boxing, a fan.

CROSS   A punch delivered with either hand, though usually the right, as the opponent leads with his opposite hand. It is so called because the blow actually crosses the opponent's leading arm; also, in the early days, a fixed fight.

CROSS BUTTOCK   A maneuver in wrestling (and, before the Queensberry era, in boxing also) whereby one man grasps his opponent under one arm and across the back, takes a step forward with the near foot, and, using his own buttock as a pivot, tosses him.

CUCKOO   Condition of being punchy.

CUTEY   A defensive, safety-first boxer.

DECISION   The official verdict at the termination of a bout. A decision can be on points, by a knockout, by disqualification, by a referee's verdict, by the combined verdict of referee and judges, or in consequence of a fighter's being stopped by injury or by quitting of his own accord.

DOUBLE-CROSS   Two-way skulduggery, whereby a fighter who has been fixed for a barney crosses his opponent and wins the fight. See Fix, Barney.

DUKES   Fists. (Eighteenth-century British slang.)

ELBOWING   Placing the elbow against the throat of an opponent.

FAN   An ardent enthusiast of boxing (or other sport).

FANCY DAN A boxer with good footwork and impressive gestures who lacks real hitting power.

FEATHERWEIGHT A fighter who does not exceed 126 pounds.

FEINT To lead toward one part of the body with the intention of striking another part if the opponent shifts his guard to protect against the original motion.

FIX A prearranged fight. To fake a fight.

FLASH a. A fast puncher. b. A fighter without much substance.

FLYWEIGHT A fighter who does not exceed 112 pounds.

FOUL In modern boxing, any act by a boxer that may incur a penalty, from loss of a round to disqualification. The following are officially designated as fouls:

Hitting below the belt.

Hitting an opponent who is down or in the process of getting up.

Elbowing an opponent.

Holding an opponent or deliberately maintaining a clinch.

Holding with one hand and hitting with the other.

Butting with head or shoulder, or using the knee.

Hitting with the inside, or butt, of the hand, the wrist, or the elbow.

Hitting or flicking with an open glove.

Wrestling or roughing at the ropes.

Going down without being hit.

Employing the pivot or rabbit punch.

Hitting deliberately over the kidneys during a clinch.

Using profane or abusive language.

Failing to obey instructions of the referee.

Employing any sort of tactics beyond the bounds of fair and sportsmanlike boxing.

GLASS JAW A boxer is said to have a glass jaw if he is easily knocked out by a punch in the vicinity of his chin.

GO INTO A TANK See Take a dive.

HAM An extremely poor fighter, a bum, a stiff, a tramp.

HANDLERS A fighter's seconds.

HAYMAKER A knockout punch.

HEAVYWEIGHT A fighter who exceeds 175 pounds. (There is no top limit.)

HEEL To push the inner side of a glove into an opponent's face.

HIT OUT OF DISTANCE To miss.

Hook A punch delivered at close range from the side, with the elbow hooked.

Horizontal fighter One frequently knocked out.

In-and-outer A fighter who fails to show consistent form.

Infighting Fighting at close range.

Jacobs Beach An area close to Madison Square Garden, New York City, named for Mike Jacobs, the promoter. It is the principal market place for fighters, managers, promoters, and their satellites.

Jab A straight punch, normally (in the case of right-handed boxers) delivered with the left hand, to either head or body.

Kidney punch A blow in the back over the kidneys. During a clinch, such a blow is not permitted.

Knockout A blow that floors a fighter for ten seconds, thereby giving victory to his opponent.

Lightweight A fighter who does not exceed 135 pounds.

Light heavyweight A fighter who does not exceed 175 pounds.

Lug A bum, a ham. (The word is also sometimes used to describe a dirty fighter.)

Mark The pit of the stomach.

Mary Ann A knockout punch delivered by a full swing of the arm, or a punch that "comes up from the floor."

Mauleys (mawleys) The fists. (Eighteenth-century British slang.)

Middleweight A fighter who does not exceed 160 pounds.

Mill A fight, to fight.

Mouse A swelling under the eye.

Mouthpiece a. A rubber device which a fighter normally clamps between his teeth to prevent chipping and breaking. b. Authorized spokesman for a fighter.

Mufflers Gloves. (Eighteenth-century British slang.)

Mug A dull or awkward fighter.

Nobber A punch to the head.

Noggin The head.

On the fret Not feeling well.

One-two punch Landing two punches almost simultaneously, the left hand normally striking first.

Pacing oneself Working according to a definite plan.

Palooka A clumsy, inexperienced, or incompetent fighter.

Parry To stop a straight blow by meeting it with the open glove in a brushing motion.

Peeper in mourning A black eye.

PEPPER To land punches frequently and effectively.

PIER SIX BRAWL A very rough fight.

PILLOWS Very large, heavily padded gloves used in training.

PIVOT BLOW A blow to the jaw or head delivered with a straight-arm movement as the striker pivots on one foot, turning halfway round while doing so.

PUG A pugilist or fist fighter.

PUNCH DRUNK A dazed condition, usually temporary, occasionally permanent, brought about in consequence of many blows to the head.

PUNCHY Same as punch drunk.

PUT THE LUG ON To borrow money.

RABBIT PUNCH A sharp blow at the base of the brain, so called because rabbits are easily killed by such a blow.

REACH The distance from the tip of the middle finger of one hand to the other, measured when the arms are fully extended in opposite directions. In addition to this "official" reach, there is the "practical" reach, which is the distance from the shoulder to the tip of the forefinger. In ordinary parlance, a boxer's reach is the distance from his shoulder to his knuckles.

RING See Squared circle. (The word ring is a misnomer, strictly speaking, yet it continues to be universally employed to designate the area of fighting.)

ROUNDHOUSE A punch delivered with a full swing of the arm.

RUSTY Out of condition.

SCRATCH Under London Prize Ring Rules the mark in the center of the ring to which the fighters had to come at the beginning of the fight and at the beginning of each succeeding round. A fighter who failed to "come to scratch" in time automatically lost the bout.

SENT TO THE CLEANERS Knocked out.

SHARPSHOOTER A clever boxer and accurate puncher.

SKIN GLOVES Unpadded leather gloves that were frequently worn by fighters in "bare-knuckle" days.

SKINTIGHT GLOVES Same as skin gloves.

SLIP A PUNCH To avert a blow by moving the body to either side.

SMASH A hard punch.

SMOKING UP A FIGHT Exciting public interest in a fight.

SOLAR PLEXUS PUNCH A blow that lands over the nerve center in the diaphragm immediately below the ribs.

SOUTHPAW A left-handed, or deliberately unorthodox, boxer who fights with his right foot forward and guards with his left hand.

SPAR To make offensive or defensive gestures without coming into contact with an opponent's head or body.

SQUARED CIRCLE The square area, twenty-four feet to a side, with posts at each corner connected by three strands of heavy rope, within which a fight takes place. The ring.

STAB A stinging jab.

STIFF An extremely poor fighter, a bum, a ham, a tramp.

STRAIGHT LEFT A jab to head or body with the left hand.

STRAIGHT RIGHT A jab to head or body with the right hand.

STUMBLEBUM A low-grade, incompetent fighter.

SWING LIKE A GATE To miss repeatedly with wide, swinging punches.

TAKE A DIVE To pretend to be knocked out. To go into a tank. To take a splash.

TAKE A SPLASH See Take a dive.

TEASER A light punch.

TECHNICAL KNOCKOUT If a fighter quits, or if the referee stops a bout because a fighter is injured or unable to protect himself, his opponent is awarded the fight as if he had won by a knock-out. In many states there is no distinction between knockout and technical knockout.

THROW IN THE SPONGE To quit.

THROW IN THE TOWEL To quit.

TINHORN SPORT A flashy and pretentious gambler with little money to back his opinions.

TOE THE SCRATCH See Scratch.

TRAMP An extremely poor fighter.

UPPERCUT A punch delivered with an upward movement, with either hand, to jaw or body. It is used in close fighting.

WEAVING Moving the body from side to side.

WEIGH-IN Taking the weight of contestants on official scales on the day of a fight. The official weigh-in usually takes place about noon, thereby permitting the boxers to eat a substantial meal some hours before fighting and to spend the rest of the intervening time in complete relaxation.

WELTERWEIGHT A fighter who does not exceed 147 pounds.

INDEX